Digital Guide to Developing International Software

Digital Guide to Developing International Software

Corporate User Publications Group / Digital Equipment Corporation

Digital Press

9 8 7 6 5 4 3 2 1

Printed in the United States of America.

Order Number EY-F577E-DP
ISBN 1-55558-063-7

Author: Cynthia Hartman Kennelly
Editor: Jacqueline Unch
Illustrator: Andrea Thurber
Compositor: Corporate User Publications (CUP/ASG)
Digital Equipment Corporation

This document was prepared with VAX DOCUMENT, Version 1.2.

Contents

EXAMPLES

FIGURES

TABLES

Foreword

With new opportunities in an open world, it is now more evident than ever that the freedom of exchange between countries provides for a unified and profitable international market. And with the communication capabilities provided by modern-day technology, such as satellite earth station networks and plans for undersea fiber-optic cables to China, it is time to design with the world in mind. Competition is fierce in foreign markets. Products sold internationally will not be successful unless they meet the needs of local users.

Digital is an international company with worldwide commitments. Our international products are accepted in world markets because they support local languages, conventions, and cultures. The revenue Digital generates outside of the United States has reached 56 percent and is growing significantly. We have invested significant resources in understanding how to create globally competitive products, which are sought-after locally in the countries where we do business. To maximize the return on an engineering investment, it is important to take advantage of this knowledge.

This guide demonstrates how companies today can ship products that support local languages and customs. To do otherwise is to run the risk of alienating international consumers. Users prefer products that provide information in their local languages and according to their local customs. Creating international products can be complicated. *The Digital Guide to Developing International Software* simplifies this process by describing the strategies, guidelines, and the product model that Digital considers when designing new software products to sell in strategic markets.

This guide includes information on standards such as the International Organization for Standardization (ISO) alphabets, which provide a framework that designers can use to create products of uniform quality and usability. It includes data formats for 18 countries, from Austria to the United States. It explains how you can create software that sells abroad successfully and design it right the first time.

David L. Stone
Vice President, Software Product Group
Digital Equipment Corporation

Preface

Competition in today's global computer industry demands the shortest possible time to market for software products. The delays usually associated with the redesigning of software for international release are no longer acceptable. For an international product to obtain optimum market share, the delay between its release at home and its release abroad must be minimal.

Although no definitive standards exist for the design of international software products, teams within Digital have developed strategies for producing software so that it can be efficiently adapted for particular markets. The guidelines offered here can help companies to make the right design decisions early in the software development cycle and thereby reduce costs.

This guide deals primarily with the early design decisions that determine whether efforts to develop international software variations are simple and efficient or complex and time-consuming. It offers a product model that allows designers to isolate components that don't need to be adapted from those that do. Developing software that is truly international also requires attention to a special requirement of Asian processing environments: multi-byte character sets. This guide points out the differences between single-byte and multi-byte environments and explains how to support and manipulate multi-byte data.

Developing guidelines for internationalization is an ongoing and difficult task. The guidelines included here present procedures that work for creating products at Digital Equipment Corporation. If these guidelines cannot be adopted directly for use in your company, perhaps they can be adapted to suit your business needs.

The second guide in a series, *The Digital Guide to Developing International Software* is intended for anyone involved in designing or developing software for an international market. This audience includes product managers, software designers and engineers, documentation writers and project leaders, editors, illustrators, course developers, human factors analysts, and quality assurance managers. It is also of interest to the consumers of international products and students of international business and engineering.

This guide is organized in two parts: Chapters 1 through 10 offer general guidelines for various aspects of the internationalization process; Appendixes A through J provide specific reference information for creating international software. Special terms, which appear in italic type when first introduced, are explained in the Glossary.

Writing this guide about the development of international software was itself an international effort. Thanks to Digital's communication system, manuscript reviews were transmitted over the network from many countries, allowing us to bring together the most up-to-date information about Digital's international software development efforts. The following reviewers made substantial contributions to this process: Dee Anderson, Jürgen Bettels, Michael Collins, Bob Dray, Pierre Gillespie-Kerr, René Haentjens, Ian Johnston, Scott Jones, Yoshi Kiyokane, Neil Keefe, Lilian Lai, Daniel Ostergren, Claude Pesquet, Wendy Rannenberg, Barbara Russell, Yoichi Suehiro, Robert Tedford, Bill Thomas, Clement Yeung, and Michael Yau.

Chapter 1

The Concept of Internationalization

To succeed in *international* markets, a software product must be adapted, or localized, to the different languages, customs, and product requirements of another locale. The term *locale* includes several aspects of the environment in which a product is used:

- Language
- Dialect
- Keyboard layout
- Data input and display conventions
- Collating sequences

These aspects and others affect the way users in various locales interact with the product. The boundaries for a locale do not necessarily match country borders: a single country might include several different locales; a single locale might include more than one country.

Given enough time, engineering expertise, and resources, any product can be localized. But a product that requires *reengineering* or a time-consuming *translation* effort will be more difficult and more costly. By choosing wisely from among several seemingly equal design alternatives, software designers can create an *international product* that keeps the *localization* process simple.

1.1 International Software

A truly international software product is one that can be localized easily and cost-effectively to suit a number of international markets.

At Digital, the success of an internationalization effort is measured according to two criteria:

- How many markets can the product serve?
- How much does it cost to localize the product to serve those markets?

The cost of localization depends not only on how many local variants are created, but also on how easily changes can be made to the original product. When the user interface and associated text can be translated or modified easily, software can be localized easily. Likewise, when software functions can be modified or extended to meet specific requirements of the market and culture, localizing the product becomes easier and more cost-effective.

Digital uses these criteria to determine where a software product falls on a scale of adaptability. At the bottom of the scale is a completely local product that must be reengineered for international markets at considerable cost in time and effort. At the top of the scale is a global software product that, without modification, meets all international needs. In between are the two types of software products for which Digital has developed general design guidelines: *localizable software* and *multilingual software*.

As its name suggests, localizable software minimizes the cost of localization. Modular in design, this software isolates all code that must be changed to suit other markets. As a result, core functionality need not be recoded. Functions that are not appropriate for a market can be eliminated, and appropriate functions can be substituted. In this type of software, all user-visible text is separated from the source code. Thus, only the text displayed by the user interface need be translated. Digital's DECwrite software provides an example of a localizable software product (see Chapter 2). Guidelines for designing localizable software are presented in Chapter 4.

Multilingual software allows the user to select from a number of interface and functionality options. For example, a user may interact with the software in more than one language, moving from one language to another during program execution. Multilingual capability allows two users of the same software on the same system to use different interfaces. These interface and functionality options may be bundled with the software or ordered for installation at a later time. Digital's ALL-IN-1 software provides an example of a multilingual software product. General guidelines for creating multilingual software, or localized software that can become multilingual, are presented in Chapter 5.

Whether to produce localizable software or multilingual software depends on the needs of the user. For instance, if the application is to be used in an office in Geneva, where different users interact with the software in different languages, multilingual software is the answer. Of course, making software localizable is the first step to making it multilingual. Multilingual software is an extended form of localizable software. Section 6.6 provides an example of localizable software created using the DECwindows interface. Section 7.6 presents an example of a multilingual software product based on the VMS operating system.

In addressing the task of designing localizable or multilingual software, Digital applies an international product model. This model enables all groups involved in developing an international product to share a common understanding of the product components. This conceptual framework provides several benefits. The model separates the product into modules, which, as we've seen, makes it easier to develop local variants. This modular approach also reduces development costs by reducing the need for reengineering. The model also makes ordering and packaging of the product more flexible. Chapter 2 explains Digital's international product model.

Digital provides various interfaces and operating systems offering features that assist in developing international software. Chapter 6, Chapter 7, and Chapter 8 provide information on developing international software using Digital's DECwindows interface, VMS operating system, and ULTRIX operating system.

Designing a software product for Asian markets requires special steps to deal with the Asian character formats. Asian languages such as Chinese, Korean, and Japanese require complex *ideographic characters* and very large character sets. The size of the character sets ranges from 6,000 characters for simplified Chinese, Korean, and Japanese to more than 30,000 characters for traditional Chinese. Products destined for Asian markets must allow for multi-byte processing since the character set for Asian languages far exceeds the 256 characters addressed by the single-byte character format used in the standard ASCII computing environment of European and English-speaking countries.

This guide discusses the internationalization of software in both single-byte and multi-byte environments. Chapter 9 focuses on input, output, and editing of Asian ideographic characters. Chapter 3 discusses the different levels of natural language text processing support required in international products. Chapter 10 describes how Digital's central engineering groups work with engineering groups located in other countries in their effort to produce international software.

The appendixes of this manual provide reference information on specific topics, including Digital's Asian localization products, collating sequences, national data formats, and symmetric programming techniques.

Chapter 2

Digital's International Product Model

The international product model used at Digital enables all groups involved in internationalization to share a common understanding of the components that make up an international product. This conceptual framework provides a number of benefits:

- Ease of localization

  Separating a product into modules makes it easier to develop local variants: country teams can focus on only those modules that must be adapted for their locale.
- Common terminology

  The model and its components provide a common terminology for different groups involved in creating products for the international market.
- Metric for modular software

  The model stresses the need to modularize software and serves as a metric for proper design.
- Reduced costs

  The model separates the product into modules, which helps to reduce the cost of developing product variants by reducing the need for reengineering.
- Flexibility in packaging

  The model provides for flexible ordering and packaging of the product for worldwide delivery, which in turn helps to increase sales.

2.1 Components in Digital's International Product Model

Digital's international product model[1] consists of the following four components:

- International base component
- User interface component
- Market-specific component
- Country-specific information component

2.1.1 The International Base Component

The *international base component* is the part of a product that is sold worldwide without modification. While the international base component is itself invariant, it can feature built-in variants that are selected by a user, perhaps by switch selection in the case of hardware, or by a parameter setting in the case of software. For a product in the Asian market, this base component must support characters of at least 16 bits (2 bytes) for multi-byte processing.

The international base component contains an application's basic functional code: the procedures responsible for processing information and performing computations. This globally applicable code may include user-selected variants, or may be externally conditioned by other components to provide the variations required for a particular locale. The code in this component can be supplemented by shared data as long as the shared data is not going to be translated.

This component could contain:

- Executable images
- Internal data files
- Command procedures without text

[1] For ease of reference, Digital often uses the letters A, B, C, and D to refer to the model's components and calls the entire model the ABCD model.

2.1.2 The User Interface Component

The *user interface component* is the language and text processing component. It is language-specific and must be localized to meet the linguistic and cultural requirements of a specific group of users. The user interface component typically contains the user interface code including messages, text and language processing routines, format specifications, online help, and documentation. When a local variation of a software product is created, all files in this component are translated, replaced, and sometimes deleted. Additional files may also be created. This component could contain:

- Message files
- Forms and menus
- Command procedures with text
- Data structures

The data structures can take several forms:

- Natural language text displayed by the user interface code. When the language of the target locale is other than the language of the original locale, this text is typically translated.
- Text used to interpret user input, such as *Yes* and *No* responses. Such input must be recognized by the system in its translated form.
- Text used in command and programming languages.

Two examples of products that Digital currently supports with various user interface components are shown in Table 2–1.

Table 2–1. Sample User Interface Components

Product	Available User Interface Languages
DECwrite	Chinese (traditional and simplified), Danish, Dutch, English, Finnish, French, German, Italian, Japanese, Korean, Norwegian, and Swedish
ALL-IN-1	Chinese (traditional and simplified), Danish, Dutch, English, Finnish, French, German, Hebrew, Icelandic, Italian, Japanese, Korean, Norwegian, Portuguese, Spanish, and Swedish

2.1.3 The Market-Specific Component

The *market-specific component* is added to meet special requirements of a specific region or business that shares a language and set of cultural conventions, such as the Netherlands and Dutch East Indies. The market-specific component adds specialized functions to the international base component, extending it without changing it.

Like the contents of the user interface component, some files in this component may be translated, replaced, and sometimes deleted when a local product variant is created. Additional files may also be created.

This component is most often used to solve implementation problems unique to a particular dialect, market, or country. The creation of the component usually involves independent design and implementation efforts for each market, leading to significant amounts of special coding. In some cases, a capability present in the base version of the product must be removed for a specific local market. This requirement may be due to an export restriction in the originating country, or to a prohibition or custom in the local market.

The following types of information are included in this component:

- Keyboard maps
- Telecommunications controls
- Printer controls
- Natural language lexicons

2.1.4 The Country-Specific Information Component

The *country-specific information component* is the set of required documentation produced to meet all the regulations for selling the product in a specific country. This component contains no software. This component does not include special functions or code supporting a country's unique requirements. These functions would be included in the market-specific component.

Examples of information included in this component are:

- License certificates
- Service and ordering information
- Warranty information
- Product descriptions

- VDE postcards (cards used in Germany for registering high-frequency equipment with the telecommunications authority)

2.2 Applying the Model to Software Development

In the development of software products, Digital's international product model provides a framework for modular design. Figure 2–1 illustrates the structure of an international product developed according to this model.

Figure 2–1. The International Product Model

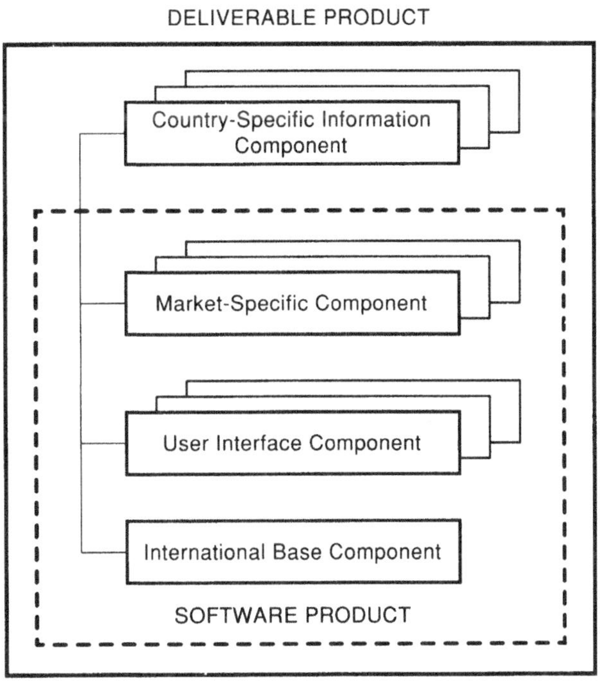

Figure 2–1 shows that the international base component is the foundation of the software, with the user interface and market-specific components added in layers as appropriate. The country-specific information component is a part of the product as a whole, but is not included in the software portion of the product.

To apply the model, application developers must define:

- The contents of each component

  All user-visible text should be eliminated from the international base component and placed in the user interface component of the international product. If there is any functionality that is appropriate for one market only, it should be placed in the market-specific component.

- Interfaces between components

  The international product must include interfaces between the different components. For example, the international base component must include interfaces to the text and data in the user interface component, as well as interfaces to the market-specific component.

- Installation requirements

  The installation procedure must allow the different components to be installed in different combinations.

- Testing requirements

  There may be special testing requirements. For example, if the software supports multiple user interfaces, the test procedures must allow for testing of multilingual operation. Refer to Chapter 5 for information on multilingual software.

2.2.1 Applying the Model to Asian Software

For the Asian market, multi-byte processing capabilities are needed and should be included in the international base component, as shown in Figure 2–2.

Since two or more bytes are required to represent a single Asian character, this multi-byte processing capability must signal the system software when a multi-byte Asian character is being entered or displayed, instead of two or more ASCII or 8-bit characters (see Chapter 9).

When you include the multi-byte processing capabilities in the international base component, the other components of the product model remain unchanged. The user interface component for an Asian market could contain information geared for users in Taiwan, Korea, Japan, or the People's Republic of China (PRC). The market-specific component would contain support features for the appropriate user interfaces. The country-specific information component would contain any warranty, packaging, or licensing information required specifically for release in Asian countries.

Figure 2–2. Applying the Product Model to Asian Software

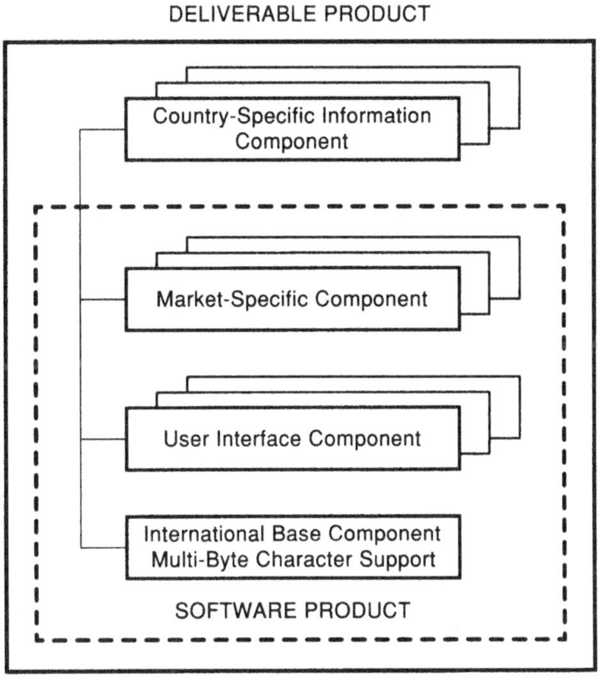

2.2.2 DECwrite Software: A Sample Product

The international product model was used in the design of Digital's DECwrite software. Available on both VMS and ULTRIX operating systems, DECwrite is an application that allows users to create and format documents that contain text, graphics, images, and supported application data.

DECwrite software combines several desktop publishing capabilities:

- Word processing
- Graphics creation

- Data-driven charting
- Image integration
- Live links to supported application data

The international base component of DECwrite software consists of the invariant base code. This code does not change, whether it is distributed in Tokyo, Japan or Pittsburgh, Pennsylvania, USA. Because the international base component does allow for multi-byte processing capabilities, DECwrite software can be localized for Asian markets. The base component contains executable images, internal data files, and any command procedures that do not contain text.

The user interface component consists of the code that determines the screens, messages, and online help. This component contains all of the application's message files, all of the forms and menus, any command procedures that do contain text, as well as symbols, icons, and documentation. When a user presses the Help key, an overview of the application is displayed on the screen along with additional topics for which help is available. All of this information is coded in the user interface component of the product.

The market-specific component consists of the information added to DECwrite software to meet the special requirements of a specific market, such as natural language lexicons and keyboard maps. The market-specific component contains the necessary printer controls to print DECwrite output on the appropriate printer, whether it is a Japanese LN03 or an English LN03.

The country-specific information component does not contain any software; rather it includes the product delivery document, which states where the package is to be shipped. This component also contains the software bill of materials shipped with each software package and the DECwrite software product description, as well as the warranty and licensing information.

2.2.3 The Independent Aspects of International Software

In designing localizable and potentially multilingual software products, it is important to avoid coupling one localizable feature with another. For example, Digital does not assume that a French user interface implies that the French layout keyboard will be used, or that the user will want the date and time formats that are preferred in France, or even that the French user is actually located in France. Each of the following aspects of a software product should be treated independently:

- Language
- Data formats
- Keyboard mapping
- Conversion functions
- Character sets
- User interface
- Collating sequences

To achieve this flexibility, developers should use a table-driven design, with externally modifiable control and text. It is easier to couple components after design to meet packaging and support goals than it is to redesign software that has made invalid coupling assumptions in the first place.

Figure 2–3 shows an international product that uses two market-specific components. Depending on the language, country, and market requirements of the locales where the international product will be sold, the product may use any number of market-specific components, or none at all.

Figure 2–3. International Software Model

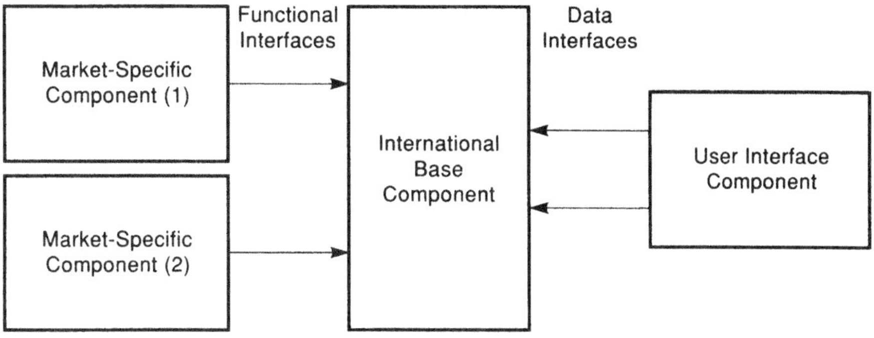

2.3 The Importance of Market-Specific Components

At Digital, decisions about what to include in the market-specific component rather than the international base component are made at the beginning of the design phase. Market-specific components are generally used to solve three types of implementation problems:

1. Problems related to natural language

   User interface text sometimes requires slight modifications to reflect differences between the dialects of a single language. For example, differences between French, Canadian French, and Belgian French might require modifications to the French version of a product before it can be sold in Canada or Belgium. For a localizable software product, the base French version of the product could be modified by market-specific components to produce Canadian and Belgian versions. For a multilingual software product, using a market-specific component in this way is not always the best solution. See Section 5.1 for details.

   Languages such as Chinese, Japanese, and Korean are characterized by complex ideographic fonts and large character sets presenting different implementation problems. Because these languages are all based on Chinese ideograms, a common architecture will address all of the Asian market requirements. Even though the use of Chinese ideograms varies a great deal in the three languages, certain rules generally apply to the ideograms themselves:

   — Root radicals are combined with other characters and strokes to form complex characters

   — There are no uppercase or lowercase characters

   — Blank spaces are not used to delineate words

2. Problems related to market requirements

   The problems addressed in the market-specific component often stem from the special requirements of a particular market. For example, the market for CAD/CAM products in Europe or Asia has established practices and preferences that must be supported by any product that is to be competitive in that market.

Linguistic aids for local languages provide another example. The following features are often located in the market-specific component:

- — Spell-checking
- — Hyphenation and word wrapping
- — Grammar and style analysis
- — Voice recognition
- — Speech synthesis

The market-specific component for a compound document editor, for example, can provide spell-checking tools and hyphenation algorithms in the language of the target market.

3. Problems related to country requirements

   Because legal requirements and accounting practices vary from country to country, a product may need to be modified to conform to the regulations of the country in which it will be sold. In this case, local field support groups in other countries can report these requirements to the corporate engineering groups, who can provide the facilities that will allow future additions to local versions of the product.

   Country-specific requirements affect primarily

   - — Financial and accounting functions
   - — Communications
   - — Security

   Legal requirements might also necessitate the omission of certain kinds of information from a product. For example, the United States Department of State requires licenses for the export of software that contains certain encryption algorithms or other security provisions. Such encryption functions should be placed in market-specific components so that they can be easily removed from the product.

Chapter 3

International Text Processing

Different levels of natural language text processing support are required depending on the type of application being designed. A traditional data processing application may require only one monospaced font and support for the input of simple one-dimensional text strings, such as names, addresses, and phone numbers. The application may use this text to annotate forms and reports.

Similarly, a graphical application such as a CAD/CAM system may only need to support input of simple text and annotation of graphical diagrams with that text. Basic word processors must support a more complicated level of natural language text processing. Electronic publishing and language analysis systems must provide full text processing support, supplying many fonts, sophisticated typeset-quality output, formatters, linguistic aids, and so on.

This chapter provides background information on the character sets and collating sequences used to support the various languages.

3.1 Character Sets

There are many different character sets in existence. Normally, a character set covers only one language or group of languages, such as Arabic or the languages based on the Latin alphabet. To date, there is no universally accepted character set that holds all the characters used in all languages.

The following list gives brief descriptions of the most widely used character sets.

- ASCII (American Standard Code for Information Interchange) character set

  The ASCII character set uses seven bits to code a character. It includes the standard 26 letters of the English alphabet but none of the national characters used by non-English-speaking countries.

- NRC (National Replacement Character) Set

  A National Replacement Character set is a 7-bit character set that is built on the national-use rules of ISO Standard 646. This standard specifies a basic character set that is almost the same as ASCII, but allows the less commonly used symbols, such as [, @, and \ to be replaced with characters used by non-English-speaking countries. Different countries use different variants of the basic character set. For example, Germany replaces \ with Ö, while France replaces the same character with ç.

- DEC MCS (Digital's Multinational Character Set)

  DEC MCS is an 8-bit character set. It includes most of the characters required by Western European languages. However, it does not include the additional characters used by Iceland, or any characters not based on the Latin alphabet.

- ISO (International Organization for Standardization) Latin alphabet character sets

  The ISO Latin-1 character set was developed by the International Organization for Standardization as the standard character set for Western European languages. It will eventually supersede DEC MCS. Other ISO character sets cover European languages that are also based on the Latin alphabet, but use characters not included in ISO Latin-1. They cover Eastern Europe (ISO 8859-2), Southern Europe (ISO 8859-3), the Northern European Countries (ISO 8859-4), and Turkey (ISO 8859-9).

- Arabic character sets

  There are a number of Arabic character sets, some of which use 7 bits per character and some of which use 8 bits. The most common Arabic sets are ASMO-449 and ASMO-662 (defined by the Arabic Standards and Metrology Organization) and ECMA-114 (defined by the European Computer Manufacturers Association). ISO Latin-Arabic (ISO 8859-6 and ECMA 114) is the standard character set for mixed Latin and Arabic text.

For computerized text processing, 8-bit coding is adequate, but the font and formatting requirements are unique. Each character has four different shapes depending on its position within a word.

- Hebrew character sets

  The Hebrew language is written and read from right to left, except for numbers, which are written from left to right. The Hebrew alphabet consists of 27 letters. Numbers in Hebrew are written as Arabic numerals (as in English). Hebrew is a single-case language; that is, all characters are in one case and cannot be changed.

  Although Hebrew is a right-to-left language, Hebrew documents usually contain some left-to-right portions. The simplest case would be a number included in a Hebrew sentence. More complicated cases might be quotations from a left-to-right language or even a number of left-to-right paragraphs embedded within the document.

  All Hebrew character sets have their own collating sequences. In general, the Latin portion is collated according to the rules of the parent character set. The Hebrew portion is collated in order of the numeric value of the character.

  Three Hebrew character sets are currently in use:

  — DEC Hebrew 7-bit character set

    The DEC Hebrew 7-bit character set, based on ASCII, was created by replacing character positions 96–122 with the Hebrew alphabet. This character set is equivalent to Israeli Standards Institute Standard 960. The character set has a DEC prefix because Digital standardized it before it became internationally standardized.

  — DEC Hebrew 8-bit character set

    The DEC Hebrew 8-bit character set is based on DEC MCS; it was created by removing characters from positions 192–223 and 251–256 and placing the Hebrew alphabet in positions 224–250.

    At Digital, as a result of a migration to the ISO Latin-Hebrew character set, new applications and DECwindows environments do not support the DEC Hebrew 8-bit character set. Only traditional applications that need to operate in both character cell-oriented and DECwindows environments require DEC Hebrew 8-bit and ISO Latin-Hebrew support.

— ISO Latin-Hebrew

The ISO Latin-Hebrew character set is a member of the family of ISO 8-bit character sets; some characters were removed or relocated, and Hebrew characters were placed in positions 224–250. This character set is defined in ISO 8859-8 and Standard SII 1311 of the Israeli Standards Institute.

- Greek character sets

For the *monotoniko* form of writing, now widely used in Greece and Cyprus, Digital has defined DEC-Greek, an 8-bit character coding set. Since then, an ISO Latin-Greek character set has been defined (ISO 8859-7) and has been taken over as standard by the European Computer Manufacturer's Association (ECMA) and the Hellenic Organization for Standardization (ELOT). The *polytonic* form of writing requires more than 8 bits for coding all characters; these characters will most probably be included in the future ISO 10646.

- Cyrillic character sets

Digital is evaluating the feasibility of supporting the ISO Latin-Cyrillic character set, ISO 8859-5.

- Ideographic character sets

Asian languages such as Japanese, Chinese, and Korean use ideographic characters. Ideographic characters symbolize a specific thought or idea without actually expressing the name of the thing they represent. They generally consist of many elements, some contain over 30 strokes of the pen or brush.

Because so many characters must be represented in these languages, a 2-byte character set is normally used.

— People's Republic of China

The People's Republic of China (PRC) National Standard Code of Chinese Graphic Character Set for Information Interchange (GB2312-80) is a 2-byte character set standard that specifies 7,445 characters and symbols, of which 6,763 are Chinese characters (2,435 are simplified Chinese characters). Over 14,000 additional characters have also been defined, but not yet published.

— Taiwan

The existing Taiwan Standard Interchange Code for generally used Chinese Characters CNS 11643 (in Taiwan) has 141,376 possible characters, which is more than the 17,672 available in the Digital mixed 1-byte/2-byte encoding; thus, 4-byte encoding for the additional characters is provided.

— Korea

The Korean Industrial Standard (KS C 5601-1987) consists of over 8,224 characters and symbols. There are 7,238 ideographic characters defined, consisting of 2,350 Hangul (Korean) and 4,888 Hanja (Korean Chinese). Korean Hangul consists of 10 vowel and 14 consonant symbols that account for 40 phonetic variations. Hangul characters are clusters of symbols that define the pronunciation of the cluster, and are modeled after Chinese characters.

— Japan

The Japan Industrial Standard (JIS) X0208 Levels I and II Kanji character set defines 6,877 characters and symbols, of which 6,353 are Kanji characters and 524 are Kana (Japanese phonetic characters) letters and symbols. At the end of 1988, 7,000 additional Kanji characters were also announced.

— Thailand

The Thailand Industrial Standard TIS 620-2529 (1986) defines 87 characters, 69 of which are Thai letters for building Thai characters.

Table 3–1 summarizes the ideographic character sets and their standards.

Table 3–1. Asian Character Set Standards Summary

Country	Standard	Ideographic Characters	Total Characters
PRC	GB2312-80	6,763	7,445
Taiwan	CNS 11643 SICGCC-1986	13,051	13,735
Korea	KS C 5601-1987	7,238	8,224
Japan	JIS X0208	6,353	6,877
Thailand	TIS 620-2529 (1986)	N/A	87

Currently, national and international standards committees are working together to produce a single, multi-byte code that will contain all characters used in all languages. Some 90,000 characters have already been identified. These include the characters for the ideographic languages and the sets of special symbols for technical and publishing use. In order to represent all of these characters, a code of at least 3 bytes (24 bits) will be needed. Digital is contributing to the different standards committees, with the goal of adopting this universal code.

3.2 Guidelines for Coding Multilingual Data

Digital's architectural foundation for the coding of multilingual data streams is the *Digital Data Interchange Syntax (DDIS)*. DDIS is Digital's internal version of the ISO Abstract Syntax Notation One (ASN.1), which provides a means for Type-Length-Value (TLV) encoding of structured data. DDIS is a collection of notation and encoding rules for data, with a standard data type notation (analogous to C structure declaration), a standard data value notation (analogous to a C initialization statement), and standard data value encoding rules (analogous to CPU data representation). An author of a standard based on DDIS uses the type notation to define data types, and uses the value notation to provide examples. Application developers use the DDIS access routines: create-and-put routines to store data, and open-and-get routines to read data.

The *Digital Document Interchange Format (DDIF)* is a syntax based on DDIS that serves as a document interchange format and conversion hub that is application- and system-independent. DDIF can express most known document semantics and combinations of text, graphics, images, and data.

DDIF data access routines call DDIS access routines to read and write compound documents. The access routines provide for:

- Separating device control instructions for line feeds, carriage returns, backspacing, and tabs from character data. This rule helps accommodate Hebrew, Arabic, and Asian requirements.
- Identifying a character set from a large and growing set of standards specifying 1-byte and 2-byte character sets and the forthcoming ISO multiple-octet character set.
- Identifying language.
- Identifying fonts.
- Separately specifying presentation attributes, including writing direction and emphasis.

Guidelines

At Digital, the following guidelines are used to standardize the coding of multilingual data streams.

- Build ISO Latin-1 character set support into all new applications.
- Migrate existing applications that support DEC MCS toward ISO Latin-1.
- Accept ISO Latin-1 characters in data, including string literals in programming and command languages.
- Support either the ISO Latin-1 character set or the DEC MCS if migration to ISO Latin-1 cannot be considered.

  This support means accepting ISO Latin-1 or DEC MCS alphabetic characters in identifiers such as names of files, documents, folders, fields, records, variables, and procedures.

  Command and programming languages cannot be expected to meet this requirement unless the international or national standard defining the language also reflects this requirement. Languages can be designed so that the support required for this feature is minimal.
- If the product is destined for the Asian market, provide interim support for the Digital mixed single-byte and multi-byte text data stream, which supports ideographic characters for Japanese, Chinese, and Korean (requiring 2 bytes) and also includes the 7-bit ASCII set. Digital's terminals and printers use this mixed data stream for multi-byte character sets.
- Use DDIS and DDIF for encoding simple and complex structured text. This practice allows the language, character set, font, writing direction and other presentation attributes to be identified independently for each unit of text, even to the level of single character units. Applications should be able to accept input and produce output in ISO Latin-1 or DEC MCS if they are not operating in a DECwindows environment. But applications should do conversions and internal processing in ISO Latin-1 since DDIS does not support DEC MCS.
- Use generalized table-driven routines for all text conversions and comparisons. Allow for the recognition of character set and selection of appropriate conversion function and collating sequence tables based on DDIF and DDIS encoding.
- Select linguistic aids such as spell-checking or hyphenation for formatting based on the language attribute of DDIF segments.

- Use standard converters to transform text to and from external and internal text processing environments. For example, transform input text from the 7-bit NRC environment used in France to ISO Latin-1 for internal processing; transform it back to the NRC environment for display.
- Identify character set, language, writing direction, and font independently. DDIF includes text attributes that provide this information for each text segment, which can be as small as a single character of information.
- Provide natural language-sensitive editors that recognize the mixed input requirements of multilingual environments.
- Use the recommended workarounds listed below for the alphabetical sorting problems until databases and indexed files support customized collating.
  - Do not make sorting dependent on the order of indexed keys in Indexed Sequential Access Method (ISAM) files or on database products that do not allow customized collation. Sort or select the keys in the application using National Character Set (NCS) routines controlled by collating sequence or an equivalent algorithm for comparison.
  - Add functions that can sort Asian text in a market-specific component.
  - Construct an invisible key from an artificial character set that has a binary value order yielding the desired collating sequence. On input, transform the original ISO Latin-1 or DEC MCS key into this artificial key used as the Record Management Screen (RMS) or relational database (Rdb) key. On output, transform the artificial key back to the original key. If storage space is not a problem, the original key can also be stored in the file or database relation. The transformations to and from the artificial key should be table-driven so that they can be customized.
- Remove *diacritical marks* and convert characters to uppercase and lowercase. All conversion techniques should be table-driven and not computed by formula as was frequently done in 7-bit ASCII processing. In the VMS environment, Digital recommends NCS routines with conversion function tables for this purpose.
- Design for a common architecture, and identify Asian symbols that are common to Japanese, Chinese, and Korean. Designing the product for a generic character set will facilitate migration to all Asian markets.

3.3 Text Processing Requirements

A common text processing function could be designed to support the requirements for each language group. For example, formal (traditional) writing of Japanese and Chinese is vertical. Until now, it has been acceptable to support only a left-to-right, horizontal writing style for computerized text processing and data processing applications. However, to be successful, an electronic publishing system for Japanese or Chinese must also support the traditional writing style. Table 3–2 summarizes international text processing requirements. The devices and peripherals associated with these languages are listed in Appendix A and Appendix B.

Table 3–2. Text Processing Requirements

Language Group	Writing Direction	Script	Bits/ Char	Input Method
Western Europe The Americas Eastern Europe Southern Europe Northern Europe	Left to right	Latin	8	Direct
Arabic	Right to left	Arabic	8	Direct
Hebrew	Right to left	Hebrew	8	Direct (LK201AT)
Japanese	Left to right Right to left	Kanji Kana	16	Phonetic (LK201AJ) (LK201AY)
Chinese	Left to right Right to left	Simplified Traditional	16 16/32	Phonetic Radical
Korean	Left to right	Hanja Hangul	16	Phonetic Composed

The preferred phonetic methods for Japanese are based on the 52-character Kana phonetic alphabets. Katakana requires the AJ keyboard; Hiragana requires the AY keyboard.

Table 3–3 lists the character set standards planned for use in Digital hardware and software engineering development.

Table 3–3. Character Set Standards Used in Digital Engineering

Language Group	Character Set Name	Standard Number	No. of Bits	No. of Characters Defined
English and W. Europe	DEC MCS ISO Latin-1	ISO 8859-1	8	94 + 96 [96]
E. Europe	ISO Latin-2	ISO 8859-2	8	94 + [96]
S. Europe	ISO Latin-3	ISO 8859-3	8	94 + [96]
N. Europe	ISO Latin-4	ISO 8859-4	8	94 + [96]
Hebrew	ISO Latin-Hebrew	ISO 8859/8	8	94 + 58 [96]
Arabic	ASMO-Arabic-8 Arabic/Latin Arabic/Latin ISO Latin-Arabic	ASMO-662 ASM0-708-85 ECMA-114 ISO 8859-6	8 8 8 8	94 + 51 [96] 94 + 51 [96] 94 + 51 [96] 94 + 51 [96]
Simplified Chinese (PRC)	DEC Hanzi	GB 2312	7/16	7,445
Traditional Chinese (Taiwan)	DEC Hanyu	CNS 11643	7/16/32	13,735
Japanese	DEC Kanji	JIS X0208	7/16	6,877
Korean	DEC Korean	KS C 5601	7/16	8,224

3.4 Collating Sequences

The sequence in which characters are collated is one area of software functionality that varies among different languages. Developers creating products for the international market need to be aware of the different country requirements and of the need to allow for these requirements in their products.

Whenever characters need to be sorted with respect to other characters to produce an alphabetic or alphanumeric list, they are sorted according to a collating sequence. The collating sequence defines the value and position of each character relative to other characters. Characters to be sorted include:

- Letters
- Numbers
- Punctuation characters
- Additional symbols, such as #, &, *, @

Software routines often use collating sequences as a basis for organizing characters into alphabetic or alphanumeric lists. The following are some examples of alphanumeric lists:

- A directory listing of filenames at operating system level
- The output from a sort utility
- An index produced by a text processing application
- The lists output by a database product, such as lists of names, addresses, or components

When designing software products that contain sorting functions, developers need to design their products so that they are flexible enough to allow for the use of individual country-specific collating sequences.

To achieve this flexibility, developers should avoid hard-coding collating sequences into the software. Instead, the software should refer to a table containing the collating sequences. The table to which the software refers can then be varied, depending on the country in which the application is being used.

The National Character Set (NCS) Utility available in Digital's VMS Version 5.0 Run-Time Library assists developers writing software that uses collating sequences. This utility, which supports the ISO Latin-1 character set, allows specific collating sequences to be defined and then stored in an NCS library (see Chapter 7).

3.4.1 Complicating Factors in Collating Sequences

Although the task of specifying the sequence in which letters should be ordered within an alphabetical list seems to be straightforward and unambiguous, a number of factors can complicate this process:

- Numerous character sets can be used; it can be difficult to decide which set of characters a collating routine will need to handle.
- For languages based on the Latin alphabet, there may be specific collating requirements that are unfamiliar to English-speaking people, such as:
  - To treat character variants as equivalent, such as *ç c* in French
  - To provide for additional letters, such as *ñ* between *n* and *o* in Spanish
  - To treat character combinations as one letter, such as *ch* in Spanish

  Sophisticated and flexible processing is necessary to process multinational characters correctly.
- Numbers, punctuation, and additional symbols can be treated in a variety of ways when producing ordered lists. It may be a requirement to allow for different ways of treating them if the software is to be used in different application domains. For example, a space between characters is ignored for some applications but observed for others. If the space is ignored, the resulting list would be

  Daniels
  Da Silva
  Dauxois

  However, if the space is not ignored, the resulting list would be

  Da Silva
  Daniels
  Dauxois
- Different countries may treat the same character differently. For example, the character *Ä* is treated as a variant of *A* in Germany and is sorted as equivalent to *A*. However, in Sweden, *Ä* is treated as a distinct character and is sorted after *Z*. Thus, different collating sequences must be used for different countries.

- Languages not based on the Latin alphabet have their own special requirements for collating, which vary from language to language. For example, with Asian languages, users must define additional characters outside the standard character set. This means that software must be able to collate text that contains both standard and user-defined characters.
- If software must collate multilingual text containing words or names from more than one language, more than one country-specific collating sequence must be applied to the text.

3.4.2 Collating ASCII Characters

The ASCII collating sequence, which is based on the ASCII character set, orders characters according to their numeric code value. This method of collating characters provides unsatisfactory results where text must be organized in alphabetical order, according to dictionary rules.

Each character within a character set has a unique numeric code. The value of this numeric code depends on where the character is positioned within the code table. For example, within the ASCII code table, uppercase *A* has a decimal value of 65. Lowercase *a* comes later in the table and has a decimal value of 97.

When the ASCII collating sequence is used, characters are collated in the following sequence:

1. Numbers
2. Uppercase letters
3. Lowercase letters

The ASCII character set does not contain national characters, that is, characters with diacritical marks and additional characters, such as *Æ*. However, some applications that use the ASCII collating sequence accept national characters. In this case, the national characters are sorted at the end of the sequence.

The following list shows a series of words sorted by the VMS SORT utility that uses the ASCII collating sequence:

Aegean
Column
Colón
Flute
Flußpferd

Noël
Zero
aegean
chasse
column
flüssig
zero
zuträglich
zéro
åsna
étude
öde

Note that all words that begin with lowercase letters appear after the words that begin with uppercase letters; words that begin with national characters are sorted after the lowercase *z*. To produce correct alphabetical output, a more sophisticated method of processing should be used.

3.4.3 Digital's Multinational Collating Sequence

For characters to be organized in a fully alphabetical list, a more complex series of comparisons needs to be performed on the characters.

The principles by which characters are collated in the DEC Multinational Collating Sequence (DEC MCS) are as follows:

- The alphabetic characters within DEC Multinational Collating Sequence are viewed as being grouped into sets of characters. Each set consists of all the variants of a basic alphabetic character. For example, all the forms of *e* comprise one set. All variants of a character have the same basic collating value.
- When alphabetic characters are collated, all members of one particular set are positioned in the same position relative to other sets. This means that all forms of *C* are sorted as if they are a *C* relative to other letters of the alphabet.
- Within any particular set, the variants are ordered in a specified way. The lowercase letters are always collated by numeric code value, and each uppercase letter immediately follows the corresponding lowercase letter. For example, the character *ç* comes after the lowercase *c* in the code table and has a higher numeric code value. Therefore, within the set of *C*'s, the order of the letters is *c*, *C*, *ç*, and *Ç*.

- The characters *æ, Æ, ø, Ø, å, Å, ñ, Ñ* form an exception to these general rules. They are treated as separate characters, not as variants of A, O, or N. The characters *æ, Æ, ø, Ø, å,* and *Å* are collated in that order after Z. The characters *ñ* and *Ñ* are collated after *N* and before *O*.

DEC Multinational Collating Sequence solves many problems associated with collating multinational characters correctly. For example, if the series of words listed in the previous section was sorted by using the Multinational Collating Sequence, the resulting list would be as follows:

aegean
Aegean
chasse
Colón
column
Column
étude
flüssig
Flußpferd
Flute
Noël
öde
zero
Zero
zéro
zuträglich
åsna

However, even with these rules, it is still not possible to provide a single, standard collating sequence for all Western European languages. Each country has different rules for sorting. The rules are to be used in contexts where alphabetization is required and the user does not, or cannot, specify the language in which the text is written.

For the Multinational Collating Sequence to be used successfully, additional rules must be applied for different countries. For example, the same character may need to be sorted at a different position in the sequence, depending on the language. The character *Ä* or *ä* is sorted as equivalent to *A* or *a* for the German language, but for Swedish and Finnish the character is treated as distinct from *A* or *a*, and must appear after *Z* in the collating sequence.

3.4.4 Collating Arabic Characters

Arabic is a single-case language, so the problems of collating uppercase and lowercase characters do not occur. The following guidelines apply to the Arabic collating sequence:

- The Arabic connecting character, the *tatweel* has no significance in a word and should be excluded during collation.
- Words are first sorted in code order with the Arabic vowels characters excluded.
- Groups of words having the same consonants are then sorted in code order including the vowel characters.
- In the common Arabic codesets, all ligatures such as *lam-alef* are represented as the character codes of their component letters so they present no special problems for sorting.
- Further guidelines for Arabic sorting are included in the text of the ASMO-449 character set standard.

3.4.5 Collating Hebrew Characters

Hebrew is also a single-case language, so the problems of collating uppercase and lowercase letters do not occur. However, all three Hebrew character sets contain both Latin and Hebrew characters. This means that collating rules must exist for both types of characters.

Latin characters are collated according to the rules of the parent character set. For example, Latin characters within the DEC Hebrew 7-bit set are collated according to the ASCII sequence, whereas Latin characters within the DEC Hebrew 8-bit set are collated according to the DEC Multinational collating sequence.

In each Hebrew character set, Hebrew characters are collated in alphabetical order. This order is the same as their numeric code order, since Hebrew characters are listed in alphabetical order in the different Hebrew character sets. Hebrew characters always appear after Latin characters in the collating sequence.

3.4.6 Collating Ideographic Characters

Collating ideographic characters is more complex than collating Latin characters. The Chinese Hanzi version of the VMS SORT/MERGE utility supports three different methods of collating:

- By radicals

  Radicals are the root forms of a character that give the character its basic meaning. The radical collating sequence sorts according to the radicals that make up the character. If there is more than one character with the same radical, then these similar characters are further sorted by the number of strokes that make up the character.

- By number of strokes

  Characters are sorted by the number of strokes that make up the character. If more than one character has the same number of strokes, these characters are further sorted by radicals.

- By phonetic sequence

  Characters are sorted according to the sequence in which they appear in a phonetic alphabet. In this phonetic alphabet, the characters are organized according to their romanized (western) spelling.

Within the Chinese Hanyu version of VMS, which is used in Taiwan, the situation is even more complicated, since the Hanyu SORT/MERGE utility must handle characters with different lengths (one, two, and four bytes).

The Japanese Kanji VMS SORT/MERGE utility supports radical and stroke collating sequences, plus additional sequences, such as those based on phonetic alphabets. Dictionaries give the collating value for each Kanji character. If the user wishes to use user-defined characters, which is a very common requirement, the user has to modify the dictionary. To date, no systematic solution for dealing with user-defined characters exists.

Chapter 4

Designing Localizable Software

The primary goal in designing international software is to isolate any functional code, text, or control that must be modified for different international markets. The following guidelines provide specific methods for accomplishing this separation.

Guidelines

- Design the code for flexibility by using table-driven algorithms and modular replacement techniques.
- Separate all user-interface text, together with its position and size control, from the code that presents it. In this way, the text can be easily accessed for translation. Include the text used for comparison against user input, as well as the text displayed by the user interface.
- Use standardized coding procedures for all processing and storage of text and data. It is best to use standardized data formats, such as registered data types or standards developed by the following groups:
    - The American National Standards Institute (ANSI)
    - The International Organization for Standardization (ISO)
    - The Institute of Electrical and Electronics Engineers (IEEE)
    - The Consultative Committee of the International Telegraph and Telephone (CCITT)

  Data interchange formats based on DDIF and DDIS, which are important parts of the Digital Compound Document Architecture (CDA) strategy, are recommended since many converters from DDIF to external standard formats are being developed.

- Transform stored data from its internal form to a user-viewable display at the latest possible time, for example, at run time. Supply the language- and locale-sensitive parts of the display. This approach allows two users on the same system to view different versions of the same internal data.
- Do all processing, storage, and interchange in the internal encoding format, using standardized processing algorithms.
- Use standardized encoding to handle any user-supplied text that will become a part of the metadata exchanged between applications. Never store such metadata in natural language text in the interchange format.
- Design your product so that it can be localized, packaged, and ordered in accordance with the international product model described in Chapter 2.
- Design for consistency across the various operating systems on which distributed software will be used.

4.1 Application and User Profiles

A user interface can be tailored to a locale by adding specialized data structures that condition underlying function and user interface services. Digital recommends two such data structures, or *profiles*. A profile is a data structure that defines parameters to localize and otherwise condition the execution of the application. A profile establishes, selects, or points to all locale-specific text that is required to execute the application.

- Application profile

  The application profile is a data structure that establishes values for application attributes that are the same regardless of the locale the application is being used in. Some examples are the character set and collating sequence for shared text databases, default display formats, and default messages.

- User profile

  A user profile is a data structure that defines or selects the locale-specific attributes characterizing an interaction with the software. The user profile can characterize an interaction with the application that does not require a human user; that is, it can describe a call from one program or process to another (a usage interaction).

Taken as a whole, an application profile and a single user profile can define the attributes needed for a single locale-specific application; and an application profile and a set of user profiles can describe a multilingual, integrated, internationally distributed application. Such distributed applications can span multilingual, multinational, and multivendor environments. For example, an international banking application might be designed to accept an international audience of users as described in Table 4–1.

Table 4–1. Sample International Audience of Users

User	User Interface Language	User's Country	Keyboard
Data Entry Operator	French	Switzerland	Swiss/French
Data Entry Operator	English	USA	North American
Teller	German	Germany	German
Data Base Administrator	French, English, and German	USA	North American

4.1.1 Defining Attributes of Profiles

A major difficulty in defining application and user profiles is deciding what attribute goes where, and when an attribute is allowed to change. User requirements for an application should dictate what needs to be in the profiles. Thus, the major uses of the application must be recognized before the profiles are defined. Many application-specific questions do arise in defining the user requirements. Often these questions do not have simple answers, and indicate the need for additional research.

These are some of the international usage questions that must be answered when defining the profiles:

- Is the character set for all text data fixed application-wide, or must it vary in order to handle the mixed multilingual requirements?
- Are the fonts available to print and display the text data encoded by the character sets?
- Is the collating sequence considered a property of the language, country, character set, database, or field? Is it allowed to vary only on a database-wide basis or on an individual key-by-key basis? Can the collating sequence in the user profile be changed by the

user? Performance characteristics of the application may determine whether an attribute is specified in the application profile and set only once or specified in the user profile and highly variable.

- Are date and time formats allowed to vary on a field-by-field basis in the user interface, or are they specified once throughout an application? What about currency and number formats? What about applications used to convert to and from different formats and which thus must refer to multiple definitions of collating sequence, format, and so on?

Digital's experience in developing international products has provided information about both the international requirements for certain applications and the characteristics of the users of such products. From this experience, Digital recommends developing general guidelines that answer the following questions:

- What application-specific features are required and need to be placed under profile control?
- What attributes should be included in the application and user profile data structures?
- How often and when are the attributes allowed to change?

Table 4–2 lists possible attributes for user and application profiles.

Table 4–2. Possible Application and User Profile Attributes

Language:[1]

  Alphabet (minimal character set and fonts)

  Primary writing direction[1]

  Month/day names and abbreviations

  Ordinal abbreviations (rule or table)

  Spell-checking, hyphenation, other linguistic aids

Writing direction[1]

Common text processing function:[2]

[1]Language determines many other aspects of the locale. Because writing direction may vary independently of language, it is convenient to have a separate attribute for writing direction.

[2]Conversion functions and collating sequence tables to be used by NCS routines are assumed here for illustration purposes.

(Table 4–2 continues on next page)

Table 4–2. Possible Application and User Profile Attributes (cont.)

Character sets and associated fonts[2]

Conversion functions:[2]
Upper/lowercase, diacritical/accent removal
between character sets (for example, between NRC
and MCS)

Collating sequence[3]

User interface (dialog) text and control:

Error/help/dialog/prompt/tutorial text, flow control

Artificial language/command parsing tables

Recognition logic for commands, replays, searches (depends on language and character set)

Country: (controls some market-specific functions)

Keyboard control:
Key sequence-to-function mapping[4]
Driver (character set) mapping (for example, NRC
to/from MCS)

Other device control:
Print control mapping
Timeouts, other external control sequences, and so on

Time transformation:
Calendar (Gregorian or Julian) offset from
Greenwich Mean Time
Zone name, zone abbreviation
Daylight savings time

Currency transformation: (exchange rates)

[2]Conversion functions and collating sequence tables to be used by NCS routines are assumed here for illustration purposes.

[3]Collating sequences can have multiple definitions in a multilingual distributed application. The collating sequence for shared data should be set only once.

[4]Key (or multi-key sequence) mappings to the internal meaning, or software interpretation of the function. Digital's VMS and ULTRIX operating systems use special TERMCAP files for this purpose and allow you to define a virtual keyboard.

(Table 4–2 continues on next page)

Table 4–2. Possible Application and User Profile Attributes (cont.)

Local display formats/conventions:
- Currency symbol (international, local)
- Negative currency indicator
- Fraction separator
- Three-digit group (thousands) separator
- List separator
- Default formats for:[5]
  - Time, date, currency, phone number, and addresses

[5]An application often requires multiple data formats for both input and output.

4.1.2 Implementing Profiles

Profiles can be implemented in a wide variety of ways. Digital's VAX RALLY software supplies examples of most of them. It uses the following techniques:

- An application profile, which is a global block of the AFILE that defines the application, contains default data formats, collating sequence, and other application-wide parameters.
- Defined logical names point to the keyboard mapping desired, application-specific error and help messages.
- The command definition for the RALLY command is provided in Command Language Definition (CLD) format.
- The product makes various database references.

The profile should be easily accessible to the software designer at run time and at application build time for easy modification. The message file is an acceptable place to collect this information, which may be employed at startup time to define logicals, open files for initializing control, and so on.

Once an application or user profile is standardized—that is, encoded, named, and registered—it can call out attributes such as collating sequence by name. References to other sites, such as the library containing all collating sequence tables for the system, provide more detailed definition of attributes. The necessary standardization for collating sequence and conversion function tables and name tables for months and days began with VMS Version 5.0 and ULTRIX Version 3.0.

4.2 Developing an International User Interface

In order to localize a product effectively, the user interface presentation services should accommodate user interface text that changes in length and positioning when it is translated.

Text Expansion

Input text such as names and addresses may require more field space when translated for other markets. User interface services should provide for flexible sizing of fields through the external control of locale-specific data. Although vertical and horizontal scrolling have been used to manage text expansion, horizontal scrolling may not be acceptable for all markets. Vertical scrolling, in a help window, for example, is acceptable. Abbreviations and *icons* can be used when appropriate and when tested by the target market.

Text Positioning

Text positioning should not be hard-coded. User interface presentation services should provide for flexible, externally-controlled positioning of labels and fields.

Depending on the user interface tools you choose, planning for extra space initially may not be necessary. For example, DECwindows software provides user interface *widgets* that can automatically adjust for text expansion. See Chapter 6 for information on DECwindows software.

Guidelines

At Digital, the following guidelines are used in developing user interface presentation services:

- Where possible, use a form system such as Digital's DECforms software to provide the user interface services and as much editing, formatting, validation, and conditional field branching as possible.
- Use screen formatters that can automatically rebuild menus and forms after translation and optimally position the expanded text. Form editors are useful for final manual adjustments to user interfaces. Such editors enable translators to view the text and fields just as they will appear during use of the software.
- At run time, allow for dynamic mapping to the modifiable locale-specific data structures stored in the user interface component.

- Plan for the text positioning changes that result from translating the original language into many target languages. Allow space for text to expand 100 percent in data fields and in single lines of text, 50 percent in a full screen, and 30–40 percent in text files. For text presented in tables, leave five spaces between table columns to provide for expansion.
- When text requires a particular format:
  - Allow the translator to reformat the text with a word processor. For example, if a Help screen is right-justified, do not store each line as a separate text string that must be justified by hand.
  - Use a utility that reformats the text automatically at either compile or run time. If a line is to be centered, the program should center it correctly. Use relative positioning rather than absolute positioning when possible.
  - Use table-driven formatting routines that do not require code changes for localization.
  - Document the method used.
  - Give some consideration to text positioning alternatives. Don't make the engineering groups in other countries manually count spaces to reposition text. If you cannot avoid manual repositioning, store the coordinates to be changed with the text, apart from the procedural code.
- Provide a mechanism to allow for the presentation of more text than appears in the original version. For example, allow for horizontal scrolling of single lines, or a "Press any key for more" routine for vertical scrolling.
- Ensure that the software does not depend on string length. Avoid arbitrary restrictions on the length or positioning of output text. Document unavoidable restrictions for translators.
- Allow the translator to easily change the order of alphabetically arranged options. This guideline ensures that the order after translation remains the same as the order the program expects.

4.2.1 Analyzing User Input

International software products must provide text that the application can use to interpret user input. When an application requests input from the user, the user's response, often a *Yes* or *No*, must be recognized in the translated form.

Guidelines

The following guidelines are used at Digital in determining how user input will be analyzed.

- Let generalized table-lookup and recognition algorithms analyze user responses, command names, qualifier names, qualifier values, and so forth. When a typed-in keyword, menu selection, or command is allowed, be prepared to match it under all of the following conditions:
  - Exact match.
  - Match that ignores diacritical marks. Remove diacritical marks before matching.
  - Match that ignores case. Use uppercase text.
  - Match that ignores diacritical marks and case. Remove diacritical marks and use uppercase text before matching.
- Do not assume that a one-character response always differentiates between responses in different languages.
- Do not require menu options to begin with a single letter. It may not be possible to find translations in the target language that begin with different letters.
- Do not assume that your product will use only ISO Latin-1, or any one character set exclusively. Design the product to handle all supported character sets.
- Do not assume that one byte represents one character when handling user input. Asian character sets use multiple bytes to represent a character. The example below shows a line of input text in English (one byte, ISO Latin-1 character set) in response to a computer prompt:

  ```
  Enter
  ```

  The next example shows a line of input text in Japanese (two bytes per character, DEC Kanji character set) in response to a computer prompt:

  入力

- Do not make assumptions about word delimiters when handling user input; delimiters may not be used between words.

- Avoid using letters as mnemonics for an option. If this approach is unavoidable, allow the translator to change mnemonics easily. For example, if a product used *df* as a mnemonic in English for *Delete a file*, the German version would need to use *dl* as the mnemonic for *Datei löschen*. Document the meaning of all mnemonics for the translator.
- Consider enabling the use of one or more of the following techniques to choose a menu entry:
  - Position the cursor or mouse pointer on the choice and click.
  - Choose a numbered menu choice.
  - Choose an indicated letter, or letters, of the menu choice.

    When using letter matching, check the letter against a table of valid commands; do not hard code it. Allow the translator to change the letters to be selected.

4.2.2 Displaying User Output

An international product must provide the text used in all user output displays. How you store text and later prepare it for display directly affects the translatability of that text. Text should be stored so that it can be modified by someone with no technical knowledge of the product function or its supporting code. Digital recommends, for example, that this text be entered and edited with a text editor.

In Digital applications, the text is placed in one or more of the following places:

- DECwindows User Interface files
- ULTRIX Message Catalogs
- Message files maintained by the VMS Message Utility
- Source files for DECforms IFDL files
- Text libraries maintained by the VMS Librarian

Syntax Differences

Message parameters may need to occur in a different order when they are translated from English to another language. For example:

English: Found “abc” when expecting “xyz”.

French: “xyz” attendu; “abc” reçu

Spelling Differences

English nouns do not indicate gender (masculine or feminine). In many languages, however, noun gender can influence the spelling of the other words in a sentence. For example, consider the following messages:

The file is locked

The printer is locked

In English, only the noun changes; it is therefore possible to design the output of error messages by inserting the appropriate noun into the message at the time the message is needed.

In French, a change in the gender of the noun affects the spelling of other words. When the preceding messages are translated into French, the word *verrouillé* changes when the masculine noun is replaced with a feminine noun.

Le fichier est verrouillé

L'imprimante est verrouillée

As this example demonstrates, an error message assembled from parts at run time may work in English, but it may not be possible to assemble the message in the same way in other languages.

Pluralization Differences

Developers sometimes use facilities to add an *s* to a word in a message if a message parameter is not equal to one. This can cause difficulties because many languages do not form a plural by adding an *s* to the noun, as the following table shows.

In English:	In German:
0 blocks deleted	0 Blöcke gelöscht
1 block deleted	1 Block gelöscht
3 blocks deleted	3 Blöcke gelöscht

Messages that use English-language pluralization facilities may be difficult or impossible to translate by the same algorithm.

Guidelines

Digital recommends the following guidelines for writing all natural language text that the user sees on line.

Organize and structure all user output, including text for menus, prompts, error messages, and online help in the following ways:

- Do not construct messages from text segments. This practice may save space, but causes many difficulties in translation because languages may have widely varying syntactic structures. This rule may necessarily be ignored when space is at a premium, for example, when messages are in ROM for firmware controllers.
- In general, avoid or minimize the use of parameters in messages. For example, the following message may present difficulty in translation because of the varying syntactic structures of targeted languages and the often limited capabilities of the message presentation services.

    Expected *parameter1* found *parameter2*

  Break the message into two separate messages with one parameter each, such as the following:

    Expected: *parameter1*
    Found: *parameter2*

- Do not use natural language text strings as message parameters. Artificial language text strings, such as identifiers for files, printer queues, and folders may be used as parameters. These strings are not translated and do not share the syntactic properties of the natural language message parts.
- Do not use a pluralizing feature such as the VMS Formatted ASCII Output ($FAO) directive that adds an *s* to base text whenever a parameter of the message is other than 1. Instead, explicitly test for and provide different messages for various situations such as equal to zero or equal to one. In VMS Version 5.2 and later, you can use $FAO directives to produce conditionalized messages using a single message string. See Section 7.2.3 for more information about the VMS $FAO facility.
- Provide comments in the text to clarify the state and function of the software at the time the text appears. This translation markup is needed because the translator may not have the working product to verify the state. This is especially critical for highly technical information. See Chapter 10 for more information about translation markup.

- Give the translator the full context of a message. Where a word has more than one meaning, indicate which meaning is required. For example, *cabinet full* may refer to a physical cabinet or a disk structure.

4.3 Local Data Conventions

Conventions for the following types of data and data format vary widely from country to country:

- Thousands separators
- Decimal separators
- Grouping separators
- Paragraph numbering
- Positive and negative values
- Currency
- Dates
- Time
- Telephone numbers
- Addresses
- Proper names and titles

See Appendix C and Appendix D for lists of specific data formats by country.

Any data format used should be modifiable and independent of any other. Do not cluster attributes based on assumptions about country or language. For example, do not link the French currency with the language French. French Canadians, for example, would use the Canadian dollar. Also, individuals or corporations may deviate from national standards or customs.

Guidelines

Digital recommends the following guidelines for writing code to format data:

- Use a single internal format for storage and active processing, regardless of the display or input format.

- Use the same default format for user input and display. However, a product might allow just one output format, while accepting several input formats. For example, a menu may show a date in the format that is customary (for example, 15-AUG-1990), but the product may accept dates input as 15-Aug-1990 or 1990-8-15, or may even accept the word *today*.
- Make any format modifiable. Do not impose arbitrary formats.
- Do not tie the formats to any other feature.
- When separators are used in formats, they should be modifiable independently.
- The default format for all numbers, currencies, and dates should be modifiable by the translator or installer to suit the user's needs.

Guidelines

The following sections offer guidelines for handling specific types of data formatting issues:

Separators

- Make the thousands separator user-definable, or design for the following formats:

2,143,526	2'143'526
2.143.526	2143526
2 143 526	

- Allow for the decimal separator to be user-definable, or design for the following formats:

3.141	3 141
3,141	3 141
3	

- Allow digits to be grouped in alternative ways, as follows:

  100,000.00
  10,0000.00

Positive and Negative Values

Positive and negative indicators differ in various countries. When writing code for positive and negative values, observe the following guidelines:

- The symbols + and –, when used to express a positive or negative number, must be valid either before or after the number.

- In accounting applications, allow negative amounts to be represented as a number enclosed in parentheses.

Currency

When formatting currencies, allow

- The comma, period, colon, and currency symbol as valid separators
- The currency symbol to be placed before or after the numerical value, or to be used as a decimal separator
- The currency separators to be modified independently of separators used for other values

  For example, *1,251.76*, expressed as a currency value might be *BF 1.251,76*.
- Currency symbol switching, and related change of space requirements, from one to four characters long. Examples are $, £, Ptas, or DM.
- A space or no space between the currency symbol and the amount

  For example, design for all of the following formats:

F 134,50	SFr 1.–
134,50F	75 c
134F50	1200 Pts
Kr 25.75	25F75
F25,75	

An ISO standard (ISO 4217 Codes for the Representation of Currency and Funds) establishes the formats for all international currencies, but earlier country abbreviations are still in use. In some instances, the European Economic Community (EEC) symbol is different from the ISO and the local symbols.

Dates

When coding for date formats, observe the following guidelines:

- Allow alternative characters to separate the day, month, and year. Date separators should include at least the hyphen, comma, period, space, and slash.
- For products that display the name of a day or month with letters, allow sufficient storage and display space to accommodate these names in other languages. Table 4–3 shows the maximum number of characters required for storage and display for French, German, Dutch, Portuguese, and Greek. These can be used as typical values for other languages.

Table 4–3. Length of Character Strings in Day and Month Name

	Number of Characters	
Language	**Longest Day**	**Longest Month**
French	8	9
German	10	9
Dutch	9	9
Portuguese	13	9
Greek	9	12

- Allow for the use of non-Gregorian calendars.
- Allow the position of each component in a date to vary, or allow the component to be omitted. The date components are listed below:
  - Year

    Allow two or four digits (two digits are frequently used).
  - Month number

    Allow numbers ranging from 1 to 12.
  - Month name

    Allow enough space for the full name of the month. Do not assume the use of abbreviations. In French, a three-letter abbreviation of month names results in confusion between juin and juillet.
  - Ordinal number of days

    Allow for the day number to be ordinal. For example:

    1st 2nd (English)
    1er 2me (French)
    1. 2. (German)
  - Ordinal numbers as words

    Allow for the day number as an ordinal in words. For example:

    first, second (English)
    premier, deuxième (French)
    den ersten, den zweiten (German)
  - Article

    For example: the, le, der

— Day name

Allow for the name for each weekday:

Sunday through Saturday (English)
Dimanche through Samedi (French)
Sonntag through Samstag (German)

— Day number

Allow numbers 1 through 31.

— Date separators

In date formats, various characters are used to separate the day, month, and year. Date separators must include at least the hyphen, comma, period, space, and slash.

Design for any of the following formats:

Date:	**Usage:**
lundi, premier mars 1990	French
14/12/90	European
90.11.17	ISO Standard
1990-11-17	ISO 8601
1999-W14-5	ISO 8601
6/27/90	USA
March 1990	
Thursday 3rd March	
1.2.'90	Iceland
900102	Swedish Standard

- Allow for changeable date formats

  If the product displays the date in a figures-only format, allow the month and day fields to be reversed, so that, for example, the fifth of December 1990, can be displayed as either 5/12/90 or 12/5/90. Ensure that the format for entering the date can be changed to match the display format.

- Allow for variation in punctuation, including the comma, colon, slash, hyphen, and space. Design for the following formats:

10/7/90	Jul 10, 1990
10:7:1990	1990-7-10
10 juillet, 1990	10 July 1990
7/10/90	10-7-90

Alternatively, prompt for each field of the date separately. Allow the separators to be changed, and allow for the use of different separators in the same date. Other possible separators are the slash, colon, backslash, hyphen, and period.

Times

- Characters used to separate hours, minutes, and seconds values must include at least the colon, period, and blank space. The letter *h* must be valid for use between hours and minutes.
- For 24-hour notation, in the 4-digit format only, allow the use of a separator or no separator. For example, for five o'clock in the afternoon, permit either 17:00 or 1700.

  In the following example, an asterisk is used to represent any separator:

  12-hour notation: *h*mm*ss S h*mm S*
  24-hour notation: *hh*mm*ss hh*mm*

  — *h* represents numeric hours, one or two digits in 12-hour notation, two digits in 24-hour notation
  — *m* represents minutes, two digits
  — *s* represents seconds, two digits
  — *S* represents the symbol A.M. or P.M., and is normally separated by a space from the time
- Allow for the use of a variable separator.
- Design for arbitrary formats. For example:

9.15 am	09:15
0915	09:15:25
09 15	21:15
9.15 pm	09h15
2115	2:04:03.50
21 15	23.15.30,75

On their own, hundredths of seconds are normally displayed in the form 00.nn. Keep in mind, however, that a comma may also be used as a decimal fraction separator. Used with the other components of time formats, hundredths of seconds follow the seconds component, separated by a variable separator. For example, four minutes and three and a half seconds past 2:00 may be displayed as 2:04:03.50.

Time Zones

- In German, at least four characters are needed to denote the time zone. For example, the Central European Daylight Saving Time in Germany is Mitteleuropäische Sommerzeit, abbreviated MESZ.
- Allow for the time zone variations to be in fractions: they are not always an integer number of hours from Greenwich Mean Time (GMT).

  For example, Newfoundland is three and a half hours behind GMT and Central Australia is nine and a half hours ahead of GMT.

Telephone Numbers

The format for telephone numbers varies, ranging from 5 to 21 digits arranged in groups. Not all telephone numbers are the same length, nor do they have the same format, even within the same country.

Telephone numbers often include special characters to separate different components. Also, the same number could be represented in different ways, depending on whether it is for national or international use.

For example:

National number: (089) 9591-2323

International number: + 49 89 9591 2323

- For international numbers, the plus sign (+) is frequently used in Europe to indicate that a number is a country code. There can also be a period (.) or a hyphen (-) between the domestic parts of an international phone number.
- For national numbers, any separator can occur. It is common but not universal to put the city code or area code in parentheses. Slashes, dashes, and periods are common separators.
- A blank space, hyphen, period, and comma must all be valid separators. Avoid invalidating any characters for use in a phone number field. The dash, plus sign, asterisk, pound sign, and other characters might be needed in some formats.
- Design for arbitrary formats. For example:

1-617-897-9111	49 89 9591 2323	(0734)-868711
(617) 897-5111	1-800-DIGITAL	081-337 8195
(1) 617 897 5111	617-897-5111	(34)-3-123456

Lexical Formats

In different countries, names and addresses are formatted using different conventions. For example, the order of elements in an address differs from country to country. When writing code for these lexical formats, observe the following guidelines:

- Allow sufficient space for different address layouts.
- Allow nonalphabetic characters, accented characters, apostrophes, hyphens, and spaces to appear in proper names and title fields. This practice allows for names such as de la Bassetière, D'Agostino, and Torres-Ferrer.
- Minimally, design for all of the following examples:

United States	
Patricia L. Blickstein Jr.	[name]
Customer Service	[department]
American Computers, Inc.	[company name]
654 Commercial Boulevard	[number] [street name]
Maynard, Massachusetts 01754	[town name] [state name] [postal code]

United Kingdom	
Mr. L. M. Turner	[title] [initials] [surname]
55, High Street	[number] or [house name] [street name]
Grantham	[postal town]
Lincolnshire, GR1 OBT	[county], [postal code]
England	[country]

Germany	
Ingrid Boderke	[name] [surname] [degrees]
Stolbergerstrasse 90	[street name] [number]
D-2000 Hamburg 95	[country code] [postal code] [postal town]
Germany	[country]

France	
Madame Dupont Claudette	[title] [surname] [first name]
17, rue Louis Guérin	[number] [street]
Thoué	[town]
F-38560 Le Versoud	[country code] [postal code] [postal town]
France	[country]

Not all postal codes are completely numeric. For example, the U.K. uses this form: RG2 0SU. For more examples of specific data formats, see Appendix D.

4.4 Local Devices

Devices used to provide user input and output vary from country to country. Therefore, international software products should be adaptable for different devices. Device adaptation can be done in numerous ways depending on the windowing system, the operating system device driver support, or other interposed virtual device definition such as that provided by a forms system.

Guidelines

Digital follows these guidelines for writing software that can be adapted to various devices:

- Support 7-bit ASCII/NRC terminals like the VT200, where feasible within the functional requirements of the product, using the Terminal Fallback Facility (TFF). This external-table-driven driver can be used to convert from NRC input to DEC MCS or ISO Latin-1 for internal processing, and from DEC MCS to NRC for output.
- Use keyboard key-to-function relationships that are completely redefinable. In other words, use a completely soft or virtual keyboard. Be aware that legends on keys may be translated too. Thus the function may need to be moved to a different alphabetical or nonalphabetical key.
- Remember that the software may be used with non-Digital devices such as IBM AT, IBM PS/2, and Apple Macintosh computers and with non-Digital terminals and printers. Each of these cases requires special study and may require testing for things like interface conformance and utilities for building control tables.
- Use a virtual device interface such as the one provided by Screen Management (SMG) from the VMS Run-Time Library instead of direct terminal input and output for character-cell terminals.

The following sections provide more specific recommendations for localizing applications used in an international network and with different terminals, keyboards, printers, and telecommunications services.

Networks

An individual computer system in an international network can have links (such as DECnet, TCP/IP, and token ring links) to other computer systems running user interfaces in different languages. Many products, such as Digital's DECmail and network management, display text strings within error and status messages. A user may try to use a French MAIL program to send a message to someone on a German node and receive a German error message.

This type of problem can be reduced by designing network applications to use numeric codes, instead of text strings, within network messages and translating the codes to text on the local system.

Terminals

Digital's VT200- and VT300-series terminals are used in all countries where Digital does business. Variants of these terminals are used in Japan (VT282), the Middle East, Greece, and Yugoslavia, where languages are not based on the Latin alphabet. In countries such as China and Korea, software is used with terminals supplied by outside vendors.

VT300 series terminals support both DEC MCS and the ISO Latin-1 character set and keyboards.

Escape Sequences

Different terminals use different device identification reports. If a product is localized to support terminals other than the VT200 series terminals, the terminal-identifying escape sequences should also be modified. Therefore, the recognition of, and action taken on, terminal-identifying escape sequences should occur in the locale-specific, customizable portions of the product.

Start and End of Area

For languages that are read from right to left, the top of the screen is the top right, and the bottom of the screen is the bottom left. The beginning of the line is at the right, and the end of the line is at the left. Customers in the Arabic countries and in Israel use a variety of terminals. Some markets use a left-to-right terminal and allow the software to reverse the direction of text. In others, the terminal is a right-to-left terminal, which also has a left-to-right mode for insertion of Latin-based text and numbers. The terminal type determines the localization required for escape sequences. However, the following guideline always applies: Do not hard code escape sequences to position or delete text.

See Chapter 3 for more information about languages that use the right-to-left writing direction.

Do not associate a keyboard with any specific language. International products should be designed without making assumptions that link a localizable feature of the software with another product feature.

Keyboards

Keyboard layouts vary throughout the world. The layout used in the United States is called QWERTY, which refers to the first six alphabetic keys in the upper-left corner of the keyboard. Germany uses a QWERTZ, and France uses an AZERTY keyboard.

The various Digital LK201 keyboards differ only in the engravings on the keys. Internally, all the keyboards work the same way. The keyboard sends a scan code indicating which key is pressed. The scan code is converted to a character code by software or firmware inside the terminal or computer. For the software to recognize the keyboard, the user must indicate the variant. The software then stores this information.

Keyboard Selection

The user selects a keyboard from a menu of possible choices at initial startup. The choice is recorded, and the user need not repeat the selection at each start. However, a method of allowing the user to reselect a keyboard should be provided.

Design Issues

When designing software that interacts with Digital keyboards, consider the following keyboard characteristics:

- Keyboard usage mode

  Some keys on the LK201 have three or four characters inscribed. The selection of the appropriate character is governed by whether the terminal is in typewriter or data processing mode. Applications should allow for certain characters not being available, depending on the user's configuration of the keyboard. All Level 3 and higher terminals allow the keyboard usage mode to be changed from the host system.

- Keyboard character set

  The terminal is capable of generating characters coded in different character sets depending on the state of the keyboard usage mode and two other values: the National Replacement Character mode (7-bit or 8-bit characters), and the User Preference Supplemental

(UPS) set. The combination of these three values controls which characters may be generated by the keyboard and how they will be coded by the terminal, as shown in the following table:

Keyboard Usage Mode	NRC Mode	Keyboard Character Set
Typewriter	7-bit	NRC set based on keyboard variant
Data Processing	7-bit	ASCII
Typewriter or Data Processing	8-bit	ASCII + UPS set DEC MCS ISO Latin-1 or locale-specific set (for example, ISO Latin-Hebrew)

Applications should recognize the keyboard character set in use so that data is properly interpreted.

- Compose mechanisms

  Digital defines two compose mechanisms that allow terminals supporting DEC MCS, ISO Latin-1, or both, to produce any character in that set, even if the character is not directly available from the keyboard. The two methods are:

  — Explicit or three-key compose: Every character that is not available on all the keyboards has one or more two-character compose sequences associated with it. For example, the compose sequence for é is [e] ['] or ['] [e]. To start a three-key compose sequence, the user presses the Compose key and the two characters of the compose sequence. The composed character is sent to the program. This compose method is similar for all LK201 keyboards on systems supporting DEC MCS.

  — Implicit or two-key compose: On certain keyboards some keys, such as the apostrophe, circumflex, and quotation mark are *dead keys*. When the key is pressed, the character is not sent to the program, but a compose sequence is started. If the next character completes a valid compose sequence, the composed character is sent. This method, which is only available with certain keyboard languages, mirrors the actions of typewriters in those languages.

  At present, DECwindows does not support a Compose key, but uses the Alt key and space bar for this purpose. The LK401 keyboard has separate Alt and Compose keys.

- Gold keys

  Digital produces eight national versions of the LK201-Bx gold key keyboard, seven versions of the LK201-Px, and one version of the LK201-Fx keyboard.

- Shift lock and capitals lock

  French and Italian versions of the LK201 keyboard have the numeric characters in the shifted position and alphabetic or other characters in the unshifted position. Users with these systems expect the lock key to produce the same character as the shift key. In other systems the lock key is expected to act as a capitals lock and only operate on the alphabetic characters.

- Kana lock

  On the Japanese version of the LK201 keyboard, the alphabet keys have both Latin and Kana characters (Japanese phonetic characters) inscribed. The Compose key and the compose indicator are labeled "Kana" (in Japanese). Pressing the Kana key puts the terminal in Kana lock mode and causes the Kana indicator light to go on. The terminal is then ready to produce one-byte Kana characters.

Telecommunications Devices

Telecommunications is highly regulated in the international market. If a software product controls a modem or interfaces with public telecommunications lines, specific national regulations apply. Many products require certification by the various telecommunications authorities. Certification of the complete product, including both the hardware and the software that drives it, is usually required. Both hardware and software must be tested for compliance with internal standards before any attempt is made to have a system certified.

4.5 Programming and Command Languages

The majority of programming languages, although derived from English, are established artificial languages and are not localized to reflect other natural languages. The few languages that are localized, such as some variants of BASIC, LOGO, PASCAL, and COBOL, tend to translate keywords only, leaving the syntactic structure constant.

A command language, however, is recognized across the industry as a special case. When designing a command language for an application or an operating system, do not rule out a possible translation. The more the language resembles a natural language, the more steps should be taken to allow for an accurate translation.

For example, a database interrogation language based on natural use of English should be designed so that the verb-object order can be altered for another language.

For example, in English:

> Find all parts with cost greater than $20

In German:

> Finde alle Teile, die mehr als $20 kosten
> Find all parts that more than $20 cost

Both the verb and object change position. The sentence structure changes when the sentence is translated and the various concepts are reordered.

As international character sets are defined, language standards organizations are beginning to adopt them. Software developers should plan to migrate to systems that can handle these character sets.

Artificial language processors should provide a flexible table-driven syntactic and semantic analysis. Because such languages are standardized and because of the training and investment in their use, translation of artificial language keywords is not often necessary. However, a good design should allow for this possibility.

Guidelines

Digital observes the following guidelines in developing artificial language processors:

- Command languages, programming languages, and expressions such as arithmetic expressions of a spreadsheet, should be compiled or interpreted by generalized, table-driven lexical scanners and parsers. These techniques should allow:
  - Substitution of translated keywords and function or procedure identifiers
  - Substitution of operator symbols, since some special characters may not be available in local keyboard layouts

- — Full support of DEC MCS or ISO Latin-1 characters in keywords and identifiers
  — Full support of all DEC MCS characters in string literals
  — Alternate formats for numeric literals and date/time literals
- Where the language provides string processing semantics, do any conversions and comparisons using routines controlled by collating sequence tables, or by equivalent algorithms. For example, the record selection expression of a database query language might provide selection based on a string value range for a particular field in a particular relation. Such a record selection expression might state, "retrieve all records between string-literal-1 and string-literal-2" and "ignore underscores, hyphen-minus, and blank spaces in comparisons." The table-driven NCS routines or equivalent algorithms should be used to provide such locally correct semantics.
- Where the language processor or its supporting utilities provide a list of named objects, such as a list of all variables used in the program, follow the guidelines for sorting lists of names provided in Section 4.2.2.
- Free-form input from the user must also be translatable. Follow the guidelines presented in Section 4.2.1.

4.6 Localizing Source Code: An Example

The following example shows how to use Digital's Command Language Interface Utilities to create a program for an international product. Listed is a three-step process by which a program can be revised to suit the international market:

1. Remove embedded user-visible text.
2. Allow command table definition at run time.
3. Allow message file definition at run time.

4.6.1 Sample Program Before Internationalization

The program shown in Example 4–1 is written in VAX-C and called EXAMPLE.C. It is important to note that this example describes one approach and should not be construed as a recommendation for coding techniques. The command definition file, COMMANDS.CLD in Example 4–2, contains the definitions of the verbs *send*, *search*, and *exit*. Each verb invokes a routine in the sample program EXAMPLE.C.

Example 4–1. EXAMPLE.C

```
#include stdio    /*** VAXC System definitions */
#include descrip
#include climsgdef

globalvalue commandtable; /*** external value assigned by SET COMMAND*/

unsigned int cli$dclparse(), cli$dispatch(), /*** External routines */
        cli$get_value(), cli$present(), lib$get_input(), SYS$EXIT();

$DESCRIPTOR(prompt, "command>"); /*** Static String Descriptor setups*/
$DESCRIPTOR(edit, "edit");
$DESCRIPTOR(filespec, "filespec");
$DESCRIPTOR(search_string ,"search_string");

#define $DYNAMIC_D(name) struct dsc$descriptor_d name = \
                           { 0, DSC$K_DTYPE_T, DSC$K_CLASS_D, NULL };

$DYNAMIC_D (file_value);
$DYNAMIC_D (search_value);  /*** Dynamic String Descriptor setups. */

int sendcommand()              /*** Action routine for SEND */
{
printf("   send command\n");

if ( cli$present(&edit) & 1)
  printf("   /edit is present\n");

if ( cli$present(&filespec) & 1)
  {
  cli$get_value(&filespec, &file_value);
  printf("   filespec = %*.s\n", file_value.dsc$w_length,
                                file_value.dsc$a_pointer );
  }
}
int searchcommand()            /*** Action routine for SEARCH */
{
printf("   search command\n");

if ( cli$present(&search_string) & 1)
  {
  cli$get_value(&search_string, &search_value );
  printf("   search string = %*.s\n", search_value.dsc$w_length,
                                search_value.dsc$a_pointer );
  }
}
int exitcommand()              /*** Action routine for EXIT */
{
SYS$EXIT(1);
}
main()                         /*** Main entry point */
{
for (;;)                       /*** loop until user types EXIT */
```

(Example 4–1 continues on next page)

Example 4–1 (Cont.). EXAMPLE.C

```
    {
    if (!(cli$dcl_parse (0, commandtable, lib$get_input,
                        lib$get_input, &prompt) & 1) )
        break;              /*** dcl_parse failed, so quit */
        else
          cli$dispatch();   /*** do another command */
    }
}
```

Example 4–2. COMMANDS.CLD

```
Module   CommandTable

Define   verb   send
         routine sendcommand
         parameter p1, label = filespec
         qualifier edit

define   verb   search
         routine searchcommand
         parameter p1, label = search_string

define   verb   exit
         routine exitcommand
```

The following DCL commands build the sample program, EXAMPLE.C.

```
$ cc   example
$ set   command commands.cld /obj
$ link   example,commands,sys$input/opt   /notrace
sys$share:vaxcrtl.exe/share^Z
```

The commands to execute the EXAMPLE.EXE command file are shown in boldface type in the following example.

```
$ run EXAMPLE
Command> search
   search command
Command> search filename
   search command
   search string = FILENAME
Command> send/edit filename
   send command
/edit is present.
filespec = FILENAME
Command> exit
```

4.6.2 Removing Embedded User-Visible Text

It would be difficult for a localization team to translate this program, as written, to make it a local language version. Ideally, the translation team should need only to translate a set of text strings in a separate file, not to recompile source code.

Use the following procedure to remove embedded text strings:

1. Search the source code for **printf**[1] statements to find lines that contain text.
2. Move the text associated with the **printf** statements to a message file.
3. Replace **printf** statements with calls to **lib$sys_getmsg** to get the text, then print out this text.

Removing One Text String

Here is the original print command:

```
printf("send command\n");
```

To remove this line from the source code, create a new message in a message file:

```
sendcmd    < send command >
! Output by the search command to show current routine
```

The old source code would then be modified to look like this:

```
text_only = 1;
lib$sys_getmsg( &msg_sendcmd ,0, &message_value , &text_only )
printf("%*.s\n", message_value.dsc$w_length,
                        message_value.dsc$a_pointer);
```

The call to **lib$sys_getmsg** extracts the text associated with the **sendcmd** message, and places it into the string **message_value.** The **printf** statement then prints out the new string. The **text_only** variable is used so that **lib$sys_$getmsg** retrieves only the message text and ignores items such as the facility name and severity level.

Example 4–3 shows the complete file MESSAGE.MSG, which replaces all **printf** lines that appear in EXAMPLE.C.

[1] Lowercase C terms appear in boldface type in the text of this chapter.

Example 4–3. MESSAGE.MSG File Contents

```
.Facility   example,1/prefix=msg_
.Ident   'Version x1.0'
.Severity   informational

sendcmd   < send command >
! Output by the send command to show current routine

editpresent   </edit is present. >
! Output by the send command to indicate that the
! edit qualifier was given on the command line
sendfile   <filespec = !AS >
! Output by the send command to show
! the value of the filespec parameter on the command line
! The !AS will be replaced by the actual run-time value.
searchcmd   < search command >
! Output by the send command to show current routine

search_string   < search string = !AS >
! Output by the search command to show the value of
! the search_string parameter in the command line.
! The !AS will be replaced by the actual run-time value.

.end
```

Using LIB$SIGNAL

Another approach would be to use LIB$SIGNAL to signal the **sendcmd** message:

```
LIB$SIGNAL(msg_sendcmd);
```

This would generate a VMS signal that looks like this:

```
%EXAMPLE-I-SENDCMD, ' send command '
```

In a real product LIB$SIGNAL would likely be the desirable means of signaling the user.

Including String Descriptors in the Signaled Text

The following example shows how to place a string descriptor into a string that is fetched from the message file. The **sendfile** message was defined with a !AS in the text of the message. This FAO parameter tells VMS that a string descriptor will be inserted here.

```
cli$get_value(&filespec, &file_value);
lib$sys_getmsg(&msg_sendfile , 0, &file_value , &text_only );
lib$sys_fao( &sendfile_txt, 0, &full_sendfile_txt, &file_value );
printf("   %*.s\n", full_file_value.dsc$w_length,
                              full_file_value.dsc$a_pointer );
```

In this section of code, the user's filename is stored in **file_value.** The message text, with FAO directive is stored in **sendfile_txt.** LIB$SYS_FAO then parses **file_value** into the message text, and copies this new string into **full_sendfile_txt.** This last string can then be printed as before. The output from this example is identical to the output in the first example, but now the internationalization team need only change the message file, not the source code.

Removing Remaining Text Strings

The source code contains four additional text strings that might need translation:

- edit
- filespec
- search_string
- Command

However, only the last string is ever seen by the user, and should thus be translated. In fact, translating the first three strings would break the program, because they provide links between the parameters and qualifiers specified in the .CLD file and the program itself.

To remove Command, add a new message to MESSAGES.MSG:

```
prompt    "Command> "
!   string used as the command prompt
```

This string is retrieved as above.

Another DCL statement is now needed to build the new EXAMPLE.EXE, as shown.

```
$ cc   example
$ set   command commands.cld /obj
$ message messages /obj
$ link   example,commands,sys$input/opt   /notrace
sys$share:vaxcrtl.exe/share^Z
$
```

The program output is the same as before; the only difference is in the internal structure of the program.

4.6.3 Allowing Message File Definition at Run Time

Example 4–4 shows how the program's messages can be changed without changing the source code; however, relinking the program is still required. The original .EXE file can be used if a logical name is used to bind the program to an external shareable image of message text. It is sometimes useful to create a set of detailed messages for new system users and a set of more concise messages for users familiar with the system. Example 4–4 shows the detailed messages.

Example 4–4. LONGMESSAGES.MSG File Contents

```
!+
!   The file contains the message for the "example" program.
!--
.Facility   example,1/prefix=msg_
.Ident   'Version x1.0'
.Severity   informational

prompt   "I await your command> "
!   string used as the command prompt

sendcmd   < I am performing the send command routine !/>
! Output by the send command to show current routine
! The !/ inserts a new line

editpresent   < The Edit qualifier was provided.!/
   Edit does nothing.>

! Output by the send command to indicate that the
! edit qualifier was given on the command line
! you can not split messages across lines

sendfile   < !AS should be sent, but will not be. >
! Output by the send command to show
! the value of the filespec parameter on the command line
! The !AS will be replaced by the actual run-time value.

searchcmd   < I am performing the search command routine !/ >
! Output by the send command to show current routine
! The !/ inserts a new line

searchstring   < I am too tired to look for !AS >
! Output by the search command to show the value of
! the search_string parameter in the command line.
! The !AS will be replaced by the actual run-time value.

.end
```

The additional DCL commands that are required to build the example are:

```
$ cc   example
$ set   command commands.cld /obj
$ message   messages   -
   /file_name=example$msg - ! Logical name to a shareable image
   /object=messages.obj   ! Note that this command is only done once
$ message   messages    /nosymbols /obj=short_msg
$ message   long_messages  /nosymbols /obj=long_msg
$ link/shareable long_msg.obj    ! Link into shareable image
$ link/shareable short_msg.obj    ! Link into shareable image
$ link   example,commands,sys$input/opt    /notrace
sys$share:vaxcrtl.exe/share^Z
$
```

The resulting image contains the program, its command table, and message pointers. However, the message text is external to the program.

Sample Session

EXAMPLE$MSG is the shareable image that contains the message text. Before running the program, you must define the logical name EXAMPLE$MSG to point to the appropriate shareable image of message text. In the sample terminal session that follows, the DCL DEFINE command causes messages from the **long_messages** message file to be selected as the user-visible text.

```
$ define EXAMPLE$MSG example$directory:long_msg
$ run example
I await your command>   search
I am performing the search command routine
I await your command>   search file_name
I am performing the search command routine
I am too tired to look for file_name
I await your command>   send/edit file_name
I am performing the send command routine
The Edit qualifier was provided.
Edit does nothing.
file_name should be sent, but will not be.
I await your command>   exit
$
```

Thus, shareable images that contain message text can be switched by a logical name switch.

4.6.4 Changing the Command Table Definition

The translation team must also modify the commands that activate the program. This requires an added level of indirection in the way the program references the information in the .CLD file. To change the command table definitions:

1. Write a new .CLD file.
2. Add a level of indirection to a specified qualifier.
3. Define a logical name that points to the correct shareable image of message text.
4. Rebuild the program.

Writing a New .CLD File

In Example 4–5, the verbs *search, send,* and *exit* are replaced by *look_for, throw,* and *bye,* respectively. In Example 4–1, *edit* is the qualifier for *send* and is embedded in the code at line 20. To switch the qualifier *edit* to *change,* rewrite the .CLD file and the program, substituting the word *change* where *edit* originally appeared. A means for switching from the qualifier *edit* to *change* without modifying EXAMPLE.C is needed.

Adding a Level of Indirection

Add a level of indirection to a qualifier specified in a .CLD file by using the label = construct. The old .CLD file is:

```
qualifier edit
```

This is now written as:

```
qualifier change, label = edit
```

The program can then search for the qualifier with the label *edit* without worrying about the qualifier's actual name.

Example 4–5 shows the NEW_COMMANDS.CLD file with new logical name definitions.

Example 4–5. NEW_COMMANDS.CLD File Contents

```
!+
!   File: new_commands.cld
!
!   The Command Language Definition file
!-
Module    command_table

   Define      verb   throw    ! replaces send
               routine send_command
               parameter p1, $    filespec
               qualifier change, label = edit

   Define      verb   look_for    ! replaces search
               routine searchcommand
               parameter p1, label = search_string

   Define      verb   bye   ! replaces exit
               routine exit_command
```

The DCL commands needed to rebuild EXAMPLE.EXE are:

```
$ set    command new_commands.cld /obj
$ link   example, new_commands,sys$input/opt   /notrace
sys$share:vaxcrtl.exe/share^Z
$
```

Sample Session

Make sure that you have defined the logical name EXAMPLE$MSG to point to the correct shareable image of message text as in this sample terminal session. Then run the program.

```
$ define EXAMPLE$MSG example$directory:short_msg
$ run example
Command> look_for file_name
search command
search string = file_name
Command> throw /change file_name
send command
/edit is present.
filespec = file_name
Command> bye
$
```

Selecting the Command Table Definition at Run Time

The translation team can select different command line text, but this change requires relinking. A more flexible solution is to allow the user to change a logical name to determine which CLI is used at run time. Switching CLIs by changing a logical name requires a different mechanism.

It is easiest to put all the command tables into the same image. However, the CDU allows no more than one module in a file. Create a separate file for each language.

With all the command tables in the same image, command definition tables can be selected at run time. The first step is to define different module names. In the previous command language definition file in Example 4–2, the same name was overlaid at image activation. The **new_commands.CLD** file must now have its own module name. The line that read:

```
Module   command_table
```

is changed to:

```
Module   new_command_table
```

Now that the two command language definition files have different module names, they can be placed into the same image. Two tables define the verbs and qualifiers, and retain the label = labelname compatibility with the program code. A new logical, EXAMPLE$COMMAND contains the values NEW or OLD to tell the VAXC program which module to use. The program is rewritten with a case statement to choose between the two possible command language definition files. The example has two command language definition files. A case statement can be used for the more general case of multiple command language definition files.

Replacing the code at line number 2 in the original program, EXAMPLE.C in Example 4–1, and for simplicity, ignoring the error-return code, the new code would be:

```
lib$sys_trnlog ( &command_logical, 0, &command_value)

if (strneq("NEW", command_value.dsc$a_pointer,
            command_value.dsc$w_length) )
    result = cli$dcl_parse (0, newcommandtable, lib$get_input,
                    lib$get_input, &prompt);
    else result = cli$dcl_parse (0, commandtable, lib$get_input,
                    lib$get_input, &prompt);
if (result & 1)
    cli$dispatch();
    else break;
```

The DCL commands to build EXAMPLE.EXE are:

```
$ cc   example
$ set   command commands.cld   /obj
$ set   command new_commands.cld /obj
$ link   example, commands, new_commands, sys$input/opt   /notrace
sys$share:vaxcrtl.exe/share^Z
$
```

Typically, the logical name EXAMPLE$COMMAND is first defined to point to the correct message shareable image. EXAMPLE.EXE is then executed.

```
$ define EXAMPLE$COMMAND "NEW"
$ run example
Command> look_for file_name
   search command
   search string = file_name
Command> throw /change file_name
   send command
/edit is present.
filespec = file_name
Command> bye
$
```

Switching Command Table Definitions Without Relinking

Any number of command language definition files can be linked together as long as their names are unique, but the program still has to be relinked.

In the following pages, a set of transfer routines is used to resolve the verb routine address. The steps are as follows:

1. Move the functions into a separate shareable image.
2. Create the shareable image.
3. Add code to resolve the address of the prompt message.
4. Tie together the command language definition file and the code.
5. Activate the command language interface image.

4.6.4.1 Moving the Functions into a Separate Shareable Image

Move the functions into a separate shareable image called FUNCTION.

This step is not required for this example, but is a common engineering practice and makes the example easier to understand. EXAMPLE.C is separated into two parts: EXAMPLE.C and FUNCTION.C. FUNCTION.C contains the **send_command, search_command,** and **exit_command** routines. The message pointer file is also included in the shareable image.

4.6.4.2 Creating the Shareable Image

Creating a shareable image requires using a linker options file and making the routine names universal:

```
!+
!   File:    function.opt
!
!   Linker Options file to create a shareable image
!
function,messages
universal=send_command
universal=search_command
universal=exit_command
universal=msg_prompt
sys$share:vaxcrtl.exe/share
```

The **msg_prompt** routine (from the message file) is made universal because EXAMPLE.EXE must locate the prompt text before it can pass control to the command language interface routines.

The following DCL commands create the shareable image:

```
$ cc function
$ link   function /opt /shareable
```

4.6.4.3 Adding Code to Resolve the Address of Prompt Message

Add the following code to EXAMPLE.C, so that the address of the prompt message can be resolved:

```
lib$find_image_symbol  ( &example_shr_log ,
                                  &msg_prompt_log,
                                  &msg_prompt  );
```

In this example, **example_shr_log** contains the name of the logical pointing towards the shareable image and **msg_prompt_log** contains the name of the logical pointing toward the entry point to the image. The **msg_prompt** routine receives the value of the image symbol so that the shareable image can be called.

4.6.4.4 Tying Together the Command Language Definition File and the Code

The technique for tying the command language definition file to the code is to point the verb addresses in the shareable image containing the command table to a set of transfer routines. The transfer routines resolve the address and transfer control to the proper code in the example. There is one transfer routine for each verb in the command table, and the set of these transfer routines is in a new file, CLI_TRANSFER.C.

In this example, **lib$find_image_symbol** and **lib$callg** locate the address of the proper routine in EXAMPLE$SHR and transfer control to it. An example of the code for the transfer of control by the transfer routine to **send_routine** follows:

```
send_routine()
{
int status = 0;

$DESCRIPTOR(example_shr_log, "EXAMPLE$SHR");
                         /* logical name of the shared image */
$DESCRIPTOR(entry_point, "send_command" );
                         /* from the universal = */
status = lib$find_image_symbol   ( &example_shr_log,
                                   &entry_point,
                                   &sendaddress);
status =  lib$callg( 0, &send_address);
}
```

Similar routines in CLI_TRANSFER.C would be written for search and exit.

An options file is needed to build the CLI shareable image as follows:

```
!   File:   commands.opt
!
commands,cli_transfer
universal=Command_Table
```

The DCL commands needed to build these new pieces are:

```
$ cc cli_transfer
$ set   command   commands.cld    /obj
$ set   command   new_commands.cld /obj
$ link   commands   /shareable /opt
$ link   new_commands /shareable /opt
```

4.6.4.5 Activating the Command Language Interface Image

When EXAMPLE.C starts up, it finds the command table. This example has two CLI shareable images, but there could be several. The following code is added to the EXAMPLE.C program to activate the correct command language interface image based on the logical name EXAMPLE$CLI:

```
$DESCRIPTOR(cli_shr_log, "EXAMPLE$SHR");
                         /* logical name of the correct CLI image */
$DESCRIPTOR(entry_point, "command_table");
                         /* module name in the CLD file */
status = lib$find_image_symbol   ( &cli_shr_log,
                                   &entry_point,
                                   &command_table);
```

The special code for selecting between command language definition files is no longer needed. The selection now takes place outside the EXAMPLE.C program. Control is passed to the command table as originally done in Example 4–1.

Because EXAMPLE.EXE performs delayed image activation of the necessary modules, the DCL commands needed to build EXAMPLE.EXE are now these:

```
$ cc   example
$ link   example,sys$input/opt   /notrace
sys$share:vaxcrtl.exe/share^Z
$
```

In summary, at run time, EXAMPLE.EXE looks at the logical name EXAMPLE$SHR and calls the **lib$find_image_symbol** routine to get the message address for the command prompt(s). The logical name EXAMPLE$MSG provides the connection between the message pointer file in the shareable image and the actual message text to be used.

A call to the **$getmsg** routine results in the prompt text. Then EXAMPLE.EXE looks at the logical name EXAMPLE$CLI and calls the **lib$find_image_symbol** routine to get the address for the command table module. The transfer functions inside COMMANDS.EXE provide the interface between the functions in EXAMPLE$SHR and the CLI shareable image. These functions are the same whenever a new image is built. EXAMPLE.EXE uses the command language routines, **cli$dcl_parse** and **cli$dispatch** to perform the command line prompt and execute loop. The output of the new program would be:

```
$ define EXAMPLE$COMMAND "OLD"
$ define EXAMPLE$SHR example$directory:function
$ define EXAMPLE$MSG example$directory:short_msg
$ run example
Command> search file_name
   search command
   search string = file_name
Command> send /edit file_name
   send command
   /edit is present.
   filespec = file_name
Command> Exit
$
```

4.6.5 Selecting Command Tables During Execution

Multiple command tables and multiple language message files can be built to allow switching while the image executes, but this makes the program significantly more complex.

Changing the logical name EXAMPLE$CLI and putting a check in the **dcl$parse** loop causes problems because

- The **lib$find_image_symbol** routine knows when the logical has been processed before and therefore has already mapped the image.
- Using a logical name means that the logical name cannot be translated and the **file_name** passed to **lib$find_image_symbol.**

However, it is possible to use a technique that has two levels of logical name translation, so that one logical name in the program actually maps to more than one name for **lib$find_image_symbol.** The **lib$find_image_symbol** routine can then switch between alternate command interfaces or message files, because it is given different logical names for each instance. For example:

1. Define two CLI logical names to point to the two command files.
2. Define a new, second-level logical to point to one of them:

```
$ define EXAMPLE$CLI1    example$dir:commands
$ define EXAMPLE$CLI2    example$dir:new_commands
$ define EXAMPLE$CLI    EXAMPLE$CLI1
```

EXAMPLE.C now contains the following code:

```
$DESCRIPTOR(cli_shr_log, "EXAMPLE$SHR");
                   /* logical name of the correct CLI image */
$DYNAMIC(cli_true_log);
                   /* receives the true logical name after running
                    cli_shr_log through sys_trn_log(). */
$DESCRIPTOR(entry_point, "command_table");
                   /* module name in the CLD file */
lib$sys_trnlog (&cli_shr_log, 0, &cli_true_log);

status = lib$find_image_symbol    ( &cli_true_log,
                                    &entry_point,
                                    &command_table);

for (;;)           /*** loop until user types EXIT */
    {
    if (!(cli$dcl_parse (0, commandtable, lib$get_input,
                    lib$get_input, &prompt) & 1) )
        break;      /*** dcl_parse failed, so quit */
        else
          cli$dispatch();      /*** do another command */
    }
```

In that code, a logical name translation function retrieves the address that the **lib$find_image_symbol** routine uses to locate the command table. To simplify this example, a new command which explicitly asks to change command tables is not added. Instead, to demonstrate that the switch occurs during execution, the **send_command** used in FUNCTION.C to change the logical EXAMPLE$CLI to the value specified on the command line is modified. The following code is added to **send_command**:

```
lib$setlogical ( &cli_shr_log, &filespec);
```

The output of the final version of the example follows:

```
$ define EXAMPLE$CLI1    example$dir:commands
$ define EXAMPLE$CLI2    example$dir:new_commands
$ define EXAMPLE$CLI    EXAMPLE$CLI1
$ define EXAMPLE$SHR    example$directory:function
$ define EXAMPLE$MSG    example$directory:short_msg
$
$ run example
Command> search filename
search command
search string = FILENAME
Command> send /edit example$cli2
send command
/edit is present.
filespec = EXAMPLE$CLI2
Command> look_for filename
search command
search string = FILENAME
Command> bye
$
```

Chapter 5

Designing Multilingual Software

A multilingual software product allows users to interact with the product using more than one language. The language options of multilingual software can be bundled into the product, or made available by order, to be installed separately at a later time. Multilingual software allows two users of the same software on the same system to use different user interfaces for that software.

Software designers must solve three primary problems when implementing multilingual software products:

- How can the components of the product be distributed on the system to facilitate switching?
- How can the switching of user interface components be implemented?
- How should the switching of culture-specific software function be implemented?

5.1 Multilingual Software

The software product model shown in Figure 5–1 expands on the international product model described in Chapter 2 and introduces a new concept: software that supports more than one locale, or multilingual software.

Figure 5–1. Multilingual Software Model

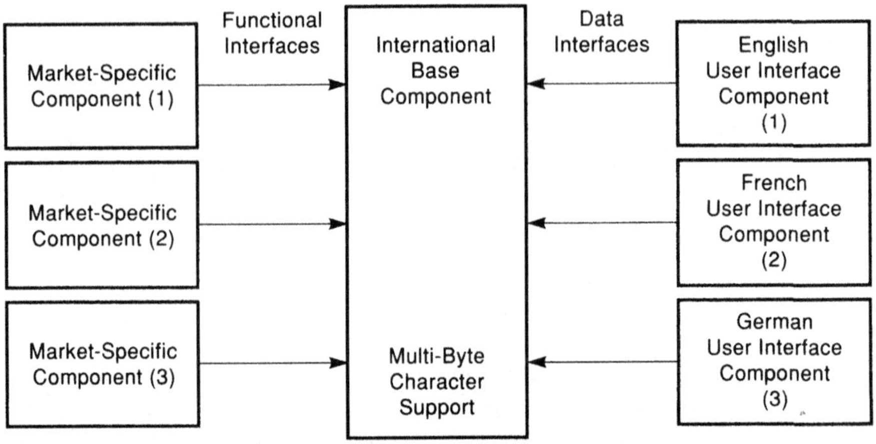

In the model shown in Figure 5–1, the software supports multilingual user interfaces supplied using multiple user interface components, and multilingual functionality supplied by three market-specific components. In this example, the software allows users to switch between English, French, and German user interface components.

A French language product variant could consist of the components shown in Figure 5–2.

Figure 5–2. French Product Variant

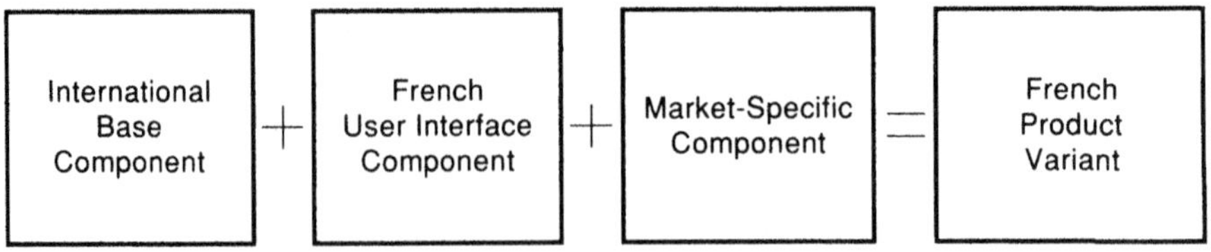

A multilingual product featuring functionality for English and German markets could consist of the components shown in Figure 5–3.

Figure 5–3. English/German Product Variant

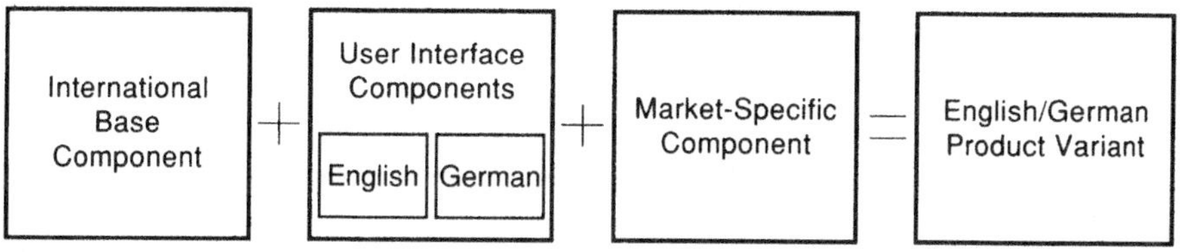

A customer can obtain a multilingual software product by adding a user interface component and optional market-specific components to an already installed product. With the addition of each user interface or market-specific component, new options are added to the product. This approach to assembling multilingual software products carries with it design ramifications, particularly for products that must support multiple dialects of the same language.

It is possible to support a dialect of a language by installing the user interface component for the primary version of that language, for example, French, and then installing a market-specific component that tailors that user interface component to suit the dialect, for example, Canadian French. The installation path for assembling such a product is shown in Figure 5–4.

Figure 5–4. Installation Path for a Product Variant

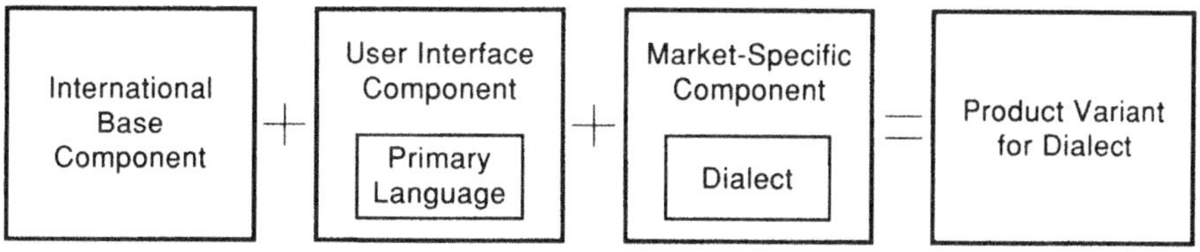

Using the market-specific component to modify the user interface component in this way means that the product can support only one dialect at a time. For example, the product created in the above example cannot support both a French interface and a Canadian

French interface because the first is lost when the second is created. To support the multilingual goal, each user interface component should provide all of the culture-specific data necessary to create a unique user interface component for one language or dialect. If each dialect is supported by its own user interface component, the installation path for a multidialect product looks like the one in Figure 5–5.

Figure 5–5. Installation Path for a Multidialect Product

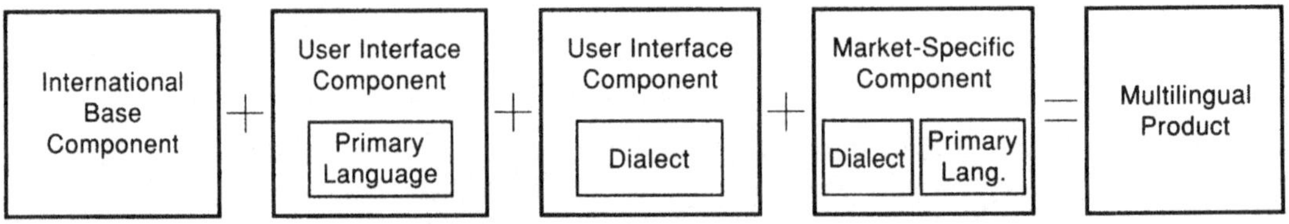

5.2 Multilingual Products Versus Localizable Products

Multilingual software products differ from localizable products in two principal ways:

- Multilingual user interfaces

  Users can interact with the software in more than one language and can switch from one language interface to another while using the product. Two users on the same system are able to work with the same application functionality simultaneously, but use two different language interfaces to that functionality. By contrast, localized software products support a single language that must be used by everyone.

- Multilingual functionality

  Users can access functionality that supports the requirements of more than one language or locale. Multilingual functionality products allow users to edit text and data, use linguistic aids, such as spelling and hyphenation checkers in multiple languages. Because it allows multiple collating sequences, users can store and retrieve text in several languages. Users may perform any of these tasks in any of the languages supported by the product, regardless of the interface they selected.

Multilingual functionality also allows users to quickly switch between languages during an editing session. Languages such as Hebrew and English, or Japanese and English, are often linked because of market demands. A multilingual product lets a user press a shift key to toggle between languages and the corresponding language environment, including character set, collating sequences, spelling and hyphenation checkers, font type, as well as writing direction. Users of localized products are limited to the language of the interface and cannot switch languages in a single session.

5.3 Planning Multilingual Applications

Applications can provide several kinds of multilingual support:

- Concurrent multilingual usage on a system
- Concurrent multilingual usage within the same application
- Concurrent multilingual usage on an integrated, internationally distributed network

5.3.1 Concurrent Multilingual Usage on a System

All software products to be adapted for several locales should be designed for concurrent usage in different languages on the same system. In the past, Digital customer systems have frequently been single CPUs. Today they are more likely to be part of an extended system such as a VMS cluster or a Local Area Network (LAN).

Figure 5–6 illustrates a central host supporting a software product that supplies concurrent multilingual user interfaces. In this scenario, a user at Terminal 1 specifies the French user interface. At Terminal 2, the user selects the Italian interface. The application uses French culture-specific data to handle interaction with the user at Terminal 1, and Italian culture-specific data to handle interaction with the user at Terminal 2. The application would use German culture-specific data to serve a user at Terminal 3, and English culture-specific data for a user at Terminal 4. All four persons use the application concurrently and each gets a different locale-specific view of the same data.

Figure 5–6. Central Host, Concurrent Multilingual User Interfaces

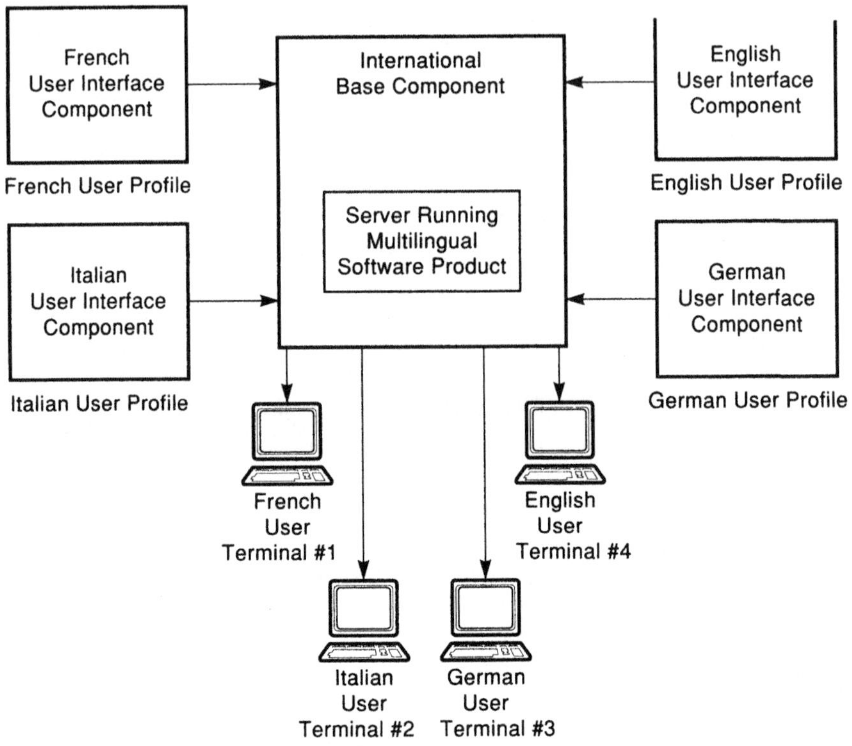

With the type of multilingual product shown in Figure 5–6, the user can change the interface only when the software is activated. The user is given a choice to override the current default language display. For example:

```
SYSTEM PROMPT> MY_PRODUCT/LANGUAGE=SVENSK
```

After this command is entered, the Swedish user interface supersedes the previous default. It is important that the default be definable to a language other than English.

A method for dynamic switching of the user interface could also be available after the software is activated. For example, a software product could have two subsystems to maintain user accounts. The first subsystem allows the user to perform limited, nontechnical changes to the user profile, such as changing their phone number. The second subsystem allows a privileged user to modify another user's system privileges. Because this second subsystem is a function typically intended for a system manager, it may not need to be translated from English.

5.3.2 Concurrent Multilingual Usage Within the Same Application

Concurrent multilingual operation within an application is a requirement for many products. In such products, the user must be able to switch language functionality and in some instances switch user interfaces while using the product.

The user must be able to switch language-specific functionality without also switching user interface, and vice versa. An example of such a product might be an editing station for language translators, allowing side-by-side editing of two language versions of the same text.

Concurrent multilingual operation is not a generic requirement for all international software products. However, the ability to switch easily by pressing a function key, for example, between language-specific functionalities is useful with frequently intermixed languages. Figure 5–7 illustrates the "multilingual within application" case.

At startup time, the user profile specifies a French user interface and French linguistic aids. At a later time, the user explicitly changes the linguistic aids attribute to English, thus selecting English functionality. Note that, while the market-specific component (with the linguistic aids attribute) has changed to English, the user interface component has remained in French. In this case, the two aspects of multilingual software (multilingual user interfaces and multilingual functionality) can be switched independently of one another.

Figure 5–7. Multilingual Functionality Within an Application

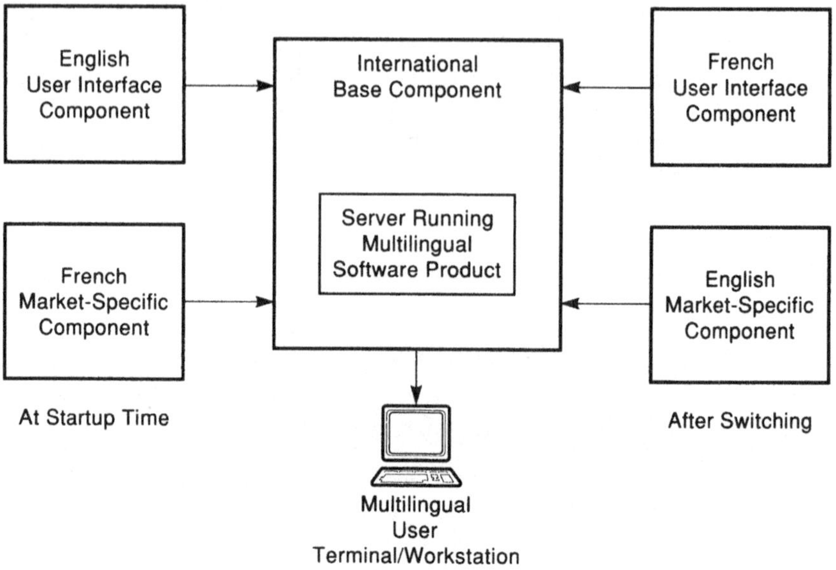

A product may require that the language-specific functions or procedures be switched within the same program. For example:

- Using a grammar checker for one language while editing in another language

  The user may be editing or creating a document in one language and wish to verify the spelling in another.

- Language switching during data entry

  A more complex problem arises if you are typing a mail message in Hebrew, where data is entered from right to left, and in that message you need to enter "Digital Equipment Corporation in 1990," which must be entered from left to right. Both the writing direction and character set must be changed, and then changed back after the English language string is entered.

Both of these situations require that user-defined function keys be made available, to either perform the language switch or to prompt the user to select a language.

5.3.3 Concurrent Multilingual Usage on an Integrated, Internationally Distributed Network

A multilingual, integrated, internationally distributed application is illustrated in Figure 5–8.

Figure 5–8. Multilingual, Integrated, Internationally Distributed Application

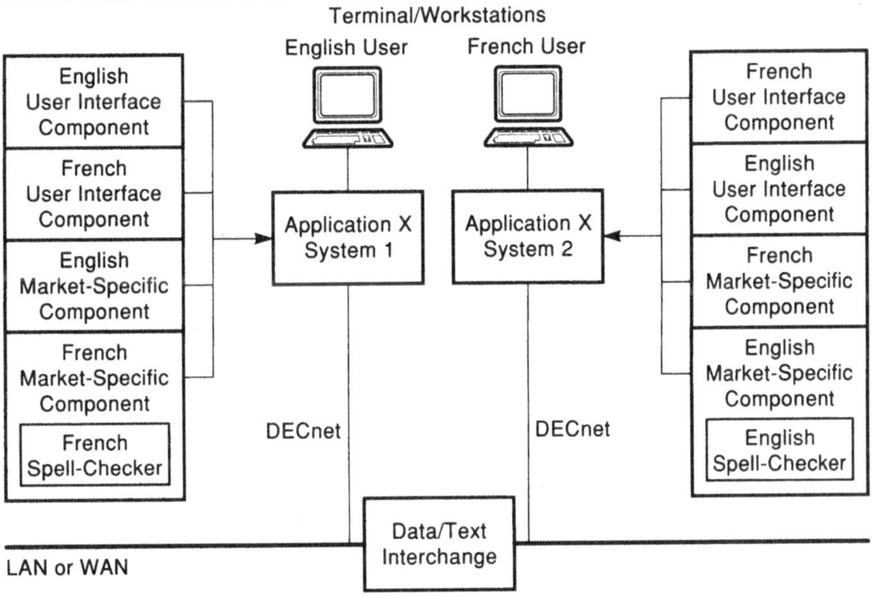

An English user running Application X on System 1 prepares a French message using an English user interface to the mail editor, but doing spell-checking with a French dictionary. The French spell-checker is provided by the French market-specific component.

The English user then sends the message to a French user who is running Application X on System 2 somewhere on the network. The French user, using a French user interface, reads the message, prints it for reading again later, prepares a reply in English using an English spell-checker, and sends it to the English user on System 1 who reads and prints it. The English spell-checker is supplied by the English market-specific component.

5.3.4 Communication Between Multilingual Applications

Applications are seldom written to operate in isolation. Increasingly, an application must be capable of linking and exchanging data with other applications to fulfill tasks for the user. A notable example is a text processing application that lets the user link with spreadsheet and graphics applications for data to be included as images in a document. In many cases, the data passed to the calling application must be stored and manipulated by the calling application as well.

Interapplication communication becomes somewhat more complex in a multilingual environment, where different applications can use different character sets, writing directions, collating sequences, and so on. In this context, using standard mechanisms for exchanging multilingual data between applications becomes extremely important. To that end, Digital has invested considerable effort in developing Digital Document Interchange Format (DDIF), Digital Table Interchange Format (DTIF), and compound strings (see Chapter 6) to facilitate the exchange of multilingual data.

Applications must ensure that the text passed to other applications contains information that the receiving application can use to derive context, such as character set and writing direction, as well as content. Applications must be capable of passing and receiving text in mixed character sets, including single-byte and multi-byte sets, and mixed writing directions.

To address these issues, developers at Digital design an application's interfaces to other applications in ways that anticipate multilingual data: applications for Digital platforms can exchange data in the form of compound strings or DDIF or DTIF definitions. Applications that do so are capable of supporting character sets and writing directions other than those supported by ISO Latin-1. If your applications do not exchange data in this way, then any attempts to provide multilingual language support in one application will have a serious impact on all other applications that use that application's resources. The impact could be so great that it precludes the addition of multilingual functionality.

5.4 Designing Multilingual Software Products

Meeting the multilingual requirement is largely a matter of following the guidelines presented in Chapter 4 with special attention to the following details.

- The user interfaces should be switchable at run time using techniques recommended later in this chapter.
- Internal data/text encodings must be locale- and language-neutral. That is, data in databases must be stored in flexible culture- or language-independent formats. The application must be able to transform or translate the data into locale-specific user interface views using language- and locale-sensitive formats at run time under user interface control. For more information, see Section 5.4.1.
- The body of text interchanges should use DDIF, DTIF, and/or compound strings to identify the appropriate character set or other content protocol language to the level of a single word and font. This level of precision is needed in switching dictionaries and algorithms for linguistic aids. For more information, see Section 5.4.1.
- Interchange formats of data and text should *not* contain language or locale-specific data in their structural and attribute encodings. For example, in a mail message TO:, FROM:, DATE:, TIME: should not appear as text but as internal codes, that is, as fields of the header record or typed objects in compound string encodings. Values for the date and time fields should be unformatted, following an external standard where appropriate.
- Error conditions reported network-wide should be locale-neutral, registered and uniquely identified error codes. They should be interpreted or translated by the user interface to the user-viewable forms. Advanced multilingual message facilities and translated technical term dictionaries will eventually be developed in support of better international messages.
- Times used for time-stamping of events should be accurate network-wide, for proper sequencing of time-dependent processing steps.

5.4.1 Storing Data for Use by Multilingual Applications

Multilingual applications must apply locale-specific conventions and language to data extracted from a database. For example, an application that presents a numeric value to a German user should use German conventions for the display of numeric values; the value should be expressed using a period as the thousands separator and a comma as the decimal separator:

```
12.998,00
```

An American view of the same numeric value should use American conventions:

```
12,998.00
```

Thus, the data must be stored in locale-neutral formats and transformed for locale-specific displays at run time. Data such as date and time values, currency values, and keywords displayed by the application should be modifiable for display as described in Chapter 4.

Special requirements apply to pure text stored in databases used by multilingual applications. In order for free-format text to be displayable, it should be stored with display instructions, that is, with specifications for the character set and writing direction needed to display the text. Compound strings (introduced in Chapter 6) are designed to provide this type of support.

5.4.2 Sorting Data Used by Multilingual Applications

Multilingual applications must be able to use multiple, locale-specific collating sequences to sort data stored in a database. A Spanish user will expect data to be sorted using the Spanish collating sequence, while a Dutch user will expect a Dutch sort of the same data.

Databases therefore must supply keyed access to files and allow the applications to apply collating sequences to the data when it is displayed. Techniques and tools that applications can use to actually sort the data are presented in Chapters 6, 7, and 8.

Chapter 6

Using the DECwindows Interface

Based on the X Window System architecture developed at the Massachusetts Institute of Technology, Digital's DECwindows software is an interface to the VMS or ULTRIX operating system. The DECwindows interface lets users divide a workstation screen into windows and design a working environment to suit specific needs. Users execute commands by selecting objects on the screen instead of typing long command lines. With DECwindows, users can run two applications simultaneously on a single physical screen and the user can switch between them using a mouse. Because DECwindows software provides an environment in which all applications have similar features, a user can use the same handful of techniques to interact with each application, avoiding the need to master several command languages.

The following features of the DECwindows interface aid localization:

- Separation of user interface form from application function
- Object-oriented, rather than language-based, interactions with the user
- User interface *widgets* that accommodate the text expansion or reduction that results from translation
- Application and library use of user interface definition (UID) files, X Resource Manager (XRM) files, and the DECwindows Help Facility
- Support for international text processing:
    - Full ISO Latin-1 font and character set support
    - Support for compound strings
- Support for local devices:
    - Startup procedure set-up of LK201 keyboard variants
    - Xlib support for Compose key and other international keyboard features

— User Interface Language (UIL) support for redefinable key bindings

6.1 International DECwindows User Interfaces

The DECwindows toolkit includes two integrated application development tools used to define the DECwindows user interface:

- User Interface Language (UIL)
- DECwindows Resource Manager (DRM)

The UIL and DRM tools allow engineering groups in various countries to replace a DECwindows interface with a translated interface without having to recompile the application program. User interfaces can be created in several languages without making any changes to the application itself.

In addition, the DECwindows user interface can use compound strings to store text and data. A compound string enables applications to specify attributes in text, graphics, images, or data. Compound strings make it possible for text in a DECwindows user interface to be translated into any language for which a DECwindows-supported font is available.

6.1.1 Object-Oriented User Interfaces

The DECwindows interface allows users to control the application by manipulating or selecting screen objects with the mouse rather than by entering text commands. To select a menu option, for example, the user points to the option with the cursor, and presses a mouse button to execute the selection.

Figures 6–1 and 6–2 show two versions of the same DECwindows dialog box, the first version in English, the second version in Japanese. The application function associated with this dialog box receives input from the user in the form of callbacks from the objects the user selects with the mouse.

Figure 6–1. Dialog Box in English

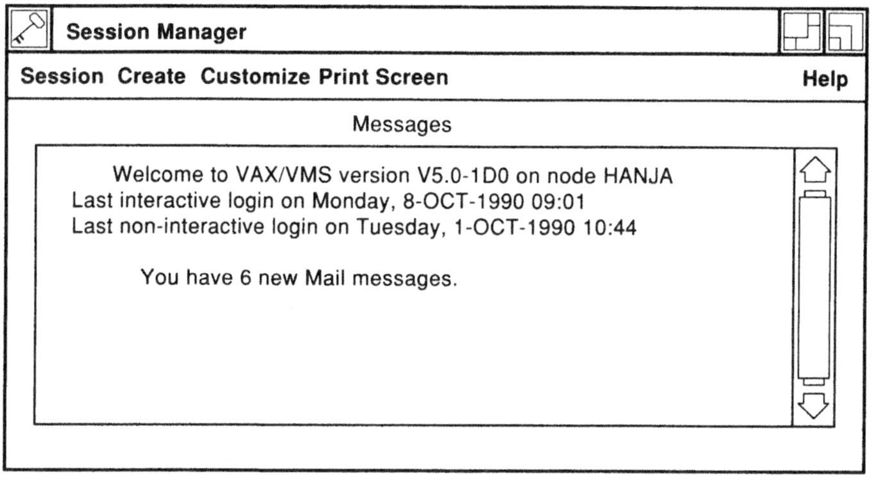

Figure 6–2. Dialog Box in Japanese

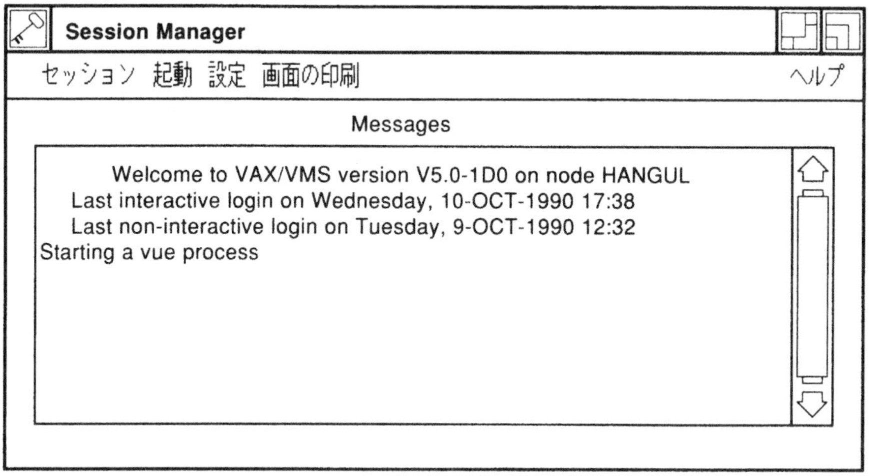

Using UIL, application designers can build menus, dialog boxes, and other user interface objects labeled with translatable text. While applications still must be able to present user interfaces in other natural languages, they do not necessarily need to interpret user input in different languages.

6.1.2 User Interface Language

The user interface language is the specification language used to describe the initial state of a user interface for a DECwindows application. UIL specifies the objects used in the interface, and the routines to be called when the interface changes state as a result of user input. The objects specified are typically these:

- Menus
- Dialog boxes
- Labels
- Push buttons

The UIL module containing this information is stored in a UIL specification file. The UIL compiler translates the UIL module into a User Interface Description (UID) file. An application uses DECwindows Resource Manager (DRM) routine calls to gain access to the UID file. When the application is executed, DRM builds the run-time structures necessary to create the user interface.

The implementation of UIL and DRM offers many benefits to international product developers. It facilitates the separation of form and function, which is one of the principal requirements of international software products. Since the UIL specifications exist as a separate file, changes in a product's user interface require few, if any, changes to the application program.

Used correctly, UIL and DRM make it possible to create user interfaces that are easily translated into other languages. Used incorrectly, UIL specification files can cause problems for translators and engineers in other countries for the following reasons:

- UIL does not prohibit placing user interface text in program source files. If translators must search through program source files to locate the text to be translated, localization becomes more difficult and time-consuming, and errors may be introduced.

- UIL specifications that control the size and position of an interface object can appear anywhere in the UIL file. These specifications often must be changed after translation. If translators must search through UIL files to locate and change specific coordinates, translation becomes more difficult and time consuming, and errors may be introduced.
- UIL is much like a programming language. It may or may not be easily understood by a translator.

The translated UID file is generally supplied in the user interface component of Digital's international product model. When country-specific data such as a currency symbol is used in an application, this data must be supplied in the market-specific component. To allow for this, two UID hierarchies have to be built into the application. The first hierarchy contains all the language-specific data; the second, all the country-specific data. Thus, all country-specific information should be contained in a UID file separate from that of the language-specific data.

Guidelines

To simplify the localization process for UIL files, Digital observes the following guidelines:

- Keep the application programs free of text.

  DECwindows interface software and applications allow programmers to include translatable text and messages in the source code of the application rather than in UIL specification files. This must be avoided. Place all translatable text in a single UIL specification file. This isolates user interface text and eliminates the need to relink the user interface to the application object files after translation. This modular approach facilitates future upgrades and revisions.
- Declare all translatable text as constants.

  The following items should be declared as constants if they are modifiable:

  — Natural language text used in prompts and messages:

```
value
   ReallyQuitText : exported 'Do you really want to quit?';
```

  In this example, text used to prompt the user is associated with a constant, and then the constant is used throughout the UIL file in place of the text. The translator has to translate this prompt only once, in the constant declaration. Also, do not use the same text string in several different contexts.

Translatable text can be declared as a constant in string tables:

```
value
   string1 : 'Print';
   string2 : 'File';

   strings : exported string_table(string1,string2);
```

In this case, the global value "strings" is read by the application program.

— Menu items:

```
list
   ItemsOfChoice : arguments {
      FileLabel = 'File';
      ReadLabel = 'Read';
      PrintLabel = 'Print';
             .
             .
             .
                 };
```

— Language-dependent keywords, which are often time-related, such as the names of months and days:

```
Monday_label    = 'Monday';
Tuesday_label   = 'Tuesday';
Wednesday_label = 'Wednesday';
Thursday_label  = 'Thursday';
Friday_label    = 'Friday';
```

— Strings used for validating user input:

```
list
   ValidAbbreviations: arguments {
      YesAbbr = 'Y';
      NoAbbr = 'N';
                 };
```

- Declare widget coordinates and sizes as constants.

  The following items must be declared as constants if they are modifiable:

  — Widget coordinates

    Interface widgets can be positioned using either explicit coordinates or relative coordinates (using attached dialog boxes as described in Section 6.1.3.2).

When using explicit coordinates, declare them as constants:

```
value
   !+
   !  This position (in pixels) is for the second button column
   !  in the radio box.
   !
   !  The position is affected by the text for the first column.
   !  It affects the right border of the radio box.
   !-
   Col2RadioBoxButtonPosX : 500;
```

In this example, the constant has been given a meaningful name; comments tell the translator how changing its position might affect the position of other widgets in the user interface.

— Widget sizes

The space required to display text often changes as a result of translation. Widget sizes, therefore, should be easily modifiable. Declare widget sizes as constants:

```
value
   !+
   ! This dimension (in pixels) represents the cancel button
   ! in the radio box.
   !  It is affected by the Okay button position
   !  It affects the Apply button position
   !-
   CancelButtonRadioBoxXsize : 40;
   CancelButtonRadioBoxYsize : 30;
```

In this example, the constants for the sizes have been given meaningful names; comments tell the translator how changing this widget size could affect other widgets in the user interface.

- Use font units to allow positioning in a coordinate system that is not pixel-based, but is sensitive to the font being used.
- Address constant values by meaningful names.

  Constants should be assigned names that indicate how they are used in the user interface:

```
!+
!  The items to be listed in the list box DisplayListBox
!_
       DisplayListBoxItem1 :
                             'First item';
       DisplayListBoxItem2 :
                             'Second item';
       DisplayListBoxItem3 :
                             'Third item';
       DisplayListBoxItem4 :
                             'Fourth item';
```

- Group the related constants.

  Constant declarations that logically belong together should be placed together in a UIL file. For example, group the constant declarations for the labels of a particular widget:

```
value
    a_box_label:
        'a_label';

    a_box_item_1:
        'first item';

    a_box_item_2:
        'second item';
               ;
```

  Also group the size and position specifications for the widget:

```
value
    a_box_x:
         50;

    a_box_y:
         250;

    a_box_height:
         500;

    a_box_width:
         400;
          .
          .
          .
```

- Never compose messages from parts.

  Messages that are assembled from two or more text strings often cause problems for translators. In the following example, four constants are used to construct a two-word message.

```
k_dis_text:       compound_string("Dis");
k_allow_text:     compound_string("allow");
k_space_char:     compound_string(" ");
k_hyphenation_text: compound_string("hyphenation");
k_stop_hyphen_message: k_dis_text & k_allow_text & k_space_char & k_hyphenation_text;
```

  The constant k_stop_hyphen_message contains the value "Disallow hyphenation" as its final text string, but, as constructed, the string is not translatable. Different syntaxes in different languages prohibit a straight translation of the text. Instead, the message will have to be restructured.

- Make full use of the option menu to accommodate syntax changes.

  When translation forces syntax changes, the option menu label and any associated text can be changed to a null string (""), and the option menu item and size can be changed to become the complete translated message. Consider the following example:

Option menu widget:	[Do this to]
Option required:	[THAT]

  These items are displayed in the original syntax as follows:

  [Do this to [THAT]]

  Translation requires the following syntax change:

  [This to [THAT] do]

  To achieve this, the option menu label should be changed from ([Do this to]) to a null string ("") and the option item should be changed from [THAT], to the complete string [This to THAT do].

- Do not use the same text string in several different contexts.

  To display the same text string in many contexts, use a separate constant for each context. In languages other than English, context can influence the spelling and syntax of a message.

  The obvious exceptions are common labels such as "help," "ok," "yes," and so on, which are used frequently and by different applications. They should be defined in a common include file that is inherited by all applications.

- Place your constant declarations in a separate file and include that file in your main UIL module.

  Your main UIL module should consist of the widget structure only. Translatable elements such as text, coordinates, and sizes, should be supplied in separate modules that are included in the main module.

  When constants are declared in a separate file, translators can easily locate the user interface text that must be translated. This supports translation both in the initial localization of your product and in any subsequent releases.

  Section 6.6 presents three examples of UIL files used to declare constants. These files are included and used by the UIL main module presented in Example 6–7, in Section 6.6.

- To assist the translator, include meaningful translation markup.

  UIL specification files are not translator-friendly. It is therefore essential to provide comments, or markup, to identify and explain translatable and customizable elements for the translator. Markup is particularly important if the meaning of messages and other text is not obvious. Use comments in UIL files to indicate

  — Values that will need to be translated or changed during localization

  — The context in which an error message is displayed

  — Any restrictions on the size or position of a text string

  See Section 10.1 for more information about translation markup.

6.1.3 DECwindows Toolkit Widgets

When used correctly, DECwindows Toolkit Widgets provide international product developers with several advantages:

- A help subsystem that supports international requirements

  The DECwindows Help Widget supplies a context-sensitive help facility that maintains application help text in a translatable form. The Help Widget is supported on both VMS and ULTRIX operating systems.

- Messages that support international requirements

  DECwindows makes it possible to store application message text in the UIL specification files used to define the application user interface. Message text is thus separated from application code, which simplifies translation. UIL also supports storing messages as compound strings.

- Ways to do relative, rather than fixed, positioning of labels and fields

  DECwindows provides ways to position user interface objects. The Attached Dialog Box widget offers a way to simplify the localization of DECwindows user interface layout.

The UIL guidelines presented in Section 6.1.2 describe how to make the text displayed by the application translatable. If the application uses DECwindows Toolkit Widgets, the text used by those widgets must also be made translatable.

6.1.3.1 Making DECwindows Toolkit Widgets Translatable

If the application uses DECwindows Toolkit Widgets such as the Help Widget, the File Selection Widget, the Caution Box Widget, or others, declare the label text used by the widgets as constants and define the constants in separate, includable UIL files.

Every widget label used by a DECwindows Toolkit Widget has a unique resource associated with it. The default English value for the resources can be overridden in the applications' UIL file. The resources that are associated with translatable text strings are easy to recognize because their names end with *label* and their type is *compound_string.*

To make a Toolkit Widget translatable, create a UIL file that contains an argument list for each widget that contains a translatable string. Include the UIL file in the application's main UIL file. Use the argument list name in each Toolkit Widget that will require translation in the application's UIL file.

Example 6–1 shows a template that can be used to create a translatable DECwindows File Selection Widget. Example 6–2 shows the UIL file that declares as constants the text used in the File Selection Widget.

Example 6–1. A Translatable DECwindows File Selection Widget

```
!=====================================================================
!+
!  This file contains object declarations for the DECwindows File
!  Selection Widget, FileSelectionBox.  The object used in the
!  application should be taken from this file and 'pasted' into
!  the applications UIL file, changing the object name for that
!  of the applications object name.
!
!  In the object declarations, anything starting with "Your"
!  should be changed to the value used by the application UIL.
!-
!+++
!       File Selection
!---
object
      YourFileSelection : file_selection
      {
       arguments
                 {
```

(Example 6–1 continues on next page)

Example 6–1 (Cont.). A Translatable DECwindows File Selection Widget

```
!+
! These are the translatable arguments
!-
                apply_label     = FileSelectionApplyLabel;
                cancel_label    = FileSelectionCancelLabel;
                filter_label    = FileSelectionFilterLabel;
                object_label    = FileSelectionObjectLabel;
                ok_label        = FileSelectionOKLabel;
                selection_label = FileSelectionSelectionLabel;
                title           = FileSelectionTitle;
!+
! These arguments can be cut out if not defined by the application,
! otherwise, the appropriate value name should be added.
!-
                accelerators         = ;
                background_color     = ;
                background_pixmap    = ;
                border_color         = ;
                border_pixmap        = ;
                border_width         = ;
                default_position     = ;
                dir_mask             = ;
                file_search_proc     = ;
                file_selection_value = ;
                font_argument        = ;
                items                = ;
                list_updated         = ;
                mapped_when_managed  = ;
                margin_height        = ;
                margin_width         = ;
                must_match           = ;
                no_resize            = ;
                resize               = ;
                sensitive            = ;
                style                = ;
                take_focus           = ;
                text_cols            = ;
                translations         = ;
                user_data            = ;
                visible_items_count  = ;
                x                    = ;
                y                    = ;
                height               = ;
                width                = ;

              };
```

(Example 6–1 continues on next page)

Example 6–1 (Cont.). A Translatable DECwindows File Selection Widget

```
!+
! paste your callbacks list in here
!-
      callbacks
              {
              };
!+
! paste your controls list in here
!-
      controls
              {
              };
     };
```

Example 6–2. Declaration of Constants for the File Selection Widget

```
!===================================================================
!+
!
!  Title:
!        FILESELECTION_XLAT_TEXT.UIL
!
! Description:
!
!  This file contains the text strings of the DECwindows File
!  Selection Widget, FileSelectionBox, for translation purposes.
!  It should be included in the application program's main UIL file
!  BEFORE any widget declarations.
!
!  Note: the character sequences %s and \n are special character
!        sequences and therefore should be left alone.
!
! Usage:
!        include file 'fileselection_xlat_text.uil';
!
!-
 value
```

(Example 6–2 continues on next page)

Example 6–2 (Cont.). Declaration of Constants for the File Selection Widget

```
!+++
!       File Selection
!---
!
!+
!  The apply button
!-
    FileSelectionApplyLabel      : compound_string
                                   ("Apply");
!+
!  The cancel button
!-
    FileSelectionCancelLabel     : compound_string
                                   ("Cancel");
!+
! The filter label
!-
    FileSelectionFilterLabel     : compound_string
                                   ("File filter");
!+
!  The object label
!-
    FileSelectionLabel           : compound_string
                                   ("Files in");
!+
!  The okay button
!-
    FileSelectionOKLabel         : compound_string
                                   ("Ok");
!+
!  The selection label
!-
    FileSelectionSelectionLabel : compound_string
                                   ("Selection");

!+
!  The title
!-
    FileSelectionTitle           : compound_string
                                   ("Open");

!+++
!   End of FILESELECTION_XLAT_TEXT.UIL include file
!---
```

6.1.3.2 Positioning Objects with DECwindows Widgets

The Attached Dialog Box Widget is a very useful tool to help reduce the work entailed in the translation process. It offers a way to accommodate translated text in user interface objects: when text lengthens due to translation, the widget positions user interface objects relative to one another. With the Attached Dialog Box Widget, developers can relate the size and position of an object to the size of the text presented within the object. The widget allows the omission of origin, width, and height coordinate specifications, in favor of relationships among the objects within the box. DECwindows software automatically manages the positioning of the object and compensates for the text expansion or compression that results when text is translated.

Use an Attached Dialog Box Widget to position and size the objects within a dialog box relative to the size and position of the dialog box itself. The widget automatically adjusts the size of the dialog box if the text labels, fields, or other objects change size after translation.

6.1.3.3 Using Icons

DECwindows supports the use of *icons* in many of the objects specified through the UIL. If designed and used with care, icons can be very effective in international products because they may not need to be changed for different international markets.

6.2 International Application Resource Databases

Application resource databases provide default values that define the basic attributes of an application user interface such as origin, height, width, background color, foreground color, and font. These values are stored in a customizable file and form a type of application profile for the software product.

Never store user interface text in an application resource database. Instead, use language-neutral values to set application defaults, and, if necessary, translate those values into user displays in UIL.

Example 6–3 provides an example of a bad application resource database, that is, a database that specifies user interface text. Example 6–4 corrects the problem by replacing the text with values that are not specific to a particular language. The application user interface can refer to these values and translate them into locale-specific user interface text at run time.

Example 6–3. A Bad Application Resource Database

```
appname.x:                                               300
appname.y:                                               200
appname.width:                                           190
appname.height:                                          240
appname*foreground:                                      Turquoise
appname*background:                                      DarkSlateGrey
appname*sqrtFontFamily:    *-*-Symbol-*-R-*-_-14-*-*-*-P-*-*-*
appname*keyFontFamily:     *-*-Times-Bold-R-Normal-_-14-*-*-*-P-*-*-*
! Define calendar order for days of the week:
appname*firstday:                                         "Sunday"
appname*secondday:                                        "Monday"
appname*thirdday:                                         "Tuesday"
appname*fourthday:                                        "Wednesday"
appname*fifthday:                                         "Thursday"
appname*sixthday:                                         "Friday"
appname*seventhday:                                       "Saturday"
```

Example 6–4. A Corrected Application Resource Database

```
appname.x:                                               300
appname.y:                                               200
appname.width:                                           190
appname.height:                                          240
appname*foreground:                                      Turquoise
appname*background:                                      DarkSlateGrey
appname*sqrtFontFamily:    *-*-Symbol-*-R-*-_-14-*-*-*-P-*-*-*
appname*keyFontFamily:     *-*-Times-Bold-R-Normal-_-14-*-*-*-P-*-*-*
!
! Define calendar order for days of the week. Identify days by number:
!
!      0 = Sunday             4 = Thursday
!      1 = Monday             5 = Friday
!      2 = Tuesday            6 = Saturday
!      3 = Wednesday
!
appname*firstday:                                         6
appname*secondday:                                        0
appname*thirdday:                                         1
appname*fourthday:                                        2
appname*fifthday:                                         3
appname*sixthday:                                         4
appname*seventhday:                                       5
```

In general, applications that allow users to modify defaults should provide a means of doing so in the application user interface, through a set-up menu, for example. Users should not have to edit default files to customize their applications.

6.3 Local Conventions

DECwindows applications must support locale-specific data formatting. For example, the application must be able to display a date and time value in the format preferred in the locale where the application is being used. Applications can use operating system services to support local conventions.

For more information about VMS and ULTRIX services available to do locale-specific formatting, see Chapters 7 and 8.

6.4 International Text Processing

DECwindows fonts and character sets, compound strings, and the text processing services and facilities resident in the operating system use the character sets listed in Table 6–1.

6.4.1 Indicating Character Sets

The UIL compiler supports each of the character sets listed, although not all of them are currently available in fonts that DECwindows software can use. Engineering groups in other countries can create user interfaces that use characters from any of the character sets in Table 6–1. Use the FONT_TABLE function to specify the character set and font used by the interface. The default character set used by UIL is ISO Latin-1.

Table 6–1. UIL-Supported Character Sets

UIL Name	Size	Description
ISO_LATIN1	8-bit	GL: ASCII, GR: ISO Latin-1 Supplemental
ISO_LATIN2	8-bit	GL: ASCII, GR: ISO Latin-2 Supplemental
ISO_ARABIC	8-bit	GL: ASCII, GR: ISO Latin-Arabic Supplemental
ISO_LATIN6	8-bit	GL: ASCII, GR: ISO Latin-Arabic Supplemental
ISO_GREEK	8-bit	GL: ASCII, GR: ISO Latin-Greek Supplemental

(Table 6–1 continues on next page)

Table 6–1. UIL-Supported Character Sets (cont.)

UIL Name	Size	Description
ISO_LATIN7	8-bit	GL: ASCII, GR: ISO Latin-Greek Supplemental
ISO_HEBREW	8-bit	GL: ASCII, GR: ISO Latin-Hebrew Supplemental
ISO_LATIN8	8-bit	GL: ASCII, GR: ISO Latin-Hebrew Supplemental
ISO_HEBREW_LR	8-bit	GL: ASCII, GR: ISO Latin-Hebrew Supplemental
ISO_LATIN8_LR	8-bit	GL: ASCII, GR: ISO Latin-Hebrew Supplemental
JIS_KATAKANA	8-bit	GL: JIS Roman, GR: JIS Katakana
DEC_TECH	8-bit	GL: DEC Special Graphics, GR: DEC Technical
DEC_KANJI	16-bit	DEC Kanji Character Set (Japanese)
DEC_HANZI	16-bit	DEC Hanzi Character Set (People's Republic of China)

6.4.2 Compound Strings

Any text string used as a label or message in a DECwindows Toolkit Widget must be passed to the widget as a compound string.

Handling text as compound strings permits the text in a UIL specification file to be translated into any language for which a character set is supported by the DECwindows interface. It also makes application support possible for multiple character sets and for character sets whose writing directions are not left-to-right.

Application developers can supply user interface text in any character set recognized by the UIL compiler, or any mixture of recognized character sets and writing directions. For example, it is possible to mix English, Japanese, and Arabic characters in a single string if that string uses the compound string format. This simplifies the modification of user interfaces to accept text from non-Latin scripts, such as Hebrew, Arabic, and Japanese. It also supports the development of multilingual applications that display characters and ideographs from several character sets at a time. Applications can support the display of multi-byte character sets without requiring explicit information about how the text must be represented on the screen.

DECwindows Toolkit support for compound strings makes possible future toolkit expansions to support multi-byte intermixed character sets and mixed writing directions. This support will be possible without any changes to the interfaces between the applications and the toolkits.

6.4.3 Collating Sequences and Conversion Functions

DECwindows applications must provide support for locale-specific collating sequences and conversion functions. For example, a DECwindows application must be capable of sorting lists of names using the Spanish or German collating sequences. Similarly, your application should be able to do case conversions on characters in the ISO Latin-1 character set, for example, the letters *ß*, *Ø*, and *Æ*.

Applications must use services available in the operating system underlying the application to provide alternative collating sequences and conversion functions. Operations like capitalizing and converting to uppercase or lowercase characters might be meaningless for alphabets that have only one case. Also, grammatical rules stating where uppercase letters are appropriate or mandatory vary from country to country. Even the assumption that capitalizing only changes the first letter of a word is not universally correct. For example, in Dutch *ijzer* is to be capitalized as *IJzer*.

For more information about VMS and ULTRIX services used to work with multiple collating sequences and conversion functions, see Chapters 7 and 8.

6.5 Local Devices

In most cases, DECwindows software provides device support, including keyboard mappings for different character sets. Keyboard mapping is needed if, for example, a German-speaking Swiss person working with a French keyboard needs a German keyboard layout. The DECwindows interface downloads software that changes the definition of some of the keys in the keyboard, and enables other characters through compose sequences. Compose sequences are two- or three-stroke sequences that create characters not available as standard keys. As far as the application is concerned, all devices are DECwindows devices. DECwindows provides startup procedure support for LK201 keyboard variants and support for compose sequences for characters in the ISO Latin-1 character set.

International software products that use accelerator keys, such as the Gold key or Control key sequences, to invoke functions must support completely redefinable keyboards. Because the name of a function may be changed during translation, for example, from *Exit* to *Sortie*, the key used to invoke a function should be translatable as well, for example, from the Gold/E keys to the Gold/S keys.

DECwindows applications can provide redefinable key bindings through the TRANSLATION_TABLE function in a UIL specification file, as shown in Example 6–5.

Example 6–5. Support for Redefinable Keyboards in DECwindows

```
!=====================================================================
!
!   APPL_KEYS.UIL
!
!+
!  This UIL file binds application functions to keys.
!
!  It is included in the main module KEYBINDING_EXAMPLE.UIL
!-
        value
         !+
         ! Set up the control key codes in an understandable
         ! form for translators
         !
         ! NOTE: this section does not need to be translated.
         !-
         Ctrl_a : 'Ctrl<KeyPress>a:      ';
         Ctrl_e : 'Ctrl<KeyPress>e:      ';
                .
                .

         !+
         ! Set up the callback name to map to the accelerator key
         !
         ! NOTE: this section does not need to be translated.
         !-
         AppendAction : 'AppendCallback()';
         ExitAction   : 'ExitCallback()';
                .
                .
```

(Example 6–5 continues on next page)

Example 6–5 (Cont.). Support for Redefinable Keyboards in DECwindows

```
!+
!  Bind the keys to the actions
!
! NOTE:  Translators - key bindings can be changed by
! changing the keycodes associated with the functions.
!
! For example, if the Exit key binding needs to be changed
! from Control/E to Control/S, then replace Ctrl_E below
! with Ctrl_S.  In this case, "Ctrl_E & ExitAction" becomes
! "Ctrl_S & ExitAction".
!-
AppendAccelerator :
                   Ctrl_S & AppendAction;

ExitAccelerator   :
                   Ctrl_E & ExitAction;


       .
       .
       .

!+
! Key event table
!
! NOTE: this section does not need to be translated.
!-
KeyTable : exported translation_table( AppendAccelerator
                                      ,ExitAccelerator
                                      );
```

The APPL_KEYS.UIL file is included by KEYBINDING_EXAMPLE.UIL, as shown in Example 6–6.

If possible, the best solution is to not use keys at all. Besides the fact that functions, when translated, may not begin with the same letter, certain functions may be positional. Therefore, the keys may not function as expected if a different keyboard is used. A keyboard-independent application allows the keyboard layout card to match different keyboards.

Example 6–6. KEYBINDING_EXAMPLE.UIL

```
!+
! Include translatable key bindings
!-
include file 'appl_keys.uil';
        .
        .
        .
object
 ApplDialogBox : dialog_box
 {
  arguments
           {
                 .
                 .
                 .
!+
! Set up the accelerators for this object
!-
            translations = KeyTable;
                 .
                 .
           };
```

6.6 DECwindows Interface: Localizable Software Example

This section shows how developers at Digital use the DECwindows interface to create a localized application. Figure 6–3 specifies the layout of the main window for an application user interface. This example shows an object-oriented user interface widget. Users interact with the application by positioning the mouse on the appropriate object (for example, the Apply button or the Cancel button) and pressing the first mouse button, MB1.

Figure 6–3. XLAT_EXAMPLE.UIL Main Window

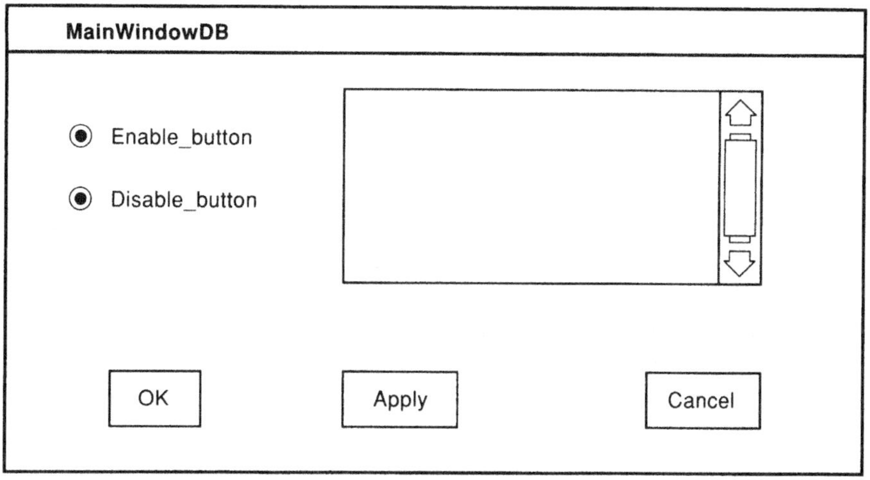

The XLAT_EXAMPLE.UIL file used to define the window shown in Figure 6–3 includes three files that declare constants:

File	Description
UIL_EXAMPLE_TEXT.UIL	Declares all translatable text strings as constants
UIL_EXAMPLE_VALUES.UIL	Declares all modifiable sizing and positioning values as constants
UIL_EXAMPLE_NONXLAT.UIL	Declares all constants that do not need to be translated

Example 6–7 shows a UIL specification file that can be translated.

Example 6–7. A Translatable UIL Specification File: XLAT_EXAMPLE.UIL

```
!===============================================================
!
!  XLAT_EXAMPLE.UIL
!
module uil_example
    version = 'v1.0'
    names = case_insensitive
!+
!  This UIL file specifies the layout of the main window for an
!  application user interface.  It also demonstrates how to
!  write UIL files in ways that  support translation.
!
!-

!+
!  Include translatable constants
!-
include file 'uil_example_text.uil';
include file 'uil_example_values.uil';

!+
!  Include non-translatable constants
!-
include file 'uil_example_nonxlat.uil';

!+
!  Main Section, builds up the widgets and their layout.
!-
object MainWindowDB : dialog_box widget
{
  arguments {
              x =       MainWindowDBXPos;
              y =       MainWindowDBYPos;
              height = MainWindowDBHeight;
              width  = MainWindowDBWidth;
            };
  controls  {
             toggle_button EnableToggleButton;
             toggle_button DisableToggleButton;
             list_box      DisplayListBox;
             push_button   OKPushButton;
             push_button   ApplyPushButton;
             push_button   CancelPushButton;
            };
};
```

(Example 6–7 continues on next page)

Example 6–7 (Cont.). A Translatable UIL Specification File: XLAT_ EXAMPLE.UIL

```
!+
!  The enable toggle button gadget
!-

object EnableToggleButton : toggle_button gadget
{
  arguments {
                x =             EnableToggleButtonXPos;
                y =             EnableToggleButtonYPos;
                label_label = EnableToggleButtonLabel;
            };
};

!+
!  The disable toggle button gadget
!-

object DisableToggleButton : toggle_button gadget
{
  arguments {
                x =             DisableToggleButtonXPos;
                y =             DisableToggleButtonYPos;
                label_label = DisableToggleButtonLabel;
            };
};

!+
!  The list box widget
!-

object DisplayListBox : list_box widget
{
  arguments {
                x =      DisplayListBoxXPos;
                y =      DisplayListBoxYPos;
                height = DisplayListBoxHeight;
                width  = DisplayListBoxWidth;
                items  = DisplayListBoxItemTable;
            };
};
```

(Example 6–7 continues on next page)

Example 6–7 (Cont.). A Translatable UIL Specification File: XLAT_EXAMPLE.UIL

```
!+
!  The okay push button gadget
!-

object OKPushButton : push_button gadget
{
  arguments {
                x =             OKPushButtonXPos;
                y =             OKPushButtonYPos;
                label_label = OKPushButtonLabel;
            };
};

!+
!  The apply push button gadget
!-

object ApplyPushButton : push_button gadget
{
  arguments {
                x =             ApplyPushButtonXPos;
                y =             ApplyPushButtonYPos;
                label_label = ApplyPushButtonLabel;
            };
};

!+
!  The cancel push button gadget
!-

object CancelPushButton : push_button gadget
{
  arguments {
                x =             CancelPushButtonXPos;
                y =             CancelPushButtonYPos;
                label_label = CancelPushButtonLabel;
            };
};

end module;
```

The files shown in Examples 6–8, 6–9, and 6–10 are included by XLAT_EXAMPLE.UIL (shown in Example 6–7).

Example 6–8. Declaration of Text Strings as Constants

```
!=================================================================
!
! UIL_EXAMPLE_TEXT.UIL
!
!+
!  This UIL file contains the text strings to be translated for the
!  application.
!
!  This file is included in the main module, XLAT_EXAMPLE.UIL.
!-
value

!+
!  The label name for the toggle button Enable_button
!-
        Enable_button :
                                'Enable the application';
!+
!  The label name for the toggle button Disable_button
!-
        Disable_button :
                                'Disable the application';
!+
!  The items to be listed in the list box DisplayListBox
!_
        DisplayListBoxItem1 :
                                'First item';
        DisplayListBoxItem2 :
                                'Second item';
        DisplayListBoxItem3 :
                                'Third item';
        DisplayListBoxItem4 :
                                'Fourth item';
!+
!  The label for the push button OK
!-
        OK :
                                'Okay';
!+
!  The label for the push button ApplyPushButton
!-
        ApplyPushButtonLabel :
                                'Apply';
!+
!  The label for the push button CancelPushButton
!-
        CancelPushButtonLabel :
                                'Cancel';
```

Example 6–9. Declaration of Position and Size Values as Constants

```
!==================================================================
!
! UIL_EXAMPLE_VALUES.UIL
!
!+
!  This UIL file contains the position and dimension values of
!  the objects used in the application program. These values
!  can be affected by the translation of the text strings found
!  in the file UIL_EXAMPLE_TEXT.UIL.
!
!  This file is included in the main module XLAT_EXAMPLE.UIL.
!-
value

!+
!  Height and width of the dialog box widget MainWindowDB.
!  These dimensions are affected by the positions and dimensions
!  of the following objects:
!            EnableToggleButton
!            DisableToggleButton
!            DisplayListBox
!            OKPushButton
!            ApplyPushButton
!            CancelPushButton
!-
       MainWindowDBHeight :
                          600;
       MainWindowDBWidth  :
                          800;
       DisplayListBoxHeight    :
                              300;
       DisplayAttachSeparation:
                              30;
!+
! X and Y position for the toggle button widget EnableToggleButton.
! This position can affect the following widgets:
!
!              DisableToggleButton
!              DisplayListBox
!-
       EnableToggleButtonXPos :
                                20;
       EnableToggleButtonYPos :
                                20;
!+
! X and Y position for the toggle button widget DisableToggleButton.
! This position is affected by the position of EnableToggleButton,
! and can affect the following widget:
!
!               DisplayListBox
!-
       DisableToggleButtonXPos :
```

(Example 6–9 continues on next page)

Example 6–9 (Cont.). Declaration of Position and Size Values as Constants

```
                              20;
        DisableToggleButtonYPos :
                              40;
!+
! X and Y position for the list box widget DisplayListBox.
! This position is affected by the position and labels of the
! following:
!
!                 EnableToggleButton
!                 DisableToggleButton
!
! This position affects the following widgets:
!
!                 OKPushButton
!                 ApplyPushButton
!                 CancelPushButton
!-
        DisplayListBoxXPos :
                         100;
        DisplayListBoxYPos :
                         20;
!+
! Height and width of the list box widget DisplayListBox.
! These dimensions affect the following widgets:
!
!                   MainWindowDB
!                   OKPushButton
!                   ApplyPushButton
!                   CancelPushButton
!-
        DisplayListBoxHeight :
                            300;
        DisplayListBoxWidth  :
                            200;
!+
! X and Y position for the push button widget OKPushButton.
! This position is affected by the list box widget DisplayListBox
! and affects the dialog box widget MainWindowDB height.
!-
        OKPushButtonXPos :
                      20;
        OKPushButtonYPos :
                      350;
!+
! X and Y position for the push button widget ApplyPushButton.
! This position is affected by the following widgets:
!
!                 OKPushButton
!                 DisplayListBox
!
! This position affects the following widgets:
```

(Example 6–9 continues on next page)

Example 6–9 (Cont.). Declaration of Position and Size Values as Constants

```
!
!                 CancelPushButton
!                 MainWindowDB (height)
!-
        ApplyPushButtonXPos :
                              200;
        ApplyPushButtonYPos :
                              350;
!+
!  X and Y position for the push button widget CancelPushButton.
! This position is affected by the following widgets:
!
!                  ApplyPushButton
!                  DisplayListBox
!
! This position affects the dialog box widget MainWindowDB height
! and width
!-
        CancelPushButtonXPos :
                                300;
        CancelPushButtonYPos :
                                350;
```

Example 6–10. Declaration of Nontranslatable Values as Constants

```
!==================================================================
!
! UIL_EXAMPLE_NONXLAT.UIL
!
!+
!  This UIL file contains the constants that do not require
!  translation.  It is included in the main module "xlat_example.uil"
!-

!+
!  The dialog box position will remain fixed (overriding any xdefault
!  position)
!-
value
```

(Example 6–10 continues on next page)

Example 6–10 (Cont.). Declaration of Nontranslatable Values as Constants

```
        MainWindowDBXPos          : 500;
        MainWindowDBYPos          : 500;
!+
! The string table of items to be listed in DisplayListBox
!-
        DisplayListBoxItemTable : string_table(
                                                DisplayListBoxItem1
                                               ,DisplayListBoxItem2
                                               ,DisplayListBoxItem3
                                               ,DisplayListBoxItem4
                                               );
```

Chapter 7

Using the VMS Operating System

This chapter describes many of the VMS features that support international product development. The VMS and Japanese VMS (JVMS) operating systems support international product development with the following system features:

- Application development tools

  New tools enable the separation of user interface text from application functions, provide means of testing translated user interfaces, and provide mechanisms for formatting local data conventions.

- VMS Message Utility

  This utility allows developers to construct informational, warning, or error messages in standard VMS format.

- Run-Time Library routines

  Routines are available to support date and time values, and other text and data formatting requirements.

- National Character Set (NCS) Utility and Run-Time Library

  These routines support ISO Latin-1 text processing requirements.

- Terminal Fallback Facility

  This facility supports terminals that use the National Replacement Character set (NRC).

7.1 DECforms User Interface

Designers working in the VMS environment can choose from several application development tools that support localization. This section describes the advantages afforded by creating a DECforms user interface for an international product.

DECforms is an application development tool used to create and manipulate fixed form interfaces. It is the preferred development tool in simple data-entry applications, which use the forms and menus as user interfaces. The forms manage the exchange of information between the user and the application program, and manage the input and output devices used by the application as well.

The use of DECforms supports a principal requirement of international product development by separating user interface form from application function. A DECforms user interface can be created and edited apart from the application program that will use the interface. Consequently, engineering groups in other countries can localize the user interface without having to modify, or even access, the international base code.

Several DECforms components support the development of international products:

- The Independent Form Description Language (IFDL) and the IFDL Translator

  The Independent Form Description Language (IFDL) and the IFDL Translator provide one method of creating a form in DECforms. The IFDL is a semi-procedural language used to describe:

  - Information displayed on a terminal screen
  - The format used to display that information
  - Interactions with a user
  - Interactions with the application program

  To create a form used in a DECforms user interface, write an IFDL source file and translate that source file into a form file using the IFDL Translator. Form files can be edited using the Form Development Environment, or invoked by an application using the Form Manager.

  An IFDL source file is a text file that can be edited using standard VMS text editors. This capability supports the important international requirement that translatable text be available to nontechnical translators in an easily editable form. An IFDL source file can also be edited in the Form Development Environment.

- The Form Development Environment

  The Form Development Environment (FDE) is a menu-driven form creation tool that enables developers to create or modify a form file or test a form file's functioning at run time. Application developers can use FDE to interactively design forms.

- The Panel Editor

  The Panel Editor enables developers to create and modify graphic form elements and their attributes, and see the results on the screen immediately. Application developers can use the Panel Editor to interactively create graphic form elements such as background text and graphics, and modify the locations and sizes of fields. The readjustment of forms when translating a DECforms application can be avoided by using widgets in applications based on the DECwindows interface (see Chapter 6).

  Engineering groups in other countries can use FDE and the Panel Editor to make adjustments to the layout of a form after the form text has been translated, and after other modifications have been made to the form.

- The Back Translator

  The Back Translator produces an IFDL source file from a form file. Thus, it performs the reverse function of the IFDL Translator. Because form files cannot be edited with a text editor, DECforms provides the Back Translator as a way of creating an editable and translatable IFDL source file from a forms file. The IFDL source file produced by the Back Translator can be translated back into a form file by the IFDL Translator.

- The Test Utility

  The Test Utility enables a form designer to check the appearance of a form before the application that will use the form is written. Engineering groups in other countries can use this utility to test the appearance of translated user interfaces before the application code is frozen or even available. The full user interface can then be tested using the FDE and enable/control text responses.

- The Form Manager

  The Form Manager is the interface between the application program and the display device. It is a run-time system that controls form display and operator input on terminals. It is the Form Manager that activates the form interface used by the application, and passes data to and from the input/output device. By placing form requests in your application program, you establish the interface between application function and form.

For more information about the DECforms system, see the following documents in the DECforms documentation set:

- *DECforms Guide to Developing Forms*, Order Number AA–LC17A–TE—Explains how to use the DECforms software to create forms.
- *DECforms Reference Manual*, Order Number AA–LC19A–TE—Provides descriptions of the DECforms DCL commands and Panel Editor Commands, and provides syntax information on the IFDL.
- *DECforms Guide to Programming*, Order Number AA–LC20A–TE—Describes calling DECforms from a program and how the program operates at run time.

7.2 Messages in VMS

The VMS Messaging Facility enables application designers to isolate the translatable message text displayed by an application by placing the text in a separate file. The application locates and uses its message text through a pointer file, which is linked to the application directly. By separating message text from the application that displays that text, designers create application programs that can use interchangeable message text files in several languages, as described in the next section.

Designers can add comments and context information for translators by subsequently editing the files generated by the VMS Messaging Facility.

7.2.1 Using Message Pointers

Message pointers allow an international product to provide different message texts for one set of messages. Using message pointers does not link the object module containing the message text directly with the facility object module. Consequently, engineering groups in other countries do not need to relink with the application executable image file to change the message text included in it. The groups can substitute message text in one language for message text in another without making changes to the application source code.

To use message pointers,

- Isolate the message text used by your product.
  1. Create a nonexecutable message file that contains the message text.
  2. Create a separate pointer file that contains message symbols and a pointer to the nonexecutable message file.
  3. Link the pointer file with your application object files.
- Create the nonexecutable message file by compiling and linking a message source file.

  For example, to create the nonexecutable message text file XYZMSGTEXT.EXE, first create the object module by compiling the message source file, XYZMSG.MSG, using the following command:

  ```
  $ MESSAGE/NOSYMBOLS XYZMSG[Return]
  ```

  Link the resulting message text object module using the following command:

  ```
  $ LINK/SHAREABLE=SYS$MESSAGE:XYZMSGTEXT XYZMSG.OBJ[Return]
  ```

  This example creates the XYZMSGTEXT.EXE nonexecutable message text file and places it into the SYS$MESSAGE system message library.
- Create the message pointer file by recompiling the message source file.

  Use the MESSAGE/FILE_NAME command. To avoid confusion, use a file name other than the name you gave the nonexecutable message text file. The resulting object module contains only global symbols and the file specification of the nonexecutable message text file.

  For example, the following command creates the object module XYZMSGPOINTER.OBJ, containing a pointer to the nonexecutable message file, SYS$MESSAGE:XYZMSGTEXT.EXE:

  ```
  $ MESSAGE/FILE_NAME=XYZMSGTEXT /OBJECT=XYZMSGPOINTER XYZMSG[Return]
  ```

  The object module XYZMSGPOINTER.OBJ contains, in addition to the message pointers, the global symbols defined in the XYZMSG message source file. If the nonexecutable message text file (in this example, XYZMSGTEXT.EXE) is not in SYS$MESSAGE, you must specify a device and directory or, better still, use a logical name in the file specification for the /FILE_NAME qualifier.

- After creating the pointer object module, link it with the application program's object module.

  For example, the following command links the pointer object module, XYZMSGPOINTER.OBJ, with the application object module, XYZCODE.OBJ:

  ```
  $ LINK XYZCODE, XYZMSGPOINTER[Return]
  ```

  When you run the resulting facility image file, message pointers direct the $GETMSG system service to retrieve message text from the nonexecutable message text file, XYZMSGTEXT.

Translating message text in the message source file, and then creating a new nonexecutable message text file allows the engineering groups in other countries to use the same message pointers used by the base version of the product to point to translated message text.

Figure 7–1 illustrates the process used to create an application that retrieves message text from a separate, nonexecutable message text file.

7.2.2 Using Logical Names to Switch Message Files

The VMS Message Utility enables you to create an application that retrieves message text from a separate message text file. The application uses a message pointer file, which is linked with the application object file.

The message pointer file can also direct the application to a logical name rather than to a file specification for the message text file. Thus, the target message text file can be changed by redefining a logical name. This method of switching message files implies that users must exit from the product, change the logical name, then reinvoke the product each time they want to switch message files.

Figure 7–1. Creating and Using a Message Pointer File

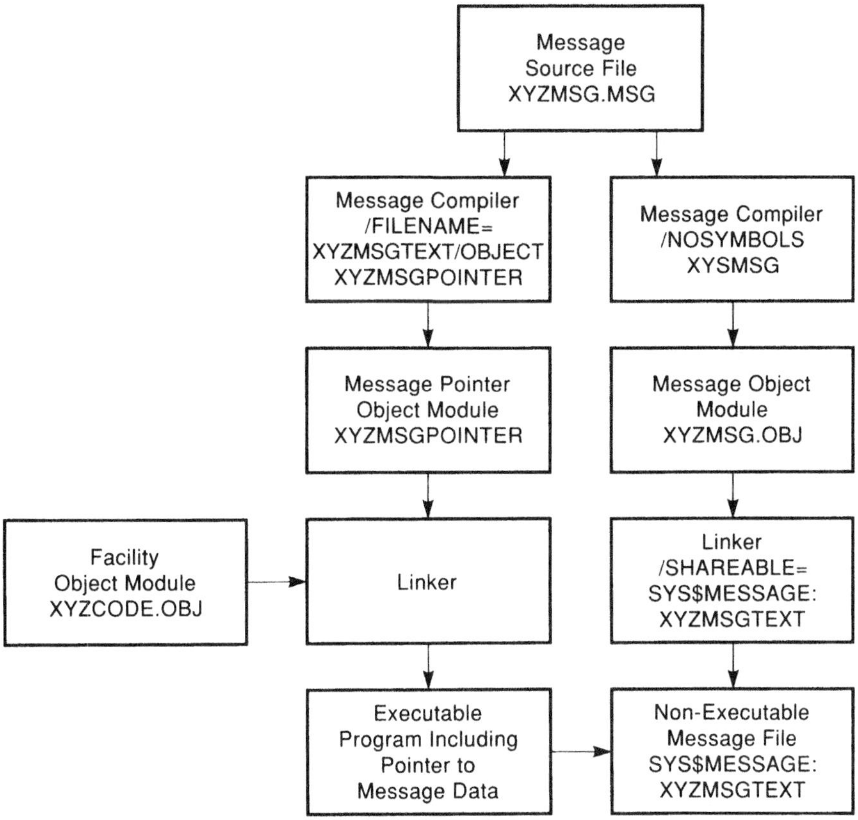

Example 7–1 shows a command file that uses three source files:

- TEST_MESSAGE.FOR
- ENGLISH.MSG
- FRENCH.MSG

Example 7–1. Command File for Switching Message Files

```
$ MESSAGE/NOSYMBOL ENGLISH.MSG          ! Compile the message files
$ MESSAGE/NOSYMBOL FRENCH.MSG
$ LINK/SHAREABLE ENGLISH.OBJ            ! Link the message files into
                                            ! shareable images
$ LINK/SHAREABLE FRENCH.OBJ
$ MESSAGE/FILE_NAME=My_messages -     ! Logical name pointing to a
                                            ! shareable image
    /OBJECT=MESSAGE_POINTERS   -        ! Note that this is only
    ENGLISH                             ! done once
$ FORTRAN TEST_MESSAGE
$ LINK/NOTRACE TEST_MESSAGE,MESSAGE_POINTERS
$ DEFINE my_messages DISK$:[DIRECTORY]ENGLISH.EXE
```

When the TEST_MESSAGE program is run, message text is extracted from the shareable image named ENGLISH.EXE, which is the file pointed to by the logical name *my_messages.* To access the French message, redefine the logical name:

```
$ DEFINE my_messages DISK$:[DIRECTORY]FRENCH.EXE
```

Use a full file specification when defining a logical name that points to a shareable image message file, unless the shareable image resides in SYS$MESSAGE. If a shareable image resides in SYS$MESSAGE, supply just the file name.

7.2.3 Using $FAO to Reorder Message Parameters

When translating software, engineering groups in other locales create foreign-language message files in which both the message text and the order of parameters may change. For example:

English: Found 'DUA1:' when expecting 'DUA0:'
French: 'DUA0:' attendu; 'DUA1:' reçu

Use parameters very selectively in application messages. Never use parameters to build a natural language sentence from parts. Because different languages use different syntax, messages built from parts may be difficult to translate. Do not use $FAO for composing messages from pieces of text. If you use artificial language parameters such as file or device names in messages, do so with care. See Section 4.2.2 for more information.

The $FAO facility provides a means for reordering parameters. For example, the following message file, ENGLISH.MSG, defines one error, whose IDENT is MSG_ORDER, "MSG_" being the prefix to all messages defined in this file. The definition specifies two parameters, whose values are provided by the $FAO parameter list.

```
.Title test_fao_messages

.Facility   efgh,1   /prefix=MSG_

.Severity   error

order   <Found   '!AS' when expecting '!AS'>/fao=2

.end
```

The following program source code signals this error message:

```
external msg_order
call   lib$signal ( msg_order , %val(2) , 'abc' , 'xyz' )
end
```

The call to LIB$SIGNAL specifies the message name, the number of $FAO parameters to be inserted in the message, and the $FAO parameters.

When the message is built, the first value, 'abc', is inserted at the point of the first $FAO directive in the message and the second value, 'xyz', is inserted at the point of the second $FAO directive. When the program is linked with the object file created by the VMS Message Utility and then executed, the following message is displayed:

```
%EFGH-E-ORDER, Found 'abc' when expecting 'xyz'
```

To use the parameters in a different order, as required by the French translation of the message, use the following $FAO directives:

!+	Causes $FAO to skip a parameter
!–	Causes $FAO to back up one parameter
!n( )	Allows specification of a repeat count for the !+ and !– directives

These directives allow access to the $FAO parameter in any order. For example, the following message file called FRENCH.MSG is phrased so that the second $FAO parameter is used first and the first $FAO parameter used second.

```
.Title test_fao_messages
.Facility   efgh,1   /prefix=msg_
.Severity   error
order<'!+!AS' attendu; '!2(-)!AS' reçu >/fao=2
.end
```

The !+!AS construction selects the second parameter in the list and inserts it into the message. After the !+!AS directives have been processed, the pointer is moved to the third directive, !2(-), needed to move the current parameter pointer two parameters to the left, or back to the first parameter, which is then output by the !AS which follows.

When this message file is compiled by the MESSAGE utility and the same program is linked with the resulting object file, the following message is issued:

```
%EFGH-E-ORDER, 'xyz' attendu; 'abc' reçu
```

This example links the program object file with a message object file, which results in a separate image for each program- and message-file combination.

7.2.4 Using $FAO for Conditional Messaging

In VMS Version 5.2 and later, you can use $FAO directives to test the value of a message parameter and create conditionalized messaging based on the result. For example, your message might include one text string that is displayed if a tested value is zero, another if the value is one, and a third if the value is anything else. This facility has obvious uses in international messages, where ways of pluralizing nouns may vary for different languages. International software products should pluralize using this approach, rather than by adding *s* to the end of a noun string.

The $FAO directives used for conditional messaging are as follows:

Directive	Function
!UL	Captures the parameter to be tested.
!n%C	Identifies the string to be displayed if the tested parameter equals the value *n*. The message can contain any number of !n%C case directives.

Directive	Function
!%E	Identifies the string to be displayed if the tested parameter is other than any of the values specified in !n%C directives.
!%F	Marks the end of the list of !n%C strings.

7.3 Local Conventions

VMS provides several facilities that enable international products to use local conventions when formatting and validating data. These facilities include:

- Run-Time Library support for date and time formatting
- Forms system support for number and currency formatting

7.3.1 Formatting Dates and Times

The VMS Run-Time Library provides routines to format date and time values and perform date and time manipulations. Applications that use the Run-Time Library date and time routines can determine a user's preferred date and time format at run time and display date and time values accordingly. Applications can also use date and time routines to transform user supplied values from the input format to an internal format for storage, processing, or transmission.

7.3.1.1 Specifying Language and Date and Time Formats

In VMS Version 5.0 and later, a system manager or someone with comparable privileges can define the SYS$LANGUAGES logical name to indicate the languages that will be used on the system. The available languages, and the logical names associated with the languages, are shown in the following table.

Language	Logical Name
Austrian	AUSTRIAN
Danish	DANISH
Dutch	DUTCH
Finnish	FINNISH
French	FRENCH

Language	Logical Name
French Canadian	CANADIAN
German	GERMAN
Hebrew	HEBREW
Italian	ITALIAN
Norwegian	NORWEGIAN
Portuguese	PORTUGUESE
Spanish	SPANISH
Swedish	SWEDISH
Swiss French	SWISS_FRENCH
Swiss German	SWISS_GERMAN

For example, if system managers need to support English-, French-, German-, and Italian-speaking users, they can define SYS$LANGUAGES as shown below:

```
$ DEFINE SYS$LANGUAGES FRENCH, GERMAN, ITALIAN
```

After defining SYS$LANGUAGES, the system manager should invoke the command procedure SYS$MANAGER:LIB$DT_STARTUP.COM. This procedure defines default date and time formats and spellings (day and month names) for the languages associated with the SYS$LANGUAGES variable. The VMS system uses the translation of SYS$LANGUAGES to select which alternate spellings and formats are to be available to applications and users.

The LIB$DT_STARTUP.COM procedure must be executed before any of the date and time routines can provide formats other than the default VMS format. Both the definition of SYS$LANGUAGES and the invocation of LIB$DT_STARTUP.COM can be done in SYSTARTUP.COM.

7.3.1.2 Defining Date and Time Formats

Users can select from a number of predefined date and time formats, or they can define new formats. Date and time formats are defined using format mnemonics. When defining a format, each mnemonic must be preceded by an exclamation point (!).

Table 7–1 lists mnemonics used to define date and time formats.

Table 7–1. Date and Time Run-Time Format Mnemonics

Mnemonic	Description	Example
D0	Day value, 0 filled	01 — first day of month 09 — ninth day of month
DN	Day value, not filled	1 — first day of month 9 — ninth day of month
MAAU	Month name, alphabetic, abbreviated, uppercase	JUL[1] — July
MAAC	Month name, alphabetic, abbreviated, capitalized	Jul[1] — July
H04	Hours, zero-filled, 24-hour clock	05 — five o'clock, a.m.
HB2	Hours, blank-filled, 12-hour clock	2 — two o'clock a.m. or p.m.

[1]Month names are presented here in English. If the user has indicated another language as the preferred language, month names are displayed in the preferred language.

Table 7–2 lists several of the predefined date and time formats.

Table 7–2. Predefined Date and Time Formats

Predefined Logical	Format	Example
LIB$DATE_FORMAT_001	!DB-!MAAU-!Y4	13-JAN-1987
LIB$DATE_FORMAT_038	!Y4.!MN0.!D0	1987.01.13
LIB$TIME_FORMAT_001	!H04:!M0:!S0.!C2	09:13:25.14
LIB$TIME_FORMAT_012	!HB2:!M0 !MIU	9:13 a.m.

7.3.1.3 Using Date and Time Formats

A system manager can select an alternative date and time format for the entire system, or individual users can create formats or select the predefined formats they prefer. You can specify date and time formats at run time by using LIB$DT_INPUT_FORMAT and the mnemonics listed in Table 7–1, for example:

```
$ DEFINE LIB$DT_INPUT_FORMAT -
_$ "!MAU !DD, !Y4 !H02:!M0:!S0:!C2 !MIU"
```

Once the SYS$LANGUAGE, LIB$DT_FORMAT, and LIB$DT_INPUT_FORMAT logicals are defined, date/time routines that format date and time values use the spellings and formats indicated by the logicals. For example, applications can use the LIB$FORMAT_DATE_TIME routine to format a VMS internal date and time in the output format indicated by the LIB$DT_FORMAT logical. Similarly, applications can use the LIB$CONVERT_DATE_STRING routine to parse user-input values against the format associated with the LIB$DT_INPUT_FORMAT logical.

Table 7–3 lists the date and time routines supplied in the VMS Version 5.0 Run-Time Library.

See the *VMS RTL Library Routines Manual*, Order No. AA–76A–TE, for more information about the VMS date/time routines used to provide international date and time formats.

Table 7–3. Run-Time Library Date/Time Routines

Routine Name	Description
LIB$FORMAT_DATE_TIME	Formats a date or time for output.
LIB$FREE_DATE_TIME_CONTEXT	Frees the date and time context.
LIB$GET_DATE_FORMAT	Returns the user's specified date and time input formats.
LIB$GET_MAXIMUM_DATE_LENGTH	Returns the maximum possible length of an output date and time string.
LIB$GET_USERS_LANGUAGE	Returns the user's selected language.
LIB$INIT_DATE_TIME_CONTEXT	Initializes the date and time context with a user-specified format.

7.3.2 Formatting Number and Currency Values

The VMS Run-Time Library provides routines to format number and currency values and perform number and currency manipulations. Applications that use the Run-Time Library number/currency routines can determine a user's preferred number and currency format at run time and display the values accordingly. Applications can also use number/currency routines to transform user supplied values from the input format to an internal format for storage, processing, or transmission.

In VMS Version 5.0 and later, a system manager or someone with comparable privileges can define the SYS$CURRENCY logical name to indicate the currency that will be used on the system. An individual user with a special need can define SYS$CURRENCY as a process logical name to override the system default. DECforms enables users to specify alternate number and currency formats.

See the *DECforms Reference Manual* for more information.

7.3.3 International Collating Sequences

The National Character Sets (NCS) are subsets of the Multinational Character Set (MCS). To convert text from a National Replacement Character (NRC) set to MCS, see Section 7.3.5. Applications using MCS can run on NRC terminals and printers with the help of the Terminal Fallback Facility (see Section 7.5).

The default NCS Library, located in SYS$LIBRARY:NCS$LIBRARY.NLB, contains collating sequence tables for the following languages and character sets:

- Danish
- Dutch
- English
- Finnish
- French
- German
- Italian
- Multinational
- Multinational_1
- Multinational_2
- Norwegian
- Portuguese
- Spanish

NCS provides routines that a VMS application can use to access the collating sequence tables. These routines are listed in Table 7–4.

Table 7–4. NCS Routines Using Collating Sequences

Routine Name	Description
NCS$COMPARE	Compares two strings using a specified collating sequence.
NCS$CONVERT	Converts a string using a specified conversion function.
NCS$END_CS	Terminates the use of a specified collating sequence by the calling program.
NCS$GET_CS	Retrieves the definition of the named collating sequence from the library. If a collating sequence is not specified, it retrieves the native collating sequence.
NCS$RESTORE_CS	Permits the calling program to restore the definition of a saved collating sequence from a database.
NCS$SAVE_CS	Permits an application to store the definition for a collating sequence in a database.

An international software product specifies a collating sequence to be used at run time in an application profile. Use NCS$GET_CS to retrieve the appropriate collating sequence and NCS$COMPARE to do all string comparisons.

In a typical application, the program performs these steps:

1. Prepares a string for comparison
2. Makes a call to NCS$GET_CS to retrieve the appropriate collating sequence
3. Makes one or more calls to the NCS$COMPARE routine to determine sorting order based on the retrieved collating sequence
4. Terminates the comparison with a call to NCS$END_CS

Example 7–2 shows a piece of code that retrieves a collating sequence from the NCS library and uses it to compare two strings.

Example 7–2. Comparing Two Strings

```
cs_name = "spanish";
lib_name = "sys$library:ncs$library";
ncs$get_cs (cs_id, cs_name, lib_name);
result=ncs$compare_cs(cs_id,str1,str2);
ncs$end_cs(cs_id);
```

In Example 7–2, each command performs its function in the following ways:

- ncs$get_cs retrieves the definition of the named collating sequence (Spanish) from the NCS library (sys$library:ncs$library).
- ncs$compare_cs compares the strings str1 and str2 using the Spanish collating sequence as the basis for comparison.
- ncs$end_cs terminates the program's use of the Spanish collating sequence.

The program may also include the use of conversion functions to prepare strings for the comparison routines. For example, conversion routines might be used to convert an entire string to all lowercase before comparison.

VMS Record Management Services (RMS), Version 5.0, support NCS routines for index files. A collating sequence can be accessed from a specified library and copied into the file during file creation. Thus, the records can be inserted according to the collating sequences embedded in the file.

Example 7–3 illustrates the use of NCS Utility collating sequence routines in a C program.

Example 7–3. C Program for Comparing Strings

```
/*********************************************************************/
/* ***************************************************************** */
/* *                                                               * */
/* *    COMPARE.C  -- An NCS demonstration program                 * */
/* *                                                               * */
/* *    This program takes two hard-coded strings and compares them * */
/* *    using a specified collating sequence.  The contents of the  * */
/* *    strings and the name of the collating sequence can be      * */
/* *    varied to see the effects of different characters in       * */
/* *    different sequences.                                       * */
/* *                                                               * */
/* *    Any bad status (such as a warning, error, or fatal condi-  * */
/* *    tion) returned by the calls is signaled immediately to     * */
/* *    the user. If the status is not fatal, execution will resume * */
/* *    with the following statement.                              * */
/* *                                                               * */
/* ***************************************************************** */
/*********************************************************************/

/* Include Files */
#include descrip
#include stdio

/* Macro Definitions */
#define CHECK_(i)     if (!((status = i) & 1)) lib$signal(status)

/* External Routines */
extern unsigned lib$signal();
extern unsigned ncs$get_cs();
extern unsigned ncs$compare();
extern unsigned ncs$end_cs();

/* The Main Procedure */
main()
{
    long        cs_id;      /* Collating Sequence Ident                 */
    int         order;      /* The order in which the strings collate  */
    unsigned    status;     /* Used by CHECK_ macro                     */
    /* Create static descriptors for the conversion function name      */
    /* and the two strings to be compared.                              */
    $DESCRIPTOR(cs_name, "German");
    $DESCRIPTOR(string1,  "Strasse");
    $DESCRIPTOR(string2,  "Straße");
```

(Example 7–3 continues on next page)

Example 7–3 (Cont.). C Program for Comparing Strings

```
    /* Get the ident of the collating sequence, compare the strings, and    */
    /* then release the resources.                                           */
    CHECK_( ncs$get_cs (&cs_id, &cs_name) );
    order = ncs$compare(&cs_id, &string1, &string2);
    CHECK_( ncs$end_cs (&cs_id) );

    /* Print the results */
    printf("\n\nThe string, \n\n\t\"%s\"\n\n", string1.dsc$a_pointer);
    printf("collates %s the string,\n\n\t\"%s\"\n\n",
            (order > 0 ?
                "after" :
                (order < 0 ?
                    "before" :
                    "equal to"
                )
            ),
            string2.dsc$a_pointer);
    printf("using the \"%s\" collating sequence.\n\n", cs_name.dsc$a_pointer);
}
```

7.3.4 Using Sort/Merge Routines

Sort/Merge callable routines use the same collating tables as the collating routines of the NCS Library. An international software product can use the Sort/Merge routines listed in Table 7–5 to sort or merge files and then continue processing the files.

Table 7–5. Sort/Merge Routines

Routine Name	Description
SOR$BEGIN_MERGE	Sets up key arguments and performs the merge.
SOR$BEGIN_SOR	Initializes sort operation by passing key information and sort options.
SOR$DTYPE	Defines a key data_type that is not normally supported by SORT/MERGE.
SOR$END_SORT	Performs clean-up functions, such as closing files and releasing memory.

(Table 7–5 continues on next page)

Table 7–5. Sort/Merge Routines (cont.)

Routine Name	Description
SOR$PASS_FILES	Passes names of input and output files to SORT or MERGE; must be repeated for each input file.
SOR$RELEASE_REC	Passes one input record to SORT or MERGE; must be called once for each record.
SOR$RETURN_REC	Returns one sorted or merged record to a program; must be called once for each record.
SOR$SORT_MERGE	Sorts the records.
SOR$SPEC_FILE	Passes a specification file or specification text. A call to this routine must precede all other calls to SOR routines.
SOR$STAT	Returns a statistic about the sort or merge operation.

7.3.5 Using Conversion Functions

The NCS Library also provides conversion function tables used to perform the following transformations:

- Convert text from NRC to DEC MCS
- Convert text from DEC MCS to NRC
- Change the case of DEC MCS characters
- Remove diacritical marks from DEC MCS characters

Table 7–6 lists the conversion function tables provided in the default NCS library.

Table 7–6. Conversion Function Tables in the NCS Library

Danish_NRC_to_Multi	EDT_VT2XX
Finnish_NRC_to_Multi	FrCan_NRC_to_Multi
French_NRC_to_Multi	German_NRC_to_Multi
Italian_NRC_to_Multi	Multi_to_Danish_NRC
Multi_to_Finnish_NRC	Multi_to_FrCan_NRC
Multi_to_French_NRC	Multi_to_German_NRC
Multi_to_Italian_NRC	Multi_to_Lower

(Table 7–6 continues on next page)

Table 7–6. Conversion Function Tables in the NCS Library (cont.)

Multi_to_NoDiacriticals	Multi_to_Norwegian_NRC
Multi_to_Swedish_NRC	Multi_to_Swiss_NRC
Multi_to_Swiss_NRC	Multi_to_UK_NRC
Multi_to_Upper	Norwegian_NRC_to_Multi
Swedish_NRC_to_Multi	Swiss_NRC_to_Multi
UK_NRC_to_Multi	

International software products can use NCS conversion tables to transform user input to a form appropriate for internal processing, storage, or transmission.

Table 7–7 lists the NCS routines that a VMS application can use to access conversion function tables.

Table 7–7. NCS Routines Using Conversion Functions

Routine Name	Description
NCS$CONVERT	Converts a string using a specified conversion function table.
NCS$END_CF	Terminates the use of a conversion function table.
NCS$GET_CF	Retrieves the definition of the named CF from the library.
NCS$RESTORE_CF	Permits the calling program to restore the definition of a saved conversion function.
NCS$SAVE_CF	Permits the calling program to save the definition of a conversion function in a database.

Example 7–4 illustrates the use of NCS Utility conversion function routines in a C program.

Example 7–4. C Program for Case Conversions

```
/***************************************************************************/
/* ********************************************************************** */
/* *                                                                    * */
/* *    CONVERT.C                                                       * */
/* *                                                                    * */
/* *    An NCS demonstration program.                                   * */
/* *                                                                    * */
/* *    This program takes a hard coded string and converts it using a  * */
/* *    hard coded conversion function.  The compiletime constant "d_size" * */
/* *    can be varied to see the effects of having a destination string * */
/* *    which is too long or too short.                                 * */
/* *                                                                    * */
/* *    Any bad status (i.e. warning, error, or fatal condition) which is  * */
/* *    returned by the calls is signaled immediately to the user.  If  * */
/* *    the status is not fatal, execution will resume with the following * */
/* *    statement.                                                      * */
/* *                                                                    * */
/* ********************************************************************** */
/***************************************************************************/

/* Include Files */
#include <descrip>
#include <stdio>

/* Macro Definitions */
#define CHECK_(i)     if (!((status = i) & 1)) lib$signal(status)

/* Constants */
#define d_size 80

/* External Routines */
extern unsigned lib$signal();
extern unsigned ncs$get_cf();
extern unsigned ncs$convert();
extern unsigned ncs$end_cf();

/* The Main Procedure */
main()
{
    long            cf_id;          /* Conversion Function Ident          */
    unsigned short  ret_length;     /* Length of the return string        */
    struct dsc$descriptor_s dest;   /* Destination string descriptor      */
    char            d_str[d_size];  /* Destination string allocation      */
    unsigned        status;         /* Used by CHECK_ macro               */

    /* Create static descriptors for the conversion function name and the  */
    /* string to be converted (source of conversion).                      */
    $DESCRIPTOR(cf_name, "EDT_VT2xx");
    $DESCRIPTOR(source,  "ctrl-A ='<ESC>', ctrl-B ='<ESC>'");
```

(Example 7–4 continues on next page)

Example 7–4 (Cont.). C Program for Case Conversions

```
    /* Initialize the destination string descriptor */
    dest.dsc$w_length = d_size;          /* The allocation of the string    */
    dest.dsc$b_dtype = DSC$K_DTYPE_T;    /* The data type: Character string  */
    dest.dsc$b_class = DSC$K_CLASS_S;    /* The descriptor class: String     */
    dest.dsc$a_pointer = d_str;          /* Address of allocation            */

    /* Get the ident of the conversion function, convert the string, and    */
    /*  then release the resources.                                          */
    CHECK_( ncs$get_cf (&cf_id, &cf_name) );
    CHECK_( ncs$convert(&cf_id, &source, &dest, &ret_length ) );
    CHECK_( ncs$end_cf (&cf_id) );

    /* Print the results */
    printf("\n\nThe source string, \n\n\t\"%s\"\n\n", source.dsc$a_pointer);
    printf("was converted to\n\n\t\"%s\"\n\n", dest.dsc$a_pointer);
    printf("using the \"%s\" conversion function.\n\n", cf_name.dsc$a_pointer);
    printf("The source string was %d characters long.\n", source.dsc$w_length);
    printf("The destination string was %d characters long.\n", ret_length);
}
```

7.4 Command Language Localization

If the application uses a command introducer, that is, a character that announces a command to the application, then that character should be modifiable. For example, if the application recognizes \P as the directive used to insert a page break, foreign engineering groups should be able to replace both the P and the backslash with characters more appropriate for the locales they support. (On some LK201 keyboard variants, the backslash character is only available through a three-keystroke Compose key sequence.) Store command introducers externally with other application control, and in a modifiable form.

Use standard encoding to handle any user-supplied text that is intended to become a part of the attributes interchanged between applications. Never store such attributes in natural language text in the interchange format.

User-supplied keywords (in the language of the user) should be recognized on input and stored in a language-neutral form in the document. These keywords may then be translated again into a different user's language at a future processing time.

7.5 The Terminal Fallback Facility

VMS provides transparent support for local terminals and keyboards through the Terminal Fallback Facility (TFF). TFF helps bridge the gap between the character set used by your application, and the character set supported by the user's terminal, relieving the application from character conversion tasks. TFF can convert characters sent to the terminal by your application to characters the terminal is capable of displaying, and it can convert characters input at the terminal into characters that your application can process. Figure 7–2 illustrates a typical configuration using TFF.

Figure 7–2. Terminal Fallback Facility

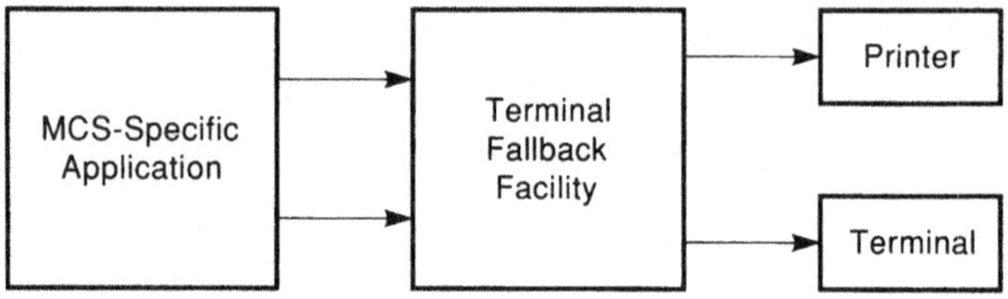

In international markets, the Terminal Fallback Facility allows users with National Replacement Character (NRC) set terminals to use applications that use the DEC Multinational Character Set (MCS). To use an NRC terminal with an MCS-specific application, characters must be converted going to and from the terminal to MCS. TFF provides this conversion using a library of conversion tables, all in a manner that is completely transparent to the application. Thus, VMS relieves an application that uses MCS of the need to provide support for NRC terminals.

If your application uses accelerator keys, such as Control key or Gold key sequences, to invoke application functionality, define your key bindings in an external, modifiable file. Your key bindings should not be hardcoded in your application source code. If you use a form management system such as DECforms, you can define your accelerator keys in the modifiable user interface source files for your product. Print control should be modifiable also, as any printing devices your product supports can vary from locale to locale.

7.6 VMS Operating System: Multilingual Software Example

This section presents an example of a multilingual software product based on the VMS operating system. This example is a menu-driven order entry system in two languages: English and French. Referred to as the Order Entry System (OES), the application demonstrates the following features:

- VMS date and time support
- DECforms (for the forms system)
- The NCS Utility
- RMS features for collating sequences and manipulation of currency and number values for an international environment

The system monitors inventories of computer components and processes orders for the components. Users can perform the following tasks:

- Place an order for a component
- Display a sorted list of components
- List a component in different languages
- Change the user profile to change the user interface
- Exit the program

The application uses two databases, one language-specific and one language-independent. The language-specific database maintains the records containing part identifiers and part descriptions in a particular language. The language-independent database maintains the records containing part identifiers, quantities, prices, order dates, and so on.

Records in both databases are accessed by using the part identifier, which is a unique, language-independent identifier. Both databases are RMS-indexed files that have specific collating sequences stored in them. Once a file is created with a collating sequence, all records inserted in the file are automatically sorted according to the stored collating sequence.

The language-specific database is ordered by using the part description as its primary key and the part identifier as its secondary key. The language-independent database uses the part identifier as its primary key, with no secondary key.

The component information is collected by using the part ID from both data files. Data formatting is based on the information stored in the form and the profile before it is displayed.

7.6.1 Sample Application and User Profiles

The OES application uses two profiles:

- An application profile

  The application profile provides two sets of information:

  — Information used by all user interfaces, regardless of locale

  — Locale-specific information used as the default (English in this case). This information includes such things as date and time formats, currency, exchange rate, and so on.

- A user profile

  The user profile contains information that is specific to a particular locale; the user profile supplements the application profile. The user profile in this example is in French.

Both profiles are text files. Example 7–5 shows a default application profile, and Example 7–6 shows a default French user profile.

Example 7–5. Application Profile

```
!* This is the application profile for the application.  User profile
!* of English is included as part of this file.
!* If there is a need for comments, add them on the line before the
!* code, NOT on the same line.
!*
!* Location of common database which includes the part ID, price,
!* quantity.
A01:$DISK2:[AVAKIAN.EXAMPLE]DATA_BASE.DAT
!* Location of description file for English
A02:$DISK2:[AVAKIAN.EXAMPLE]ENG_DESC.DAT
```

(Example 7–5 continues on next page)

Example 7–5 (Cont.). Application Profile

```
!* Location of the form file, holds the help files also
A03:$DISK2:[AVAKIAN.FORMS]ORD_ENTRY.FORM
!* Location of the message file.
A04:$DISK2:[AVAKIAN.EXAMPLE]ENGLISH_MSG.MSG
!* Location of the user profile's which will be read at start up.
B01:$DISK2:[AVAKIAN.EXAMPLE]FRENCH.UP
!* Location of the NCS library
C01:SYS$LIBRARY:NCS$LIBRARY
!* Base language
C02:ENGLISH
!* Base date/time formats and the language of use.
D01:LIB$DATE_FORMAT_011
D02:LIB$TIME_FORMAT_013
D03:ENGLISH
!* Base currency and exchange rate relative to base country
!* Make sure the currency symbol matches the one specified in
!* IFDL file.
E01:$
E02:1
!* The thousand separator and the fraction separator.
!* Make sure the separators are the same specified in the IFDL
!* form file.
E03:,
E04:.
```

Example 7–6. French User Profile

```
!* The user profile specific to French.
!* Since this file is a subset of application profile, the
!* format of the file is similar to the application profile.
!* Even the records have the same ID (for example, A01 has
!* the same kind of information in both files if they are
!* the same kind)
A02:$DISK2:[AVAKIAN.EXAMPLE]FRN_DESC.DAT
A04:$DISK2:[AVAKIAN.EXAMPLE]FRENCH_MSG.MSG
!* Location of the NCS library and the NCS language.
C01:SYS$LIBRARY:NCS$LIBRARY
C02:FRENCH
!* Date and Time format
D01:LIB$DATE_FORMAT_001
D02:LIB$TIME_FORMAT_019
D03:FRENCH
```

(Example 7–6 continues on next page)

Example 7–6 (Cont.). French User Profile

```
!* The currency and the exchange rate relative to US.
E01:Fr
!* Put the exchange rate in (rate * US $) = country money
E02:0.5
!* The thousand separator and the fraction separator.
E03:
E04:,
```

The OES application utilizes the profiles as follows:

1. At the beginning of the OES program, both profiles are read in and stored in memory as data structures, the application profile has a pointer to the user profile.
2. Some initialization is done from the information read in.
3. Logical names for date and time formatting and the language, LIB$DT_FORMAT and SYS$LANGUAGE, are set as shown in Example 7–6.
4. A language logical for forms, FORMS$LANGUAGE, is set up.
5. The language-specific database, language-independent database, and the form file are opened.
6. The menu is displayed.

7.6.2 Sample Source Code

The OES sample source code for two options is shown in Example 7–7 in detail: Placing an order and Displaying ordered list of components. The panels (from the .IFDL file) for these options appear at the end of the source code in both English and French. The other three options are described at the end of the .IFDL piece.

Example 7–7. OES Source Code

```
/*
 **
 ** Structure defined to read each line of the profile.
 **
*/

struct AP_LINE
        {
        char id[ID_LENGTH] ;
        char *data ;
        } ;

/*
 **
 **      UP_REC holds the language dependent information such as
 **      date/time formatting logicals and language, the currency,
 **      and the rate exchange.
 **
*/

struct UP_REC
        {
        char *ncs_lib ;
        char *ncs_lang ;
        char *desc_file ;
        char *msg_file ;
        char *date_format ;
        char *time_format ;
        char *dt_lang ;
        char *currency ;
        char *exchange_rate ;
        char *thousand_sep ;
        char *fraction_sep ;
        };

/*
 **      Since UP_REC is a subset of AP_REC, include the structure
 **      in AP_REC and add the AP_REC specific ones at the end.
 **      NOTE: The header of UP_REC type should be the first field of
 **      the structure.
*/

struct AP_REC
        {
        struct UP_REC header ;
        char *up_file ;
        char *neutral_data ;
        char *form_lib ;
         struct UP_REC *u_profile ;
        } ;
```

(Example 7–7 continues on next page)

Example 7–7 (Cont.). OES Source Code

```
/*
 **
 **      Record for the order item panel.
 **      The constants for length are defined earlier.
 **
*/

struct COMPONENT {
        char part_id[COMP_ID] ;
        char part_desc[COMP_DESC] ;
        long unit_price ;
        char valid_until[DATE_LENGTH] ;
        short quantity ;
        short order ;
        } ;
/*
 **
 **      Record used for listing the sorted items.
 **
*/

struct ordered_items {
        char part_id[COMP_ID] ;
        char descrip[DESC_LEN] ;
        char currency[CURR_LEN] ;
        long price ;
        short q_avail ;
        char valid_until[DATE_SHORT] ;
        } ;

struct ordered_list {
        short number_entries ;
        struct ordered_items list_items[ITEM_LIMIT] ;
        } ;

/*
 **
 **      All the external functions for DECforms, NCS calls
 **      and necessary system calls.
 **
*/
        .
        .
        .
/*
 **
 **      Global information set for accessing the forms$ calls.
 **
*/

$DESCRIPTOR (device_name , "SYS$INPUT" ) ;
```

(Example 7–7 continues on next page)

Example 7–7 (Cont.). OES Source Code

```
/*
 **
 **      Since switching between English and French occurs, save
 **      each one and then set it to the main session_id when needed.
 **
*/

$DESCRIPTOR (session_id , "                 " ) ;
$DESCRIPTOR (session_id1 , "                " ) ;
$DESCRIPTOR (session_id2 , "                " ) ;

$DESCRIPTOR ( list_items_desc, "ordered_list" ) ;

struct COMPONENT comp_info ;
struct ordered_list list ;
$STRUCTURE_DESCRIPTOR( list_desc, list ) ;


/*
 **
 **      SET_UP_LOGICALS sets up the itemlist and the other parameters
 **      and calls the system routine SYS$CRELNM to create the
 **      'SYS$LANGUAGE' and date/time formatting logicals in the process
 **      table.
 **
*/

long SET_UP_LOGICALS ( up_profile )
struct UP_REC *up_profile ;
{
unsigned long status ;

char *temp = "LNM$FILE_DEV" ;
char *logic_name = "SYS$LANGUAGE" ;
char *date_time  = "LIB$DT_FORMAT" ;
char temp_log[50] ;
struct dsc$descriptor_s table ;
struct dsc$descriptor_s log_name ;
/*
 **      Since LIB$DT_FORMAT is combination of LIB$DATE_FORMAT_nnn and
 **      LIB$TIME_FORMAT_nnn (nnn specifies a format) itemlist is an
 **      array of 3 items.  For FORMS$LANGUAGE, itemlist will be 2.
 **
 **
struct items itemlist[3] ;

/*
 **      Put the table name and the logical name in a string descriptor
 **      format, since sys$crelnm expects a string descriptor.
*/
```

(Example 7–7 continues on next page)

Example 7–7 (Cont.). OES Source Code

```
table.dsc$w_length = strlen (temp) ;
table.dsc$b_dtype = DSC$K_DTYPE_T ;
table.dsc$b_class = DSC$K_CLASS_S ;
table.dsc$a_pointer = temp ;

log_name.dsc$w_length = strlen (logic_name) ;
log_name.dsc$b_dtype = DSC$K_DTYPE_T ;
log_name.dsc$b_class = DSC$K_CLASS_S ;
log_name.dsc$a_pointer = logic_name ;

/*
 **      Fill in the itemlist with information for SYS$LANGUAGE logical.
 **
*/

itemlist[0].buf_len = strlen(up_profile->dt_lang ) ;
itemlist[0].item_code = LNM$_STRING ;
itemlist[0].buf_add = up_profile->dt_lang ;
itemlist[0].ret_len_add = 0 ;

itemlist[1].buf_len = 0 ;
itemlist[1].item_code = 0 ;
itemlist[1].buf_add = 0 ;
itemlist[1].ret_len_add = 0 ;


status = sys$crelnm (0, &table, &log_name , 0, itemlist );
if ( status == SS$_NORMAL || status == SS$_SUPERSEDE )
        {
/*
 **      When SYS$LANGUAGE is set, then set up the LIB$DT_FORMAT logical
 **      using the same procedure as above.
*/

        log_name.dsc$w_length = strlen(date_time ) ;
        log_name.dsc$b_dtype = DSC$K_DTYPE_T ;
        log_name.dsc$b_class = DSC$K_CLASS_S ;
        log_name.dsc$a_pointer = date_time ;

        itemlist[0].buf_len = strlen(up_profile->date_format ) ;
        itemlist[0].item_code = LNM$_STRING ;
        itemlist[0].buf_add = up_profile->date_format ;
        itemlist[0].ret_len_add = 0 ;

        itemlist[1].buf_len = strlen(up_profile->time_format ) ;
        itemlist[1].item_code = LNM$_STRING ;
        itemlist[1].buf_add = up_profile->time_format ;
        itemlist[1].ret_len_add = 0 ;

        itemlist[2].buf_len = 0 ;
        itemlist[2].item_code = 0 ;
        itemlist[2].buf_add = 0 ;
        itemlist[2].ret_len_add = 0 ;
```

(Example 7–7 continues on next page)

Example 7–7 (Cont.). OES Source Code

```
        status = SS$_NORMAL ;
/*
 **
 **      If the date/time logical was already set up, clear the memory
 **      block for that information so we can reset it.
 **
*/
        if ( user_context != 0 ) status = lib$free_date_time_context ( &user_context) ;
        if (status = SS$_NORMAL )
                {
                status = sys$crelnm (0, &table , &log_name , 0, itemlist) ;
                if ( status == SS$_NORMAL || status == SS$_SUPERSEDE )
                        return (SS$_NORMAL) ;

                }
        }
        return (status) ;
}


/*
 **
 **      OPEN_FORM_FILE sets up the descriptor for the form file which
 **      is a global variable set in the application profile and calls
 **      the DECforms call to perform it.
 **
*/
long open_form_file ()

{
long stat ;

struct dsc$descriptor_s form_name ;

  form_name.dsc$w_length = strlen(prof->form_lib) ;
  form_name.dsc$b_dtype = DSC$K_DTYPE_T ;
  form_name.dsc$b_class = DSC$K_CLASS_S ;
  form_name.dsc$a_pointer = prof->form_lib ;

stat = forms$enable (0,               /* form table in case of linked in */
                     &device_name,    /* Terminal to use */
                     &session_id ,    /* session ID returned by enable */
                     &form_name ) ;   /* name of the form file */

if (stat = FORMS$_NORMAL )
        stat = sys$success ;
else
        stat = sys$enable_error ;

return stat ;

}
```

(Example 7–7 continues on next page)

Example 7–7 (Cont.). OES Source Code

```
/*
 **      The information following  this  point shows steps taken when
 **      the first option, Place an order for component, is selected.
 **
 **      ORDER_ITEM puts up the order item panel and receives the user
 **      input for the part ID.
 **
*/

long order_item ( part )
struct dsc$descriptor_s *part ;

{
long stat ;
long cf_id ;

$DESCRIPTOR(comp_name_desc, "comp_info" ) ;
$STRUCTURE_DESCRIPTOR(comp_rec_desc, comp_info ) ;
$DESCRIPTOR(cf_name , "Multi_to_Upper" ) ;
$DESCRIPTOR(cf_lib , u_p->ncs_lib ) ;
struct dsc$descriptor_s dest ;
struct dsc$descriptor libr ;

stat = SS$_NORMAL ;
stat = forms$receive( &session_id ,         /* session_id */
                       &comp_name_desc,     /* name of receive record */
                       &1,                  /* number of records received */
                       0,0,                 /* receive ctl text msg/count */
                       0,0,                 /* send ctl text msg/count */
                       0,                   /* timeout */
                       0,                   /* parent request ID */
                       0,                   /* request options item list */
                       &comp_rec_desc,      /* the record */
                       0) ;                 /* shadow record */

if (stat = FORMS$_NORMAL)
{
   stat = SS$_NORMAL ;
   part->dsc$w_length = COMP_ID ;
   part->dsc$b_dtype = DSC$K_DTYPE_T ;
   part->dsc$b_class = DSC$K_CLASS_S ;
   part->dsc$a_pointer = comp_info.part_id ;

   dest.dsc$w_length = COMP_ID ;
   dest.dsc$b_dtype = DSC$K_DTYPE_T ;
   dest.dsc$b_class = DSC$K_CLASS_S ;
   dest.dsc$a_pointer = "         " ;
```

(Example 7–7 continues on next page)

Example 7–7 (Cont.). OES Source Code

```
    /*
     **   The next piece demonstrates the use of NCS conversion functions.
     **   The user can enter the part ID in capital letters, lowercase letters,
     **   or a combination of both.
     **   The piece converts the input (part ID) to uppercase characters.
     **   DECforms lets the user specify 'UPPERCASE' clause in the field
     **   attribute to capitalize the input.
     **
    */
    libr.dsc$w_length = strlen(u_p->ncs_lib ) ;
    libr.dsc$b_dtype = DSC$K_DTYPE_T ;
    libr.dsc$b_class = DSC$K_CLASS_S ;
    libr.dsc$a_pointer = u_p->ncs_lib ;

    stat = ncs$get_cf( &cf_id , &cf_name ,&libr ) ;

    if (stat = SS$_NORMAL) {
     stat = ncs$convert (&cf_id, part , &dest ) ;
     if (stat = SS$_NORMAL) {
             stat = ncs$end_cf (&cf_id ) ;

             strncpy(comp_info.part_id , dest.dsc$a_pointer , COMP_ID ) ;
             part->dsc$a_pointer = comp_info.part_id ;
             stat = SS$_NORMAL ;
       }
       else stat = sys$conv_func_f ;
     }
     else  stat = sys$cf_get_f ;
}
else stat = sys$receive_f ;

return stat ;
}

/*
 **
 **      After the language-specific database and Language-Independent
 **      Database are searched for the remaining information,
 **      DISPLAY_COMPONENT is called.  It in turn calls:
 **      CONVERT_DATE, CONVERT_PRICE, and DISPLAY_THE_COMPONENT.
 **
 **      CONVERT_DATE formats the date and time (in the internal format)
 **      passed by the 'date' to a string using the already setup logicals.
 **
*/

long convert_date ( date , date_desc )
struct quad *date ;
struct dsc$descriptor_s *date_desc ;

{
```

(Example 7–7 continues on next page)

Example 7–7 (Cont.). OES Source Code

```
date_desc->dsc$w_length = 50 ;
date_desc->dsc$b_dtype = DSC$K_DTYPE_T ;
date_desc->dsc$b_class = DSC$K_CLASS_S ;
date_desc->dsc$a_pointer = (char *) calloc(1,date_desc->dsc$w_length ) ;
return ( lib$format_date_time ( date_desc , date , &user_context )) ;

}
/*
 **
 **      CONVERT_PRICE converts the price according to the exchange rate
 **      specified in user_profile.  The price is stored in the data base as
 **      longword integer. The price_type which is kept as a field in the same
 **      data base identifies the price as decimal (fractional) or integer.
 **      If the price_type is 'I' (integer) then the price is multiplied by
 **      100 to cancel out the forms scaling down by -2.
 **      The form makes the necessary additions before displaying the information.
 **      It adds thousand separator if necessary, the decimal separator and also
 **      the currency symbol. All of this information is kept in the .IFDL file.
 **
*/

convert_price (  price , converted_price , price_type )
long *price ;
long *converted_price ;
char *price_type ;

{
float temp ;
long temp_l ;
float rate ;

rate = (float) atof(u_p->exchange_rate) ;
temp = *price * rate ;
temp_l = temp ;

/*
 **      The number is rounded up.
*/
if ( temp - temp_l >= .50 )     temp = temp + 1 ;

/*
 **      To undo the scaling down of the forms system.
*/

if ( *price_type == 'I' )       temp = temp * 100 ;
*converted_price = temp ;

}
```

(Example 7–7 continues on next page)

Example 7–7 (Cont.). OES Source Code

```
/*
 **
 **      Displays information such as quantity available, price, date the
 **      price is valid until and description of the part in specified language.
 **      The information is displayed on the same panel where ID was entered.
 **      Forms$transceive is used first to send this information to the panel,
 **      and then to receive the users input on the 'Quantity to Order' field.
*/

long display_the_component ()

{
long stat ;
$DESCRIPTOR(comp_name_desc, "comp_info" ) ;
$STRUCTURE_DESCRIPTOR(comp_rec_desc, comp_info ) ;

 stat = forms$transceive(&session_id,            /* session_id */
                         &comp_name_desc,         /* send record name in form */
                         &1,                      /* number of records sent */
                         &comp_name_desc,         /* receive record name in form */
                         &1,                      /* number of records sent */
                         0,0,                     /* receive ctl text msg/count */
                         0,0,                     /* send ctl text msg/count */
                         0,                       /* timeout */
                         0,                       /* parent request ID */
                         0,                       /* request options item list */
                         &comp_rec_desc,          /* the send record */
                         0,                       /* send shadow record */
                         &comp_rec_desc,          /* the receive record */
                         0 ) ;                    /* receive shadow record/length */

if (stat != FORMS$_NORMAL)       stat = sys$transceive_f ;
else stat = SS$_NORMAL ;
return stat ;

}
/*
 **
 **      DISPLAY_COMPONENT converts the date, price, and all the raw data to
 **      user specified values, and then calls the DISPLAY_THE_COMPONENT to
 **      display it on the panel. It also stores the date and time the order
 **      was put in.
 **
*/
```

(Example 7–7 continues on next page)

Example 7–7 (Cont.). OES Source Code

```
display_component ( id , q_avail , q_ordered , date_ordered , price ,
                   price_type , price_valid , description )
struct dsc$descriptor_s *id ;
short *q_avail ;
short *q_ordered ;
struct quad *date_ordered ;
long *price ;
char *price_type ;
struct quad *price_valid ;
struct dsc$descriptor_s *description ;

{
struct dsc$descriptor_s date_desc ;
long converted_price ;
long status ;

status = convert_date (price_valid , &date_desc ) ;
if ( status != SS$_NORMAL )      return status ;
convert_price ( price , &converted_price , price_type ) ;

id->dsc$b_dtype = DSC$K_DTYPE_T ;
id->dsc$b_class = DSC$K_CLASS_S ;
strncpy( comp_info.part_id , id->dsc$a_pointer , id->dsc$w_length) ;
description->dsc$b_dtype = DSC$K_DTYPE_T ;
description->dsc$b_class = DSC$K_CLASS_S ;
strncpy(comp_info.part_desc , description->dsc$a_pointer, description->dsc$w_length ) ;
comp_info.unit_price = converted_price ;
strncpy( comp_info.valid_until , date_desc.dsc$a_pointer , date_desc.dsc$w_length ) ;
comp_info.quantity = *q_avail ;
comp_info.order = 0 ;

status = display_the_component () ;
if ( status != SS$_NORMAL ) return status ;
*q_ordered = comp_info.order ;

/*
 **
 **      Get the date and time the order was placed, in case we want
 **      to use it later on.
 **
 **      After displaying the information, the user is expected
 **      either to enter a quantity to order or quit.  The database
 **      modification is done after the panel is processed.
 **
*/
return ( lib$convert_date_string (0, date_ordered)) ;

}
```

(Example 7–7 continues on next page)

Example 7–7 (Cont.). OES Source Code

```
/*
 **
 **      The information following this point is the second option
 **      on the menu, Listing the ordered items.
 **
 **      This routine is called when the list of ordered items is to be
 **      displayed. The components information is read from two different data
 **      files and for each component this function is called.
 **      This routine fills up the array to be displayed for index.
 **      'list' is declared globally. Also there is an equivalent structure in
 **      IFDL file (as form data and form record). Since the entries in the data
 **      base are limited to a small number in this example, the array is
 **      preallocated to 30 elements.
 **
*/

long populate_ordered_list (id, description, price_type, price,
                         q_avail, price_valid )
struct dsc$descriptor_s *id ;
struct dsc$descriptor_s *description ;
char *price_type ;
long *price ;
short *q_avail ;
struct quad *price_valid ;

{
struct dsc$descriptor_s date_desc ;
long converted_price ;
long status ;

status = SS$_NORMAL ;

status = convert_date (price_valid , &date_desc ) ;

convert_price (price, &converted_price, price_type ) ;

strncpy (list.list_items[list.number_entries].part_id, id->dsc$a_pointer,
id->dsc$w_length ) ;
strncpy (list.list_items[list.number_entries].descrip, description->dsc$a_pointer,
DESC_LEN) ;
strncpy (list.list_items[list.number_entries].currency, u_p->currency,
strlen(u_p->currency )  ) ;
strncpy (list.list_items[list.number_entries].valid_until ,
date_desc.dsc$a_pointer, DATE_SHORT) ;

/*
**      converted_price and q_avail are passed as long and short integers.
**      The form makes the final modifications to display them in the
**      user-specified format.
*/

list.list_items[list.number_entries].price = converted_price ;
list.list_items[list.number_entries].q_avail = *q_avail ;
list.number_entries ++ ;
```

(Example 7–7 continues on next page)

Example 7–7 (Cont.). OES Source Code

```
return status ;

}
/*
**
**      This routine is called after the array is filled with information
**      to blank out the array fields not filled, otherwise if the last page is
**      not full it will have the items from the previous page.
**
*/
clean_up_array ()

{
short i ;

  for (i = list.number_entries ; i < ITEM_LIMIT ; i ++ )
        {
        strcpy(list.list_items[i].part_id , "       ") ;
        strcpy(list.list_items[i].descrip , "                         " ) ;
        strcpy(list.list_items[i].currency , "  " ) ;
        strcpy(list.list_items[i].valid_until , "                          " ) ;
        list.list_items[i].price = 0 ;
        list.list_items[i].q_avail = 0 ;
        }
}

/*
**
**      DISPLAY_LIST is called when the array of ordered items is ready
**      to be displayed.
**
*/

display_list ()

{

long stat ;

stat = forms$transceive( &session_id,           /* session_id */
                        &list_items_desc ,      /* send record name in form */
                        &1,                     /* number of records sent */
                        &list_items_desc,       /* receive record name in form */
                        &1,                     /* number of records sent */
                        0,0,                    /* receive ctl text msg/count */
                        0,0,                    /* send ctl text msd/count */
                        0,                      /* timeout */
                        0,                      /* parent request ID */
                        0,                      /* request options item list */
                        &list_desc,             /* the send record */
                        0,                      /* send shadow record */
                        &list_desc,             /* the receive record */
                        0 ) ;                   /* receive shadow record */
```

(Example 7–7 continues on next page)

Example 7–7 (Cont.). OES Source Code

```
if ( stat != FORMS$_NORMAL)  stat = sys$transceive_f ;
else stat = SS$_NORMAL ;
return stat ;
}
```

Example 7–8 shows portions of code taken from the ORD_ENTRY.IFDL file. They correspond to the source code described in Example 7–7. Both layouts with their corresponding panels are kept in one file, called ORD_ENTRY.FORM. Switching between layouts is done through the FORMS$LANGUAGE logical when the user selects the fourth option, Change Profile. Example 7–8 does not display the full layouts and panels; rather, it includes only the pieces necessary to demonstrate DECforms internationalization features.

All the text relating to the screen is kept in ORD_ENTRY.IFDL. The panel and field names in the two layouts are identical to each other. The layouts differ only in the text that is displayed and the position of that text.

Example 7–8. Samples from ORD_ENTRY.IFDL

```
/*
* The data fields are defined at the beginning of the file.
* Form data is defined first, then the form records.
*/

    Form Data
        PART_ID Character(7)
        PART_DESC Character(30)
        UNIT_PRICE Longword Integer
        VALID_UNTIL Character(30)
        QUANTITY Word Integer
        DATE_TIME Character(30)
    END Data
```

(Example 7–8 continues on next page)

Example 7–8 (Cont.). Samples from ORD_ENTRY.IFDL

```
    FORM DATA
        first_page       UNSIGNED WORD
        entry_count      UNSIGNED WORD
        GROUP items OCCURS 30
                part_id CHARACTER(7)
                descrip CHARACTER(22)
                curr CHARACTER(2)
                price LONGWORD INTEGER
                q_avail WORD INTEGER
                VALID CHARACTER(25)
        END GROUP
    END DATA

    FORM RECORD comp_info
        PART_ID Character(7)
        PART_DESC Character(30)
        UNIT_PRICE Longword Integer
        VALID_UNTIL Character (30)
        QUANTITY Word Integer
        ORDER   Word Integer
    END RECORD

    FORM RECORD ordered_list
        entry_count                UNSIGNED WORD
        GROUP items OCCURS 30
                part_id            CHARACTER(7)
                descrip            CHARACTER(22)
                curr               CHARACTER(2)
                price              LONGWORD INTEGER
                q_avail            WORD INTEGER
                VALID              CHARACTER(25)
        END GROUP
    END RECORD

/*
*       Beginning of a layout - English layout.
*       Note the Language is defined here.
*/

    Layout ENGLISH_LAYOUT
        Device
            Terminal
                Type %VT300
            Terminal
                Type %VT200
            Terminal
                Type %VT100
        End Device
        Language "ENGLISH"
        Units Characters
        Size 24 Lines by 80 Columns
```

(Example 7–8 continues on next page)

Example 7–8 (Cont.). Samples from ORD_ENTRY.IFDL

```
/*
* Define External responses for this panel.
*/

        TRANSCEIVE RESPONSE comp_info comp_info
                ACTIVATE FIELD order ON order_item
        END RESPONSE

        RECEIVE RESPONSE comp_info
                RESET PART_ID
                RESET PART_DESC RESET UNIT_PRICE RESET VALID_UNTIL
                RESET QUANTITY RESET ORDER
                ACTIVATE FIELD part_id ON order_item
        END RESPONSE

/*
 * English panel for ordering a component.
*/

        Panel ORDER_ITEM
            Display
                %Keypad_Application

            /*
             *   screen where the user can enter the order
            */

            Use Help Panel
                HELP_ORDER_ITEM

            /*
            *   code for Digital Logo - NOT SHOWN
            */

            Literal Text
                Line 5
                Column 23
                Value "Order Item Menu"
                Display
                    Bold
                    Font Size Double High
            End Literal

            Literal Text
                Line 10
                Column 8
                Value "Part id :"
                Display
                    Bold
            End Literal
```

(Example 7–8 continues on next page)

Example 7–8 (Cont.). Samples from ORD_ENTRY.IFDL

```
Literal Text
    Line 12
    Column 8
    Value "Part Description :"
    Display
        Bold
End Literal

Literal Text
    Line 14
    Column 8
    Value "Price /Unit :"
    Display
        Bold
End Literal

Literal Text
    Line 16
    Column 8
    Value "Price /Valid Until :"
    Display
        Bold
End Literal

Literal Text
    Line 18
    Column 8
    Value "Quantity :"
    Display
        Bold
End Literal

Literal Text
    Line 20
    Column 8
    Value "Quantity to Order :"
    Display
        Bold
End Literal

Field PART_ID
    Line 10
    Column 18
    Output Picture X(7)
    REQUIRE part_id <> " "
            MESSAGE "INPUT REQUIRED"
End Field

Field PART_DESC
    Line 12
    Column 27
    Output Picture X(30)
End Field
```

(Example 7–8 continues on next page)

Example 7–8 (Cont.). Samples from ORD_ENTRY.IFDL

```
/*
*       W - There will be a currency sign displayed at the left side of
*           the picture.
*       R - Appearing to the right of decimal point invokes the trailing
*           replacements. And to the left of the decimal point invokes
*           the leading replacements.
*       Note - The currency sign is specified in the form and also the
*               decimal separator is specified here.
*
*/
            Field UNIT_PRICE
                Line 14
                Column 22
                Output Picture W99',''999',''99R9.9R9
                SCALE -2
                CURRENCY SIGN IS "$"
                DECIMAL POINT IS PERIOD
            End Field

            Field VALID_UNTIL
                Line 16
                Column 29
                Output Picture X(30)
            End Field

            Field QUANTITY
                Line 18
                Column 19
                Output Picture 99',''999R
            End Field

            Field ORDER
                Line 20
                Column 28
                Justification Right
                Replace Leading " "
                Output Picture 99',''999R

                VALIDATION RESPONSE
                   IF ORDER > QUANTITY THEN
                   MESSAGE "'Order' amount should be less than 'Quantity' available"
                   INVALID
                   END IF
                END RESPONSE
            End Field

        End Panel
```

(Example 7–8 continues on next page)

Example 7–8 (Cont.). Samples from ORD_ENTRY.IFDL

```
/*
*       The layout definition for French. Language is again defined here.
*/

    Layout FRENCH_LAYOUT
        Device
            Terminal
                Type %VT300
            Terminal
                Type %VT200
            Terminal
                Type %VT100
        End Device
        Language "FRENCH"
        Units Characters
        Size 24 Lines by 80 Columns

/*
 *      The external responses are defined the same way as in English layout.
*/

/*
 *       The French version of the same panel.
*/

        Panel ORDER_ITEM
            Display
                %Keypad_Application

            /*
             *   screen where the user can enter the order
            */

            Use Help Panel
                HELP_ORDER_ITEM

            /*
             *   Digital Logo
            */

            Literal Text
                Line 5
                Column 19
                Value "Menu d'articles à commander"
                Display
                    Bold
                    Font Size Double High
            End Literal
```

(Example 7–8 continues on next page)

Example 7–8 (Cont.). Samples from ORD_ENTRY.IFDL

```
Literal Text
    Line 10
    Column 8
    Value "Identification de l'article :"
    Display
        Bold
End Literal

Literal Text
    Line 12
    Column 8
    Value "Description de l'article :"
    Display
        Bold
End Literal

Literal Text
    Line 14
    Column 8
    Value "Prix unitaire :"
    Display
        Bold
End Literal

Literal Text
    Line 16
    Column 8
    Value "Prix valable jusqu'au :"
    Display
        Bold
End Literal

Literal Text
    Line 18
    Column 8
    Value "Quantité :"
    Display
        Bold
End Literal

Literal Text
    Line 20
    Column 8
    Value "Quantité à commander  :"
    Display
       Bold
End Literal
```

(Example 7–8 continues on next page)

Example 7–8 (Cont.). Samples from ORD_ENTRY.IFDL

```
          Field PART_ID
              Line 10
              Column 38
              Output Picture X(7)
              REQUIRE part_id <> " "
              MESSAGE "Entrée requise"
          End Field

          Field PART_DESC
              Line 12
              Column 34
              Output Picture X(30)
          End Field

          Field UNIT_PRICE
              Line 14
              Column 24
/*
 *       The thousand separator can be any character.
*/
              Output Picture W99' '999' '99R9,9R9
              SCALE -2
              CURRENCY SIGN IS "Fr"
              DECIMAL POINT IS COMMA
          End Field

          Field VALID_UNTIL
              Line 16
              Column 32
              Output Picture X(30)
          End Field

          Field QUANTITY
              Line 18
              Column 19
              Output Picture 99' '999R
          End Field

          Field ORDER
              Line 20
              Column 28
              Justification Right
              Replace Leading " "
              Output Picture 99' '999R

              VALIDATION RESPONSE
                      IF ORDER > QUANTITY THEN
                      MESSAGE "L'ordre le montant doit être au-dessous de la
                               Quantité existante"
                      INVALID
                      END IF
              END RESPONSE
```

(Example 7–8 continues on next page)

Example 7–8 (Cont.). Samples from ORD_ENTRY.IFDL

```
            End Field

        End Panel

/*
 * English panel for the list of ordered items.
*/

        Panel list_items
            Viewport OPTION_SCREEN
            Display
                %Keypad_Application
            REMOVE

        FUNCTION RESPONSE TRANSMIT
                REMOVE OPTION_SCREEN
                RETURN
        END RESPONSE

        LITERAL TEXT
                LINE 5 COLUMN 11
                VALUE "Ordered List of the Items"
                DISPLAY FONT SIZE DOUBLE HIGH
        END LITERAL

        LITERAL TEXT
                LINE 7 COLUMN 2
                VALUE "Part ID"
                DISPLAY BOLD
        END LITERAL

        LITERAL TEXT
                SAME LINE COLUMN 12
                VALUE "Part Description"
                DISPLAY BOLD
        END LITERAL

        LITERAL TEXT
                SAME LINE COLUMN 35
                VALUE "Price/Unit"
                DISPLAY BOLD
        END LITERAL

        LITERAL TEXT
                SAME LINE COLUMN 49
                VALUE "Quantity"
                DISPLAY BOLD
        END LITERAL
```

(Example 7–8 continues on next page)

```
        LITERAL TEXT
                SAME LINE COLUMN 59
                VALUE "Price Valid Until"
                DISPLAY BOLD
        END LITERAL

        LITERAL POLYLINE
                LINE 8 COLUMN 1
                LINE 8 COLUMN 80
        END LITERAL

GROUP items
        VERTICAL DISPLAYS 10
        FIRST first_page
        SCROLL BY PAGE

            FUNCTION RESPONSE DOWN ITEM
                IF LAST ITEM THEN
                    MESSAGE "End of the list"
                    SIGNAL
                ELSE
                    POSITION TO DOWN OCCURRENCE
                END IF
            END RESPONSE

            FUNCTION RESPONSE UP ITEM
                IF FIRST ITEM THEN
                    MESSAGE "Beginning of the list"
                    SIGNAL
                ELSE
                    POSITION TO UP OCCURRENCE
                END IF
            END RESPONSE

            FUNCTION RESPONSE NEXT PANEL
                IF LAST ITEM THEN
                    MESSAGE "End of the list"
                    SIGNAL
                ELSE
                    POSITION TO DOWN OCCURRENCE UNSEEN
                END IF
            END RESPONSE

            FUNCTION RESPONSE PREVIOUS PANEL
                IF FIRST ITEM THEN
                    MESSAGE "Beginning of the list"
                    SIGNAL
                ELSE
                    POSITION TO UP OCCURRENCE UNSEEN
                END IF
            END RESPONSE
```

(Example 7–8 continues on next page)

Example 7–8 (Cont.). Samples from ORD_ENTRY.IFDL

```
        FIELD part_id           LINE 9 COLUMN 2
                                OUTPUT PICTURE X(7)
                            END FIELD

        FIELD descrip           LINE 9 COLUMN 10
                                OUTPUT PICTURE X(22)
                            END FIELD

        FIELD curr              LINE 9 COLUMN 33
                                OUTPUT PICTURE X(2)
                            END FIELD

        FIELD price             LINE 9 COLUMN 36
                                OUTPUT PICTURE 9',''999',''99R9.9R9
                                DECIMAL POINT IS PERIOD
                                SCALE -2
                            END FIELD

        FIELD q_avail           LINE 9 COLUMN 50
                                OUTPUT PICTURE 99',''999R
                            END FIELD

        FIELD valid             LINE 9 COLUMN 57
                                OUTPUT PICTURE X(23)
                            END FIELD

    END GROUP

    LITERAL POLYLINE
        LINE 19 COLUMN 1
        LINE 19 COLUMN 80
    END LITERAL

    FIELD first_page
        LINE 20 COLUMN 2
        OUTPUT PICTURE X(50)
        OUTPUT "FIRST page of the list."
            WHEN first_page = 1
        OUTPUT "MIDDLE page of the list."
            WHEN first_page = 11
        OUTPUT "LAST page of the list."
            WHEN first_page = 21
        PROTECTED
    END FIELD

END PANEL
```

(Example 7–8 continues on next page)

Example 7–8 (Cont.). Samples from ORD_ENTRY.IFDL

```
/*
 * French panel for listing the ordered items
*/
        Panel list_items
            Viewport OPTION_SCREEN
            Display
                %Keypad_Application
            REMOVE

        FUNCTION RESPONSE TRANSMIT
                REMOVE OPTION_SCREEN
                RETURN
        END RESPONSE

        LITERAL TEXT
                LINE 5 COLUMN 11
                VALUE "Liste alphabétique d'articles"
                DISPLAY FONT SIZE DOUBLE HIGH
        END LITERAL

        LITERAL TEXT
                LINE 7 COLUMN 2
                VALUE "Ident."
                DISPLAY BOLD
        END LITERAL

        LITERAL TEXT
                SAME LINE COLUMN 12
                VALUE "Description de l'article"
                DISPLAY BOLD
        END LITERAL

        LITERAL TEXT
                SAME LINE COLUMN 35
                VALUE "Prix unitaire"
                DISPLAY BOLD
        END LITERAL

        LITERAL TEXT
                SAME LINE COLUMN 49
                VALUE "Quantité"
                DISPLAY BOLD
        END LITERAL

        LITERAL TEXT
                SAME LINE COLUMN 59
                VALUE "Prix valable jusqu'au"
                DISPLAY BOLD
        END LITERAL

        LITERAL POLYLINE
                LINE 8 COLUMN 1
                LINE 8 COLUMN 80
        END LITERAL
```

(Example 7–8 continues on next page)

Example 7–8 (Cont.). Samples from ORD_ENTRY.IFDL

```
GROUP items
        VERTICAL DISPLAYS 10
        FIRST first_page
        SCROLL BY PAGE

            FUNCTION RESPONSE DOWN ITEM
                IF LAST ITEM THEN
                    MESSAGE "Fin de la liste"
                    SIGNAL
                ELSE
                    POSITION TO DOWN OCCURRENCE
                END IF
            END RESPONSE

            FUNCTION RESPONSE UP ITEM
                IF FIRST ITEM THEN
                    MESSAGE "Commencement de la liste"
                    SIGNAL
                ELSE
                    POSITION TO UP OCCURRENCE
                END IF
            END RESPONSE

            FUNCTION RESPONSE NEXT PANEL
                IF LAST ITEM THEN
                    MESSAGE "La fin de la liste"
                    SIGNAL
                ELSE
                    POSITION TO DOWN OCCURRENCE UNSEEN
                END IF
            END RESPONSE

            FUNCTION RESPONSE PREVIOUS PANEL
                IF FIRST ITEM THEN
                    MESSAGE "Le commencement de la liste"
                    SIGNAL
                ELSE
                    POSITION TO UP OCCURRENCE UNSEEN
                END IF
            END RESPONSE

            FIELD part_id           LINE 9 COLUMN 2
                                    OUTPUT PICTURE X(7)
                                END FIELD

            FIELD descrip           LINE 9 COLUMN 10
                                    OUTPUT PICTURE X(22)
                                END FIELD

            FIELD curr              LINE 9 COLUMN 33
                                    OUTPUT PICTURE X(2)
                                END FIELD
```

(Example 7–8 continues on next page)

Example 7–8 (Cont.). Samples from ORD_ENTRY.IFDL

```
        FIELD price          LINE 9 COLUMN 36
                             OUTPUT PICTURE 9' '999' '99R9,9R9
                             DECIMAL POINT IS COMMA
                             SCALE -2
                         END FIELD

        FIELD q_avail        LINE 9 COLUMN 50
                             OUTPUT PICTURE 99' '999R
                         END FIELD

        FIELD valid          LINE 9 COLUMN 57
                             OUTPUT PICTURE X(23)
                         END FIELD

    END GROUP

    LITERAL POLYLINE
        LINE 19 COLUMN 1
        LINE 19 COLUMN 80
    END LITERAL

    FIELD first_page
        LINE 20 COLUMN 2
        OUTPUT PICTURE X(50)
        OUTPUT "Première page de la liste"
           WHEN first_page = 1
        OUTPUT "Page central de la liste"
           WHEN first_page = 11
        OUTPUT "Dernière page de la liste"
           WHEN first_page = 21
        PROTECTED
    END FIELD

END PANEL
```

The third option brings up a panel where the user must enter the ID of the desired component. As with the Placing an order option, the ID is matched with the information in two databases, and then the collected information goes through two phases:

- Modification based on the setting of the current user interface
- Modification after logical reassignment by the new values

This information is put into the array one piece at a time and is then displayed.

In this case, unlike the regular listing where the quantity and price information was passed as short and long integers, the information is passed to the form as character strings, and the separators and the currency symbol are inserted prior to display. The logicals are set to their original values at the end.

The fourth option invokes the Change Profile panel. The user enters the new profile and presses the Return key. The logicals are reset, and the corresponding language-specific database is opened. The main menu is then displayed with the new interface.

The last option, *Exit*, closes all of the open files and terminates the program.

Chapter 8

Using the ULTRIX Operating System

Digital's ULTRIX operating system supports international product development with the following system features:

- Message catalogs and associated tools

  Message catalogs are databases that make possible the separation of text strings from application code. The tools are used to assist in the following tasks:

  — Extraction of text strings from existing C language programs

  — Translation from one language to another of the message text

  — Generation of message catalogs

- A set of library routines

  The set of library routines enables programs to dynamically determine the format of cultural and language-specific data, such as date and time strings, day and month names, currency symbols, and *radix character* symbols.

- Internationalized library functions

  The internationalized library functions of standard C library routines provide:

  — Locale-dependent character type classification

  — Conversion from uppercase to lowercase characters and vice versa

  — Date and time messages

  — Floating point to string conversions

  — Text collation

- An announcement mechanism

  The announcement mechanism identifies the national language, local custom, and codeset requirements (referred to as *language* in this chapter) appropriate to each user for applications at runtime.

- Language support databases

  Language support databases contain the tables that hold the language-specific data, with one database for each supported language.

- An international compiler for the database

  The international compiler (**ic**), supplied with the ULTRIX internationalization package, compiles the source languages information into the language support databases.

8.1 International Keyboard Support

Programmers writing applications that support several languages must take into account that languages are represented by one or more coded character sets. Because of the requirements of different languages, the coded character sets may vary in both size and representation.

You can create characters that do not exist as standard keys on your keyboard by using *compose sequences*. A compose sequence is a series of keystrokes that creates a character. You can create any character from the character set currently used by your terminal or, if you are using ULTRIX Worksystem Software, by your DECterm session.

Depending on your keyboard, you can compose characters in any of the following ways:

- Using three-stroke sequences for a VT320 keyboard
- Using two-stroke sequences on all keyboards except the North American/United Kingdom, the Dutch, and the Norwegian/Danish keyboards, which all use three-stroke sequences
- Using a combination of the Compose key and the space bar to create characters in a DECwindows environment

8.2 The Message Catalog System

Digital's ULTRIX message catalog system allows users to interact with an application program in their local language. The program message text is stored in a message catalog separate from the main body of the program. Thus, message catalog source files can be translated into many languages depending on the requirements of the end users.

The access mechanism to a message catalog retrieves a message catalog at run time and binds it to a particular program. Each internationalized program contains a number of library routines. The library routines provide for retrieval of the message text from the message catalog.

The routine used for accessing the opened catalogs is **catgets**[1]. This routine retrieves messages from a message catalog opened by a call to **catopen**. The routine **catclose** closes an open message catalog.

When using the message catalog system it is recommended that message source files be suffixed by **.msf** and message catalog files be suffixed by **.cat**.

8.2.1 Creating a Message Catalog

To create a message catalog:

1. Write the program, including the program messages.
2. Use the string extraction tools to extract the message text and put it in a message text source file (see Section 8.2.2).
3. Translate the message text source file into the required national languages using the **trans** translation tool (see Section 8.2.6).
4. Pass the message text source files through the **gencat** program to create the message catalogs (see Section 8.2.4).

You can use any text editor to create the program source file.

You can combine Steps 1 and 2 if the source program includes the calls to the message catalog retrieval functions. In this case, the **catgets** or **catgetmsg** routines should be included in the source file as appropriate. The message text string can then be extracted using a stream editor and stored in the message text source file.

[1] ULTRIX terms appear in boldface type in the text of this chapter.

You can divide message catalogs into one or more sets of program messages, each set containing one or more messages. The library routines allow programs to access messages within message sets.

The internationalization tools used to create a message catalog are shown in Table 8–1.

Table 8–1. Internationalization Tools to Create Message Catalogs

Tool	Description
extract	For interactive message string extraction
strextract	For batch message string extraction
strmerge	For batch message source file merging (used in conjunction with strextract and the trans translation tool)
gencat	The message catalog generator

8.2.2 String Extraction

You can use the string extraction tools to partially automate the process of internationalizing a C program. For example, you could use the tools to change the following segment from a C program:

```
printf("hello world\n");
```

to

```
printf(catgets(cat, 1, 1, "hello world\n"));
```

The corresponding message text source file would be automatically created:

```
$set 1
$quote "
1 "hello world\n"
```

There are two ways to extract text strings from a particular program source file and to replace the extracted strings with library routines:

- Use only the interactive extraction tool, **extract**
- Use the batch extraction tool, **strextract**, followed by the batch merging tool, **strmerge**

In both cases the extracted message text is stored in a message source file with the **.msf** suffix. The message text can then be translated using the **trans** translation tool.

The translated messages in the source file are submitted to **gencat** to generate a message catalog. At run time, the library routines in the internationalized program retrieve the translated text from the message catalog.

The interactive and batch methods of string extraction use the following files:

- Pattern file

  The pattern file is used to determine which strings are matched for the program being internationalized. The default pattern file is **/usr/lib/intln/patterns**. The systemwide pattern file is used by the extraction tools.

- Optional ignore file

  The ignore file is used to instruct the string extraction tools to ignore specific strings in the source file. Each line in the ignore file contains a single string, which is compared against the strings matched by the pattern file.

- Internationalized source program file

  The internationalized source program file has a prefix of **nl_** and is generated during the internationalization process.

- Intermediate file

  The intermediate file has a **.msg** suffix and is created in your directory. This file can be referenced by other utilities.

- Message text source file

  The message text source file contains the extracted and translated text strings (with a **.msf** suffix) that are generated during the internationalization process. The format of the message text source file is described in Section 8.2.3.

The string extraction tools produce two files:

- Internationalized program source file

  The internationalized program source file has had the text strings removed and replaced with calls to a message catalog access routine.

- Message text source file

  The message text source file contains the text strings removed from the original program source file, for use as input to **gencat** after translation of the text.

8.2.3 Format of the Message Text Source File

Message text strings can be specified using either message numbers or mnemonics. The fields of a message text source line are separated by a single ASCII space or tab character. Any other ASCII spaces or tabs are considered to be part of the subsequent field.

8.2.3.1 Set and Message Numbers

Message catalogs can be divided into one or more sets of program messages that are grouped together by a set number. The set number is a parameter of the **catgets** routine.

Use the following construct to specify the set number of succeeding messages up to the next **$set**, **$delset**, or **end-of-file** command.

```
$set n comment
```

The *n* denotes the set number, which must be presented in ascending order within a single source file but need not be contiguous. Any string following the set number is treated as a comment. A message text source file must include at least one **$set** directive before any messages.

Any string following the set number is treated as a comment.

To place comments in the message text source file, type a line beginning with a dollar sign ($), followed by an ASCII space or tab character and then the comment:

```
$  comment
```

To define message numbers, use the following construct:

```
m  message-text
```

In the message catalog, **message-text** is stored with message number **m** and the set number specified by the last **$set** directive. If **message-text** is empty, and an ASCII space or tab field separator is present, a null string is stored in the message catalog.

Note the **catgets** routine does not distinguish between a null message and an undefined message; it returns a pointer to the null string. Message numbers within a single set need not be contiguous, although they must be in ascending order. The length of **message-text** must not exceed the number of characters specified in the **NL_TEXTMAX** field of the file **/usr/include/limits.h**.

You can use an optional quote character **c** to surround **message-text** so that trailing spaces are visible in a message source line. You specify this with the following command:

```
$quote  c
```

By default, or if an empty **$quote** directive is supplied, quoting of **message-text** is not recognized. If a quote character is defined, all blank space between the message number and the quote is ignored. Empty lines in a message text source file are always ignored.

Text strings can contain the special characters and escape sequences. Escape sequences recognized by the **gencat** program are defined in Table 8–2.

Table 8–2. Escape Sequences Recognized by the gencat Program

Description	Symbol	Sequence
Newline	NL (LF)	\n
Horizontal tab	HT	\t
Vertical	VT	\v
Backspace	BS	\b
Carriage return	CR	\r
Form feed	FF	\f
Backslash	\	\\
Octal value	ddd	\ddd

The escape sequence *ddd*[1] consists of a backslash followed by one, two, or three octal digits which specify the value of the desired character. If the character following a backslash is not one of those specified, the backslash is ignored. You can also use a backslash to continue a string on the following line. Thus, the following two lines describe a single message string:

```
1 This line continues \
to the next line
```

These two lines are equivalent to:

```
1 This line continues to the next line
```

1 ULTRIX variables appear in italic type in the text of this chapter.

The backslash must be the last character on the line that is to be continued. Further localization is provided by translating the strings contained in the message text source file into the required languages, and by using the **gencat** program to create the various language message catalogs.

The **gencat** utility is designed to allow for some maintenance and update of existing message catalogs if they use numeric identifiers. As already mentioned, if a catalog exists, it is possible to merge new messages or replace messages in an existing set. It is also possible to delete an entire set by using the **delset** directive. If the message catalog **foo.cat** already exists, the following message source file can be used to update it.

```
$ file: foo.msf V1.1
$ Maintenance update for foo.cat V1.0

$ Replace message 1,2 in set 2 with new version based on code changes
$set 2
$quote "
1 "A new message for the catalog\n"
2 "Another one\n"

$ Delete set 3 since routine bogus() is no longer required
$delset 3

$ Add new set for routine creative()
$set 4
$quote "
$1 "creative processing at its finest\n"
...
...
```

In this example, set 1 in **foo.cat** is not modified but the others are, as indicated by the comments in the new message source file. The following command would result in the appropriate updates:

```
gencat foo.cat foo.msf
```

8.2.3.2 Mnemonics

Sets and messages can be given mnemonic names as an alternative to set and message numbers. A mnemonic is any string that begins with an alphabetic character. Digital recommends using mnemonic identifiers since they are easier to read and maintain and because they make the C language source files easier to maintain. You cannot mix the use of mnemonic identifiers with numeric identifiers in the same message text source file.

In the following example, the mnemonic SET_GREET, HELLO and BYE are used instead of the numbers 1, 1 and 2 respectively:

```
$set SET_GREET
HELLO Hello world
BYE Goodbye world
```

The call

```
catgets (catd, SET_GREET, HELLO, "")
```

would return the message:

```
Hello world
```

A more detailed example of a message catalog can be found in Section 8.6.

The **-h** flag of the **gencat** tool forces the creation of a header file containing **#define** statements. You must include **#define** statements in the program source files when you use mnemonics. Using the previous example as a basis, the following code fragments compare two programs, one using mnemonics and the other using message numbers:

- Using mnemonics:

  ```
  #include "prog.h"
   ....
  catopen("prog.cat",0);
   ....
  catgets(catd, SET_GREET, HELLO, "Hello\n");
   ....
  catclose("prog);
  ```

- Using numerics:

  ```
   ...
  catopen("prog.cat",0);
   ...
  catgets(catd, 1, 1, "Hello\n");
   ...
  catclose("prog");
  ```

  The contents of the message text source file, **prog.msf**, used to create the message catalog, **prog.cat** would be:

  ```
   ....
   ....
   ....
   ....
  catgets(catd, 1, 1, "Hello\n");
   ....
  ```

The contents of the message text source file, **prog.msf**, used to create the message catalog, **prog.cat** and header file, **prog.h** would be:

```
$quote "
$set SET_GREET
HELLO "Hello world"
 ....
 ....
```

Only the text within the quotes should be translated.

The header file generated using **gencat -h** contains the following lines:

```
#define SET_GREET 1
#define HELLO 1
#define BYE   2
 ....
```

In all other respects, using mnemonics does not change the way you use the internationalization tools. Restrictions on the use of mnemonics do exist:

- Set and message mnemonics cannot have the same name.
- Catalogs cannot be merged using the **gencat** program. A new catalog replaces an old catalog.
- Mnemonics and set and message numbers cannot be combined in the same source file.

8.2.4 Using the gencat Program

The **gencat** program takes a message text source file and either produces a new message catalog or merges the new message text into an existing message catalog. If the message catalog has already been created, and set and message numbers are being used, **gencat** merges the set and message numbers with the existing message catalog. If the message catalog does not exist, **gencat** creates it.

If a message text source file uses mnemonics, **gencat** does not merge the files. The new file overwrites the original file. An example of the use of **gencat** follows:

```
gencat catfile msgfile
```

In this example, **catfile** is the name of the target message catalog and **msgfile** is the name of a message text source file. If **catfile** exists, then the messages and sets defined in **msgfile** are added to **catfile**.

If set and message numbers collide, the new message text given in **msgfile** replaces the existing message text contained in **catfile**. If **catfile** does not exist, **gencat** creates it.

When using mnemonic identifiers in the message text source, the **gencat -h** option creates the header file that defines the mapping between the mnemonic message identifiers and the numbers required by the **catgets** function.

For example:

```
gencat -h catfile msgfile
```

In this case, the **hdrfile** file is created in addition to **catfile**. You then have to add the include statement, **#include "hdrfile"**, to the C language source program.

The sequence of operations needed to create an internationalized source file and a translated message catalog is shown in Figure 8–1.

In Figure 8–1, the C program (**prog.c**) is changed into an internationalized source program (**nl_prog.c**) with the text strings removed. The text strings are replaced with calls to the message catalog retrieval routines. This is done by using either the interactive extraction tool **extract**, or by using the batch extraction tool **strextract**, followed by the batch merging tool **strmerge**.

The message text source file produced, **prog.msf**, can be translated using the ULTRIX translation tool **trans**. A message catalog, **prog.cat**, containing the translated messages is then produced using the **gencat** tool. The message catalog, **prog.cat**, is accessed at run-time by the application program, **a.out**.

8.2.5 Library Routines

The ULTRIX library routines are as follows:

- **catopen**
- **catgets**
- **catclose**

To compile a C program, use the **-li** option to include the internationalization library, as shown in the following example:

```
cc -o prog prog.c -li
```

Figure 8–1. Creating a Message Catalog

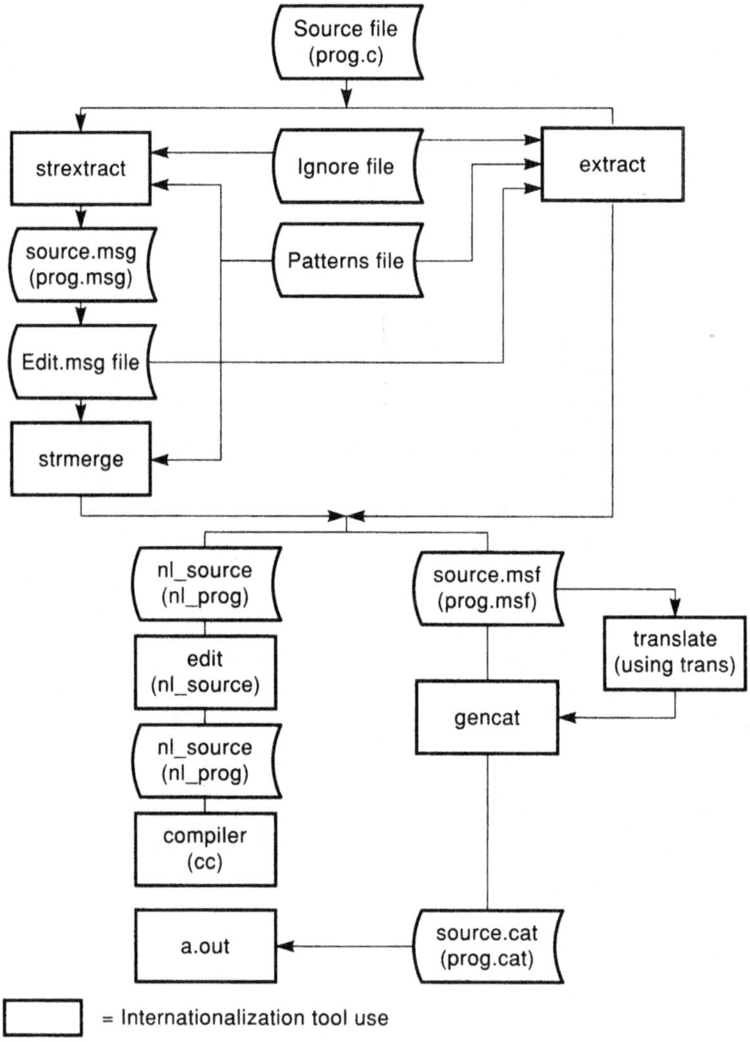

8.2.5.1 Using the catopen Routine

Message catalogs are opened for use by calling the library routine **catopen**. This routine locates the identified message catalog according to the search and naming rules defined in the environment variable **NLSPATH**. The following example demonstrates the use of the **catopen** routine:

```
catd = catopen(argv[0], 0);
```

If successful, **catopen** returns a catalog-descriptor of type **nl_catd** which is used on subsequent calls to **catgets** and **catgetmsg** to identify the prepared message catalog. Message catalogs are closed by calling the library routine, **catclose**.

Two environment variables, **NLSPATH** and **LANG**, can affect the behavior of the **catopen( )** function call.

If set, **NLSPATH** specifies the search path to be used for locating the message catalog. The syntax for setting this environment variable, shown below, is based on that of the Bourne shell PATH environment variable.

```
NLSPATH=[:][/directory][/substitution field][/filename][:alternate pathname
```

A leading colon indicates the current directory while subsequent colons act solely as field separators. The substitution fields, as shown in Table 8–3, are derived from the setting of the **LANG** environment variable and the argument passed in the **catopen( )** function call.

Table 8–3. Substitution Fields

Substitution Field	Description
%N	The value of the name argument to catopen( )
%L	The value of the LANG environment variable
%l	The language component of LANG
%t	The territory component of LANG
%c	The codeset component of LANG

If the **LANG** variable is not set, the null string is substituted into **NLSPATH**. In the following example, the current directory is searched for the message catalog **foo;**. If the message catalog is not found, the file **/usr/lib/nls/msg/FRE_FR.8859/foo.cat** is searched. If that too fails, **/usr/newapp/foo.cat** is opened. If the **LANG** variable was not set, an attempt to open the file **/usr/lib/nls/msg//foo.cat** would have been made. Note that multiple slashes in pathnames are treated as a single slash. If the message catalog cannot be opened or is not found, **catopen( )** returns an error message.

```
$LANG=FRE_FR.8859
$ NLSPATH=:/usr/lib/nls/msg/%L/%N.cat:/usr/newapp/%N.cat
$EXPORT LANG NLSPATH
      .
      .
      .
catopen("foo",0);
      .
      .
      .
```

Message catalogs should be in the directory tree **/usr/lib/nls/msg**.

8.2.5.2 Using the catgets Routine

The **catgets** routine retrieves a numbered message from a numbered message set in the message catalog identified by the **catd** argument.

```
char *catgets (catd, set_num, msg_num, s)
```

In this example, the **set_num** argument is the number of the message set containing the message **msg_num**, and **s** is a pointer to the default message string. If **catgets** retrieves the message successfully, the routine returns a pointer to the message text to the caller. If the call is unsuccessful because the message catalog identified by **catd** is unavailable, then **catgets** returns an **s**. If *msg_num* is not contained in the message catalog identified by **catd**, **catgets** returns the null string.

All buffer handling and allocation of storage space (for holding the text of a program message) is performed internally by **catgets**.

The following C source program uses **catopen** and **catgets** to retrieve messages from the message catalog identified as **prog**:

```
#include <stdio.h>
#include <nl_types.h>
#define NL_SETN 1

main ()
{
    nl_catd catd = catopen ("prog", 0);
    printf ("%s\en", catgets (catd, NL_SETN, 1, "hello world"));
    catclose (catd);
}
```

Default message strings enable the text for one language to be kept with the program to make it easier to read. Alternatively, the default message strings can be used to allow application programs to continue working predictably when specific localizations of the message text are unavailable. For example, the above program could be invoked from the shell as follows:

```
$ LANG=FRE_FR.8859; export LANG
$ prog
```

Assuming that the French message text for **prog** was undefined on the system, then the above invocation of **prog** would cause the default message string to be displayed:

```
hello world
$
```

8.2.6 Using the trans Translation Tool

The translation tool **trans** assists in the translation of source message catalogs. This utility has built-in knowledge of the source format for message catalogs. Such knowledge assists the translator by ensuring that only the appropriate text strings are modified.

The command reads input from **file.msf** and writes its output either to a file named **trans.msf** or to a file you name on the command line. The command displays **file.msf** in a multiple window screen that lets you simultaneously see the original message, the translated text you enter, and any messages from the **trans** command.

This multiple window screen is easier to use for translating messages than a single window screen. The top window in the multiple window screen displays the text in the message source file **file.msf**. The editor displays the current message in reverse video.

In the center window, **trans** displays a prompt asking the user to enter a translated message. A control key editor allows the user to move the cursor and delete text in the center window. The control key sequences are defined in Table 8–4.

Table 8–4. Control Key Sequences

Key Sequence	Meaning
CTRL/K	Display control key help
CTRL/H	Back space
CTRL/L	Forward space
CTRL/W	Back word
CTRL/F	Forward word
CTRL/E	Move to end of input
CTRL/B	Move to beginning of input
CTRL/N	Next line
CTRL/P	Previous line
CTRL/U	Delete input
CTRL/I	Insert mode (default)
CTRL/R	Replace mode
DEL	Delete previous character

If you need to span more than one line with the translated text, enter a backslash (\) and press the Return key to enable line continuation. After you finish entering the translated text, press the Return key to signal that you have finished translating that message.

The bottom window displays any messages generated by **trans**. If an error occurs, **trans** prompts you to re-enter the entire line, including the message label or number.

8.3 Creating Localized Programs

An internationalized program localizes its run-time behavior for a particular language, territory, and codeset by establishing the required localization data in the program's locale. Calling the **setlocale** library routine establishes the localization data.

```
language[_territory[.codeset]][@modifier]
```

The ULTRIX operating system allows you to define *language territory*, and *codeset* for all settings of *category*. You can also define an *@modifier* for all categories except **LC_ALL**.

The following preset values of *locale* are defined for all settings of *category*:

Preset Value	Description
C	Specifies the standard environment for the C language. The C locale is the default if **setlocale** is not invoked.
""	Specifies that the setting of the *locale* is obtained from the corresponding environment variables.
NULL	Directs **setlocale** to query *category* and return the current setting of *locale*. You can use the string **setlocale** returns only as input to subsequent **setlocale** calls.

To use **setlocale** to obtain the *locale* for all categories from environment variables, use the following command:

```
setlocale (LC_ALL, "")
```

You can also define a *locale* setting for a specific category. To define a specific category, you pass the *locale* setting directly in the **setlocale** call, as shown:

```
setlocale (LC_COLLATE, "FRE_FR.MCS")
```

This example specifies collation appropriate for the DEC MCS in France.

If you need to define a category more precisely than is possible using *language*, *territory*, and *codeset*, you can use the *@modifier*. The following example shows a category definition that uses the *@modifier*.

```
setlocale (LC_COLLATE, "FRE_FR.8859@CCOLL")
```

In this example collating is done according to the collation table, **CCOLL**, defined in the **FRE_FR.8859** database, rather than the default collation table. Preferably, you can obtain the *locale* for the **LC_COLLATE** category from the corresponding environment variable as follows:

```
setlocale (LC_COLLATE, "")
```

8.3.1 The Announcement Mechanism

When a program internationalized using the ULTRIX operating system is run, the system must be aware of the language requirements of the program.

By defining the environment variable, **${LANG}**, you can identify which *language*, *territory*, *codeset*, and *modifier* a program requires. You can define a unique value of **${LANG}** for each supported *language*, *territory*, *codeset*, and *modifier* combination. If you define **${LANG}** settings for different *language*, *territory*, *codeset*, and *modifier* settings, each definition might be associated with a different instance of collating sequence, character conversion, character classification, **langinfo** tables, and message catalogs.

The **${LANG}** variable contains the required *language*, *territory*, *codeset*, and *modifier* names in English as follows:

```
language[_territory[.codeset][@modifier]
```

The length of the entire string should not exceed the value of **NL_LANGMAX** located in **/usr/include/limits.h**. The set of characters, excluding separators, is restricted to the ASCII set of alphanumeric characters.

On its own, *language* selects the required native language. If you need to be more specific than native language, you can specify *_territory* or *_territory.codeset*. The following examples demonstrate defining the **${LANG}** variable. The first example selects a database that supports the French native language.

```
$ LANG=FRE
```

The next example selects a database that supports the French native language, as it is spoken in France (rather than Canada).

```
$ LANG=FRE_FR
```

The last example selects a database that supports the French native language, as spoken in France, and the DEC MCS. You cannot specify the DEC MCS unless you specify a *_territory*, in this case **_FR**.

```
$ LANG=FRE_FR.MCS
```

If the files **FRE** and **FRE_FR** are linked to the **FRE_FR.MCS** database, the three examples refer to the same database.

8.3.2 Announcement Categories

The environment variable **${LANG}** provides the general announcement mechanism by which users can identify overall requirements for program localization. This is sufficient when a single localization covers the user's requirements for text collation, character classification, and message presentation.

The ULTRIX operating system allows you to selectively modify the international environment by defining additional environment variables, one for each setting of the categories:

- **LC_COLLATE**
- **LC_CTYPE**
- **LC_NUMERIC**
- **LC_TIME**
- **LC_MONETARY**

You cannot define additional environment variables for **LC_ALL**.

If any of these categories are not defined in the current environment, **LANG** provides the necessary default information. The categories are also defined to accept an additional field, *@modifier*, which enables you to select a specific instance of localization data within a single category, such as selecting dictionary-ordering of data as opposed to character-ordering of data.

For example, if you want to interact with the system in French, but are required to sort German text files, you could define **LANG** and **LC_COLLATE** as follows:

```
$ LANG=Fr_FR
$ LC_COLLATE=De_DE
```

You could extend this definition to select, for example, dictionary ordering by using the *@modifier* field, as follows:

```
$ LC_COLLATE=De_DE@dict
```

8.3.3 Setting the Program Locale

There are three ways to set the program locale using the **setlocale** library routine:

- **setlocale** (*category, string*)

  This usage sets a specific category in the program locale to a specific value of *string*, for example;

  ```
  setlocale (LC_ALL, "FRE_FR.MCS");
  ```

  In this example, all categories of the program locale are set to the locale corresponding to the string **FRE_FR.MCS**, or the French language as spoken in France, using the Digital MCS. The string **FRE_FR.MCS** is used to locate the appropriate database.

  If *string* does not correspond to a valid setting of locale, **setlocale** returns a null pointer and the program locale is not changed. Otherwise, **setlocale** returns the name of the locale.

- **setlocale** (*category, "C"*)

  This usage resets the default environment for the C language.

- **setlocale** (*category, " "*)

  This usage sets *category* to correspond to the setting of the associated environment variable.

By default, the directory **/usr/lib/intln** contains the language support databases. The ULTRIX operating system allows you to place your language support databases in another directory by specifying the directory path with the **INTLINFO** environment variable.

8.3.4 Setting a Specific Category

Setlocale allows you to set the **LC_COLLATE, LC_CTYPE, LC_NUMERIC, LC_TIME** or **LC_MONETARY** values individually. For example:

```
setlocale (LC_COLLATE, "");
```

Here, **setlocale** first checks the value of the corresponding environment variable, **${LC_COLLATE}**. If the value contains the name of a valid locale, **setlocale** sets the specified category to that value and returns its name. If the value is invalid, **setlocale** returns a null pointer and the program locale is not changed.

If the environment variable corresponding to *category* is not set or is the empty string, **setlocale** examines **${LANG}**. If **${LANG}** is set and contains the name of a valid locale, that value is used to set *category*. Otherwise, **setlocale** returns a null pointer and the program locale is not changed.

When using the ULTRIX operating system, the default locale is the C locale.

8.3.5 Setting All Categories

This use of **setlocale** is similar to that described in Section 8.3 except that here **setlocale** examines all the environment variables to determine what values to set. In this case, **setlocale** is called as follows:

```
setlocale (LC_ALL, "")
```

Here, **setlocale** first checks all the environment variables. If the variables are valid, **setlocale** initializes each category to the value of the corresponding environment variable. If any environment variable is invalid, **setlocale** returns a null pointer and the program locale is not changed.

Categories are initialized in the following order, where **${LANG}** is used to initialize category **LC_ALL**:

LC_ALL
LC_CTYPE
LC_COLLATE
LC_TIME
LC_NUMERIC
LC_MONETARY

Using this scheme, environment variables corresponding to specific categories override the setting of **${LANG}**.

If a category-specific environment variable is not set, or is set to the empty string, that category is not overwritten; it assumes the setting of **${LANG}**. If **${LANG}** is not set, or is set to the empty string, **setlocale** returns a null pointer and the program locale is not changed. This is the default.

8.3.6 Supported Locales

The following language support databases are included as part of the base system on ULTRIX platforms:

Table 8–5. ULTRIX Language Support Databases

Name	Language	Territory	Character Set
ENG_GB.MCS	English	United Kingdom	DEC MCS
FRE_FR.MCS	French	France	DEC MCS
GER_DE.MCS	German	Germany	DEC MCS
ENG_GB.8859	English	United Kingdom	ISO Latin-1
FRE_FR.8859	French	France	ISO Latin-1
GER_DE.8859	German	Germany	ISO Latin-1
ENG_GB.646	English	United Kingdom	ISO 646
FRE_FR.646	French	France	ISO 646
GER_DE.646	German	Germany	ISO 646

The file names of the language support databases will be updated in the future to align with the ISO 639, ISO 3166, and other appropriate standards. For example **GER_DE.MCS** will become **de_DE.DECMCS**. File names specified here will continue to be supported on ULTRIX systems during this transition.

In the C locale, all characters are encoded in 7-bit ASCII. Also, characters are collated in machine order. The C locale is guaranteed to exist on all systems compliant with X/Open and Portable Operating System Interface for Computer Environments (POSIX). Table 8–9 shows how national language strings are returned in the C locale.

8.4 Local Conventions

In addition to using message catalogs, an application must be able to format information in a locale-specific manner. For example, a product should be capable of displaying a numeric value using the thousands separator and decimal point character preferred in the locale where the product is being used.

Specialized C routines can reference a language support database for the formats, natural-language strings, separators, and so on, needed to do locale-specific data formatting. These routines, which enable an application to format data for a specific locale at run time, are listed in Table 8–6.

Table 8–6. C Routines Supporting the Use of Local Conventions

Routine Name	Description
atof( )	Converts ASCII characters to a numeric value formatted using the thousands separator and decimal point character indicated by the **LC_NUMERIC setlocale( )** category.
ecvt( )	Converts a numeric value formatted for a specific locale into a locale-neutral ASCII character string. This routine uses the **LC_NUMERIC setlocale( )** category to identify separator and decimal point characters in the number to be converted.
nl_langinfo( )	Returns a pointer to a string containing locale-specific information for date and time formats, yes and no prompts, and monetary and numeric formats.
printf( )	Prints formatted output, optionally using natural-language strings (for example, day or month names) extracted from a language support database. Includes extensions to aid translation of message text strings.
scanf( )	Reads formatted input, interpreting and storing the input using values extracted from a language support database. Includes extensions to aid translation of message text strings.
strftime( )	Converts a date and time value to a formatted string using natural-language strings and separators indicated by the **LC_TIME setlocale( )** category.
vprintf( )	Prints formatted output, optionally using natural-language strings extracted from a language support database. Is called with an argument list as defined by **varargs**. Includes extensions to aid translation of message text strings.

The extended versions of **printf( ), scanf( ), and vprintf( )** are in **libi**. A user must link with **libi** if the extensions are desired. The extensions provide a mechanism whereby a specific argument in the argument list can be referenced in the format specification. The traditional use is to access the argument list sequentially.

The following example results in the second argument being printed first (digit-name).

```
printf("%2$d-%1$s", name, digit)
```

This can be very useful for a translator when the word order changes from language to language. A simple change in the format specification within a message text source file and re-creation of an updated message catalog is all that is required. The application program itself remains unchanged.

8.5 International Text Processing

An application should be able to sort text using multiple character sets and collating sequences, and do case conversions for multinational characters. ULTRIX software provides specialized C routines that support these international text processing requirements. Table 8–7 lists these routines.

Table 8–7. C Routines Supporting International Text Processing

Routine Name	Description
conv( )	Does character conversions. For example, *toupper( ), tolower( ),* converts a character from lowercase to uppercase, and uppercase to lowercase, respectively. The routine uses conversion tables from a language support database indicated by the **LC_CTYPE setlocale( )** category.
ctype( )	Identifies the character type (uppercase character, lowercase character, punctuation, digit, and so on) of a character. Characters are identified using a character code from the character set identified by the **LC_CTYPE setlocale( )** category.
strcoll( )	Indicates the order in which two strings should be sorted, based on the collating sequence indicated by the **LC_COLLATE setlocale( )** category.
strxfrm( )	Transforms a string into the form the **strcmp( )** and **memcmp( )** routines use to efficiently compare strings.

8.6 IDATE: A Sample ULTRIX Program

Example 8–1 is an internationalized C program. This program, **idate.c**, displays the date and time for a specified locale. The associated header and message files are shown following the source program.

Example 8–1. idate.c

```
/*
* idate: display date and time in locale specific format
*
* Sample internationalized application. This program uses the *
* mnemonic format for message catalogs to enhance maintainability *
*/

#include <sys/time.h>

#include <langinfo.h>  /* default strings for date/time *
*                         formats, etc.  */
#include <locale.h>    /* declarations used by setlocale */
#include <nl_types.h>  /* declarations for message catalog system */

#include "idate.h"     /* generated by gencat, contains message *
*                         identifiers */

nl_catd catd;
struct timeval  tp;
struct timezone tpz;

main(argc, argv)
int argc;
char *argv[];
{
  char    timestring[50];
  struct  tm *tms;

  /* open message catalog - look in current directory */

  catd = catopen("idate.cat", 0);

  /* check command line arguments */

  if (argc > 1) {
      printf(catgets(catd, IDATE_SET1, USE_MSG, "usage: incorrect\n"));
      exit(1);
   }

 /* initialize runtime locale */

 if (setlocale(LC_TIME, "") == (char *)0) {
```

(Example 8–1 continues on next page)

Example 8–1 (Cont.). idate.c

```
    printf(catgets(catd, IDATE_SET1, LOCALE_MSG, "idate: cannot change \
    locale - check environment variables\n"));
  }

    /* get time from system clock */

    time(&tp.tv_sec);
    tms = localtime(&tp.tv_sec);

    /* do I18N conversion */

    strftime(timestring, sizeof(timestring), nl_langinfo(D_T_FMT), tms);

    printf(catgets(catd, IDATE_SET1, TIME_MSG, "Local time: %s\n"), \
    timestring);

    /* close message catalog */

    catclose(catd);

}
```

Example 8–2 contains the contents of the header file for **idate**.

Example 8–2. Header File Contents

```
/*
 * idate.h: header file created by gencat -h idate.h
 * idate.cat idate.msf
 */

#define IDATE_SET1      0       /* set name */
#define USE_MSG 0
#define LOCALE_MSG      1
#define TIME_MSG:       2
```

Example 8–3 displays the contents of the message file **idate.msf** that is used in conjunction with **idate.c**.

Example 8–3. Message File: idate.msf

```
$ idate.msf

$ This is the sample message file for use with the program
$ idate.c. Note the syntax of each line with a directive.

$ Note also that blank lines are accepted as input

$ When using mnemonic format for messages you are required
$ to use a quote character and to quote each message string.

$ This file can be used as input to the trans utility.
$ trans provides a simple user interface to aid the
$ process of message text translation.

$quote "

$set IDATE_SET1
USE_MSG "usage: idate\n"
LOCALE_MSG "idate: cannot change locale, check environment variables\n"
TIME_MSG: "Local Time: %s\n"

$ End of idate.msf
```

8.7 Language Support Databases

The ULTRIX operating system's language support databases are used to hold various language dependent entities, and to free programs from national language dependencies. There is one language support database for each national language used on the system. The information in the language support databases is supplied through database language source files, which enable the national language and codeset characteristics to be defined.

The database language source file includes definitions for

- Codeset
- Property table
- Collation table
- String tables
- Conversion tables

The international compiler converts these tables into an efficient binary representation suitable for use by run-time functions.

The following general considerations apply to the database language source file:

- The database source should contain only ASCII characters.

- The source is free format; blank spaces have no significance other than as a separator for tokens in the input.
- You can use C-style comments and macro definitions, in particular the **#include** and **define** facilities.

By default, the language support database files are held under **/usr/lib/intln**. Example 8–4 demonstrates the basic structure of the source file. All definitions are terminated with the **END.** sequence.

Example 8–4. Sample Language Database Source File

```
CODESET ENG_GB.MCS :
        /*
         * codeset definition and default property table
         */
END.
COLLATION :
        /*
         * default collation table
         */
END.
STRINGTABLE :
        /*
         * default string table
         */
END.
CONVERSION toupper :
        /*
         * lowercase to uppercase conversion table
         */
END.
CONVERSION tolower :
        /*
         * uppercase to lowercase conversion table
         */
END.
```

8.7.1 The Codeset Definition

The codeset defines the valid characters and their properties within the language. For example, it could specify that *A* is a valid character in the English language, possessing lowercase and hexadecimal properties.

The definition of the codeset being used starts with the keyword **CODESET** followed by the codeset name **double** letters. For example, *é* in the ISO 6937 standard is replaced by the sequence *e'*.

Once compilation is successful, the name given to the codeset becomes the name of the binary file. In most cases, this name is in the following format:

```
language_[territory[.codeset][@modifier]]
```

You can specify the name of the codeset on the **ic** command line using the **-o** option.

If you specify a name on the command line, the name you specify supersedes the name of the codeset in the database source file. After the keyword assignment, each code is defined by assigning the value of the code to an identifier.

This identifier can be used to reference the code from then on. This assignment has the following form:

```
Identifier '=' value_list [ ':' Properties ] ';'
```

For example:

```
a = 'a' : LOWER, HEX;
```

The **value_list** is a list of values separated by commas. A value may be given as a C-style character constant (' '), in octal (0nnn), hexadecimal (0xnnn), decimal (nnn), ISO notation (mm/nn), or by giving the name of a previously defined code.

Codes may be either simple or combined. However, several restrictions must be observed when defining codes in the **CODESET** section:

- The list of simple codes must contain all codes from code value 0x0 up to and including the code with the highest value defined. The order of definition is not important, since all code values are sorted into ascending collation order after the whole codeset definition has been read.
- The list of simple codes cannot contain codes with duplicate code values.
- There may be up to 2^{15} definitions for multi-byte codes. Combined codes need not have contiguous code values and will be sorted in ascending machine collation order and will construct the double letter table in the compiled database.
- Only one definition of a codeset can exist, and that definition must be the first item in the source file.

The optional **properties** part of the definition assigns default properties to a code. If it is not given, the code is assumed to be defined but illegal. This feature is useful for languages that do not require all the letters defined in a standard code set. Properties take the form of a list of keywords separated by commas.

A third kind of statement allowed in the **CODESET** section is the assignment of default properties to an already defined code in the following form:

```
Identifier ':' Properties ';'
```

The use of the **#include** facility provided in the language is strongly recommended since most of the codes considered contain common code (for example ASCII or ISO 646) in their lower half. Using a common **include** file reduces the risk of error and provides a common name basis for the remainder of the source.

8.7.2 The Property Table

The property table contains the mapping information between characters in the codeset and classification. Each character code from the coded character set is used to index an entry in the relevant language property table. Each entry in the property table contains a series of flags identifying whether a particular language assertion is true or false. The character may possess any of the following attributes:

- Undefined
- Uppercase alphabetic
- Lowercase alphabetic
- Punctuation
- Control
- Blank

These can be accessed at run-time by the **ctype** library routines.

More than one property table can be included, and each is introduced by the keyword **PROPERTY**. The default property table, built along with the code set, has the predefined name **PROP_DFLT**. The property table must not be redefined. Names of property tables must be unique throughout the source.

A statement in the property table takes the following form:

```
Identifier ':' Properties ';'
```

where **Identifier** designates a defined code and **Properties** is a list of properties separated by commas. For example:

```
C: UPPER, HEX;
```

Some properties affect the interpretation of characters by various other internationalization library routines. For example, the property **DIPHTONG** must be set for diphthongs to collate correctly as diphthongs, and the property **DOUBLE** must be set to recognize correctly the first of a double-letter sequence.

The full list of properties is shown in Table 8–8.

Table 8–8. Properties and Character Classification

Property	Character Classification
ARITH	Arithmetic sign
BLANK	Blank character
CTRL	Control character
CURENCY	Currency character
DIACRIT	Diacritical sign
DIPHTONG	Diphthong
DOUBLE	Double letter
FRACTION	Fraction character
ILLEGAL	Illegal character
LOWER	Lowercase letter
MISCEL	Miscellaneous symbol
PUNCT	Punctuation character
SPACE	Space character
SUPSUB	Superscript or subscript
UPPER	Uppercase letter

The corresponding code to the property **DOUBLE** is constructed from two other single-byte codes, but it is treated as a single code. This treatment allows:

- The expansion of 8-bit character sets to allow double letters (for example Ll or ll in Spanish) that collate 2 to 1

- The handling of 8- or 16-bit codes like ISO 6937-1, is the character *é*

The corresponding code to the property **DIACRIT**, for ex ple, is a diacritical sign. If combined with either **UPPER** or **LOWER**, the corresponding code is a diacritical letter.

The meaning of the word *diphthong* in internationalization is somewhat different from the definition used in the grammar of languages that use diphthongs. *Diphthong*, for the purposes of internationalization, is defined as a character for which 1-to-2 collation must be used. This definition implies an interdependence with the collation tables.

The properties of a code can be redefined by the user because only the definition in effect upon reaching the end of the property table will be put in the binary file.

A code with no defined property will be listed as **ILLEGAL** in the resulting property table.

8.7.3 The Collation Table

Collation tables define the collating sequence for each supported language. The binary values of characters in the associated coded character set are used as indexes into the table. Individual entries are used to indicate the relative position of that character in the language collating sequence. The package supports the following capabilities:

- 1-to-1 character mappings, such that *a* collates before *b* and so on.
- 1-to-2 character mappings, where certain characters are treated as two characters. For example, in German *ß* becomes *ss* for collating.
- 2-to-1 character mappings, where certain character sequences are treated as a single character in the collating sequence. For example, *ch* and *ll* in Spanish are collated after *c* and *l* respectively.
- No-preference characters, where certain characters are ignored by the collating sequence. For example, if the hyphen is defined as a no-preference character, then the strings *re-locate* and *relocate* are equal.

These capabilities provide support for collating algorithms that provide for case and accent priority, where for example, two characters are first compared for equality, ignoring accents, and, if equal, are then ordered by accent sequence. Collating algorithms of this type give a dictionary ordering of data. The dictionary ordering of data within the internationalization package is the same as for a normal dictionary in the language being considered. Telephone book ordering is the same as for a telephone directory in the supported language. It should be noted that both dictionary and telephone book ordering may be subject to local variation.

The default collation table is introduced by the keyword **COLLATION**, and is named **COLL_DFLT**. The default table must exist for **ic** to compile the database. Other collation tables can be introduced by the keyword **COLLATION**, followed by the name of the table. The names of the collation tables must be unique throughout the source.

A statement in the collation section may take one of the following forms:

- PRIMARY ':' Ident_list ';'

  For example:

  ```
  PRIMARY: a, A, b, B;
  ```

  The statement PRIMARY ':' Ident_list ';' assigns the named codes ascending secondary weights from left to right.

- PRIMARY ':' Ident '-' Ident ';'

  For example:

  ```
  PRIMARY: a-z;
  ```

  The statement PRIMARY ':' Ident '-' Ident ';' assigns ascending secondary weights for ascending machine collation order to the named codes.

- PRIMARY ':' REST ';'

  For example:

  ```
  PRIMARY: REST;
  ```

  The statement PRIMARY ':' REST ';' sets the primary weight of codes not explicitly named in the collation section. The secondary weight of the codes is set to ascending machine collation order. This is a convenient notation for defaulting unspecified codes to collate after or before all others.

- EQUAL ':' Ident_list ';'

  For example:

  ```
  EQUAL: a,A;
  ```

  The statement EQUAL ':' Ident_list assigns the same PRIMARY and SECONDARY weight to all codes in the list.

- Ident '=' '(' Ident ',' Ident ')' ';'

  For example:

  ```
  PRIMARY: ae = (a, e);
  ```

  The statement Ident '=' '(' Ident ',' Ident ')' ';' is reserved for the collation of diphthongs (1-to-2 collation). It implies that the left-hand code collates as if it were the first right-hand code followed by the second right-hand code.

- PROPERTY ':' Property_table_name ';' .

  For example:

  ```
  PROPERTY: newprop;
  ```

  In order for the diphthong collation to work correctly, the code named on the left-hand side of the statement must be marked as **DIPHTONG** in at least one property table. If this property table is not the default table, the statement PROPERTY ':' Property_table_name ';' must be used to identify the property table name to the compiler. This statement allows the run-time routines to load a collation-only property table for use with diphthongs.

The order of statements in the collation section is significant. All of the statements (except the last) open a new class of codes with primary and secondary weights. The primary weight is set by the position of the PRIMARY or EQUAL statement, with all the codes named in the statement having the same primary weight. For example, the sixth PRIMARY statement in a collation section would assign the primary weight 6 to all the codes listed. Primary weights start at 1 and increase by one for each statement encountered up to a limit of 254. The secondary weight of the codes is governed by their ordering within a set, except codes with an EQUAL statement, which all have the same secondary weight. The limit on secondary weights is 255.

8.7.4 The String Table

The string table contains the language strings required for formatting date and time, *yes* and *no*, and radix characters. The default string table is introduced by the keyword **STRINGTABLE**, and is named **STRG_DFLT**. The default string table must exist for the international compiler to compile the database. Other string tables can be introduced by the keyword **STRINGTABLE**, followed by the table name. However, the names of the string tables must be unique throughout the source.

Each statement in a string table has the following form:

```
Ident '=' value_list ';'
```

In this statement, Ident is an identifier, and the name of the string and *value_list* are part of a comma-separated list of strings, character constants, and identifiers designating codes. This format allows inclusion of non-ASCII codes in any string table by giving the name of the code in **value_list**. Table 8–9 shows the strings that must appear in the string table.

Table 8–9. Mandatory Strings in the String Table

String	Meaning	C locale	Category
NOSTR	Negative response	no	LC_ALL
YESSTR	Positive response	yes	LC_ALL
D_T_FMT	Default date and time format	%a %b %d %H:%M:%S %Y	LC_TIME
D_FMT	Default date format	%m/%d/%y	LC_TIME
T_FMT	Default time format	%H:%M:%S	LC_TIME
DAY_1	Day name	Sunday	LC_TIME
DAY_2	Day name	Monday	LC_TIME
....	....	....	....
DAY_7	Day name	Saturday	LC_TIME
ABDAY_1	Abbreviated day name	Sun	LC_TIME
ABDAY_2	Abbreviated day name	Mon	LC_TIME
ABDAY_3	Abbreviated day name	Tue	LC_TIME
....	....	....	....
ABDAY_7	Abbreviated day name	Sat	LC_TIME
MON_1	Month name	January	LC_TIME
MON_2	Month name	February	LC_TIME
MON_3	Month name	March	LC_TIME
....	....	....	....
MON_12	Month name	December	LC_TIME
ABMON_1	Abbreviated month name	Jan	LC_TIME
ABMON_2	Abbreviated month name	Feb	LC_TIME
....	....	....	....
ABMON_12	Abbreviated month name	Dec	LC_TIME

(Table 8–9 continues on next page)

Table 8–9. Mandatory Strings in the String Table (cont.)

String	Meaning	C locale	Category
RADIXCHAR	Radix character		LC_NUMERIC
THOUSEP	Thousands separator		LC_NUMERIC
CRNCYSTR	Currency format		LC_MONETARY
AM_STR	String for AM	AM	LC_TIME
PM_STR	String for PM	PM	LC_TIME
EXPL_STR	Lowercase exponent character	e	LC_NUMERIC
EXPU_STR	Uppercase exponent character	E	LC_NUMERIC

8.7.5 The Conversion Tables

The conversion tables are used to convert characters within the codeset, such as to convert uppercase characters to lowercase characters. There must be at least two conversion tables within the database language source file. These are named *toupper* and *tolower* and are used to convert characters to uppercase and lowercase respectively.

A statement in a conversion table takes one of three forms in which **Ident** specifies a code defined in the codeset, and **conversion_value** specifies the code or string value that the left-hand side should be converted to.

- Ident '->' conversion_value ';'

  For example:

  ```
  a -> A;
  ```

- Ident '-' Ident '->' Ident '-' Ident ';'

  For example:

  ```
  a-z -> A-Z;
  ```

- DEFAULT '->' default_value ';'

  For example:

  ```
  DEFAULT -> SAME;
  ```

The default value for a conversion may be given using the **DEFAULT** statement. Any code without a specified conversion maps to the given value.

There are two predefined values possible in a **DEFAULT** statement:

- VOID, which means that all other codes convert to either the ASCII NUL code (in the case of a code conversion) or to an empty string (in the case of a string conversion).
- SAME, which means that a code is converted to itself if there is no explicit conversion given. This default conversion is not valid for string-type conversions.

The range notation in the conversion section implies an underlying machine collation sequence and is only valid for code conversions where such a collation sequence is always defined.

If no **DEFAULT** clause is given, the default clause is assumed to read:

```
DEFAULT -> VOID ;
```

Appendix G provides examples of both types of conversion.

Chapter 9

Supporting Multi-byte Characters

When designing the international base component of software targeted for Asian markets, it is important to address the input, output, and editing of multi-byte characters. Ensuring the ability to handle the input and output of Asian ideographic characters is a significant part of the localization effort in Chinese, Korean, and Japanese markets.

The major difference in handling Asian data versus European and American data is the difference in the processing environments. This difference is further complicated by the two- or four-byte representation of different characters in the same character set. Digital's Asian platforms have adopted a simple rule of using a 1:1 ratio between the display positions required and the number of bytes in an internal buffer. The adoption of this rule allows for easy synchronization of display positions and internal buffer pointers.

Many input and output capabilities for Asian markets have been included in Digital language-specific terminals and printers. Digital also provides utilities for Asian character input, output, and manipulation. These utilities are included in multi-byte-handling routine libraries of individual operating systems.

The prerequisite for multi-byte character support is the ability to recognize all multi-byte characters as valid data. When international software is designed, the routines in the software that validate input against Digital's Multinational Character Set (DEC MCS) must be modified to accept all valid multi-byte characters defined for a particular Asian language.

9.1 Input of Multi-Byte Characters

At Digital, the input method for Japanese characters is built into the software, while the input methods for Chinese and Korean are built into the terminals. Digital's terminals for Chinese and Korean languages can handle input methods that support multi-byte characters. When the input mode is activated in these local language terminals, the terminal uses one of its input methods to select the data character for input. The terminal then passes the multi-byte internal code that represents this character to the application.

9.1.1 Terminators and Delimiters

The recognition of terminators and delimiters in an input stream of multi-byte characters requires more handling than it does in a single-byte input stream. In a mixed single-byte and multi-byte environment, part of a multi-byte character can contain the same code as a valid single-byte terminator or delimiter.

The design of software for the Asian market should ensure that all input parsing within the software process of the input stream is based on characters rather than bytes. Digital provides a multi-byte search routine, JSY$STR_SEARCH, as a useful tool for this task.

9.1.2 Queue Input/Output

In any software performing editor-like functions, Digital's QI/O (Queue Input/Output) service is very often used to acquire input. QI/O services $QIO and $QIOW requests under the VMS operating system. The QI/O request system service prepares an I/O request for processing by the driver and performs device-independent preprocessing of the request.

The standard English QI/O service only operates on a single-byte basis. Digital recommends designing software to use QI/O that operates on a multi-byte basis in order to support multi-byte languages. QI/O ensures that all bytes required to represent the character are read into a buffer before processing begins, as shown in the following example.

```
.
.
.
Issue QIO to get BYTE1
IF hex(BYTE1) < hex(A0) THEN
         Process it as a 7-bit ASCII character
           or 8-bit control character
ELSE
     BEGIN
         Issue QIO to get BYTE2
         Process BYTE1 and BYTE2 together as a 2-byte
           Asian character
     END
.
.
.
```

9.2 Character Output

The multi-byte character output at field, line, or screen boundaries, where there is not sufficient space to accommodate the whole multi-byte character, must be properly handled in order to preserve the accuracy of the data. Digital's Asian VMS software offers localized editors such as HEDT (Hanzi, Hanyu, or Hangul EDT) or HTPU (Hanzi, Hanyu, or Hangul TPU), which can be used in the design of these output functions.

9.2.1 Character Wrapping

Because multiple display positions are required for multi-byte characters, special handling is necessary when software displays multi-byte characters. Preprocessing of the output buffer is necessary to handle proper wrapping of multi-byte characters at field, line, or screen boundaries. If a wrapping function is not provided by the software, the software should ensure that no partial multi-byte character is displayed at field, line, or screen boundaries.

In wrapping multi-byte characters, the software must determine whether sufficient space is available for the output of the multi-byte character. If sufficient space is not available, then the whole multi-byte character should be wrapped.

For screen display, the software can choose to place a special character at the last position of the field, line, or screen. When designing software for an Asian market, ensure that the display is based on characters rather than bytes.

9.2.2 Formatted Output

Formatted output also requires that the display be based on multi-byte characters. Software design should identify formatted output, and ensure that truncation at a field boundary including multi-byte characters is based on characters instead of bytes.

For example, assume the string is to be fitted into a field that can store up to a maximum of 10 bytes. In a byte-processing environment, part of the multi-byte character at the field boundary would be truncated, leaving part of the character in the field.

When designing software for Asian markets, make sure that the whole multi-byte character is truncated. A multi-byte truncate routine, JSY$TRUNC can be used for this purpose.

9.3 Editing

Line editing, as well as screen editing, requires special attention for multi-byte characters. The complexity of Asian characters makes it necessary to use more space to present each individual character.

In a multi-byte processing environment, editing should be based on characters, rather than on bytes. Methods for moving the cursor, as well as deleting and replacing characters, must be modified for multi-byte characters.

9.3.1 Moving the Cursor

A multi-byte character occupies multiple video positions. Since each multi-byte character is considered as a single logical unit, the left and right boundaries of a multi-byte character must be recognized. The software should always position the cursor at the first byte of a multi-byte character.

All functions and utilities that involve the movement of the cursor in the software should be designed so that the cursor is positioned at the first byte of a multi-byte character. This rule applies whether the cursor is moved as a result of direct positioning, editing functions (such as character insertion), or pressing the up or down arrow keys.

9.3.2 Deleting and Replacing Characters

Because a multi-byte character occupies multiple video positions, character deletion should be extended from a byte-by-byte basis to a character-by-character basis. For example, all positions occupied by the multi-byte character should be deleted by pressing the Delete key once.

Guidelines

Digital recommends the following guidelines to accomplish the character deletion.

- Modify the size of the delete buffer to allow for the storage of multi-byte characters. In most cases, this means increasing the size of the buffer.
- Because concepts of characters and words differ in different languages, the function of character deletion versus word deletion should be clearly defined.
- For software that has an undelete function, which replaces the text deleted, the software should perform the undeletion so that it exactly reverses deletion.

  Like deletion, undeletion in a multi-byte environment should be character-based.

9.3.3 Overstriking Characters

Character overstriking becomes complicated when characters of variable lengths are mixed. In a true character processing environment, a character overstrike should be a one-to-one character replacement without regard to the difference between the number of bytes in the overstriking character and the character being replaced.

Thus, if the overstriking character is a different length, the rest of the string shifts accordingly. The shift reflects the change in both the internal buffer and the character displayed.

Another condition in character overstriking is important in multi-byte processing. At times, it is not desirable to change the position in the internal buffer or display the position of the rest of the string after the overstrike character. Under these circumstances, character overstriking should be handled in one of three possible ways:

- Overstrike a character with one character that occupies the same number of bytes in the internal buffer. In this case, no additional action is necessary. Simply replace the existing character with the new character.

- Overstrike a character with one character that occupies fewer bytes in the internal buffer. Since the existing character occupies more bytes, there are unused bytes after the character is replaced. Fill these bytes with spaces.
- Overstrike a character with one character that occupies more bytes in the internal buffer. If the new character spans over a portion of another character, fill the remaining bytes of the affected character with blanks.

9.3.4 Cutting and Pasting

In most software developed for English and European markets, the cut-and-paste functions of the software work on a line-by-line basis. For the Asian market, design the software to perform cuts on a character-by-character basis. When you cut and paste a multi-byte character in a byte-processing environment, you may cut part of a multi-byte character and leave the rest, producing errors in subsequent characters.

Nor should you select a block of text containing multi-byte characters for cutting in a byte processing environment either. Multi-byte characters could be cut or pasted incorrectly during the process.

The design of software that provides the cut-and-paste functions should establish its own rule for handling these situations. For instance, depending on the situation, the multi-byte characters that span the cut-and-paste boundaries may or may not be included in the cut-and-paste action.

When performing the paste function, be sure to avoid inserting data in the middle of a multi-byte character.

9.4 Character Casing

Most of the multi-byte character sets define a set of 2-byte alphabetic characters called *full-form characters*. These full-form characters are distinguished from single-byte alphabetic characters, referred to as *half-form characters*, and make the case conversion of alphabetic characters problematic, as shown in Figure 9–1.

Figure 9–1. Case Conversion of Alphabetic Characters

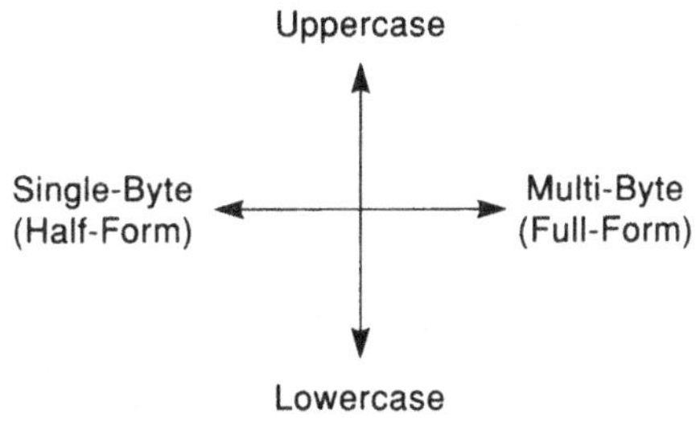

Although putting a multi-byte alphabetic character in uppercase or lowercase is recognized as a valid activity, case conversion of multi-byte ideographic characters produces undesirable results. When a multi-byte character's case is changed, a different multi-byte character is created.

During software design, parts of the software that perform casing conversion of a string or text should be designed to ensure that the casing of multi-byte ideographic characters is disabled. If the case of text must be converted, use the multi-byte routines JSY$TRA_ROM_UPPER and JSY$TRA_ROM_LOWER, located in the multi-byte library.

9.5 Character Searching

String searching and matching in standard English software is usually done on a byte-by-byte basis. However, to support multi-byte characters, the search or match should be performed character by character.

To localize software, modify all search routines so that they are performed on a character-by-character basis. You can use JSY$STR_SEARCH, a multi-byte search routine, to do this. If the software supports a wildcard search, the search should be carried out character by character.

9.6 Character Sorting

Sorting and merging of multi-byte characters is fundamentally different from sorting and merging of single-byte characters. A number of attributes unique to some Asian languages, such as Chinese, necessitate a different set of rules for sorting and merging these characters. These unique attributes include a large character set, duplicate collating values, a number of different collating sequences, user-defined characters, and characters of variable length. The sorting of multi-byte characters should be carried out character by character rather than byte by byte.

9.6.1 Collating Sequences

Languages, such as English, which are built on alphabets, have unique collating sequences. These unique sequences do not exist in languages based on ideographic characters. For most Asian languages, each ideographic character may have more than one collating sequence. For example, an ideographic character can be sorted by the number of strokes in the character, or by its phonetic alphabet. Depending on the purpose of the sort, different collating sequences may be used.

The sorting of ideographic characters is also distinguished by non-unique collating values. For a particular collating sequence, different characters can have the same collating value, such as the number of strokes. For this reason, sorting of ideographic characters based on one collating sequence is usually not enough. Thus a single key may need to be sorted according to multiple collating sequences.

The key field identified for the sort process is first sorted according to the primary collating sequence specified. If the collating values are the same, the values of the character according to the second collating sequence specified are compared. This comparison will be repeated until all the collating sequences specified for the particular sort are exhausted.

A set of commonly used collating sequences is already defined in sort utilities provided with Digital's operating systems. Users can also define collating sequences to meet their own specific needs. When defining these collating sequences, define the absolute collating value of characters instead of relative collating positions. This practice eliminates the need to reshuffle the collating sequence when characters are added or deleted, which can be inefficient due to the large size of the character set.

9.6.2 Variable Length Data

In a standard sort of alphabetic characters, the key starting position is expressed in terms of byte offset from the beginning of the record. This method does not work in the multi-byte environment. If you specify the key to start from byte two, the first byte of the second character in record one is compared with the last byte of the first character in record two, and with the second byte of the first character in record three, and so on. This does not provide for a comparison based on the logical unit of a character.

Similarly, specifying the length of the sort key by the number of bytes does not produce correct results in a multi-byte character data environment, as shown in Figure 9–2.

Figure 9–2. Sample Specification of the Sort Key

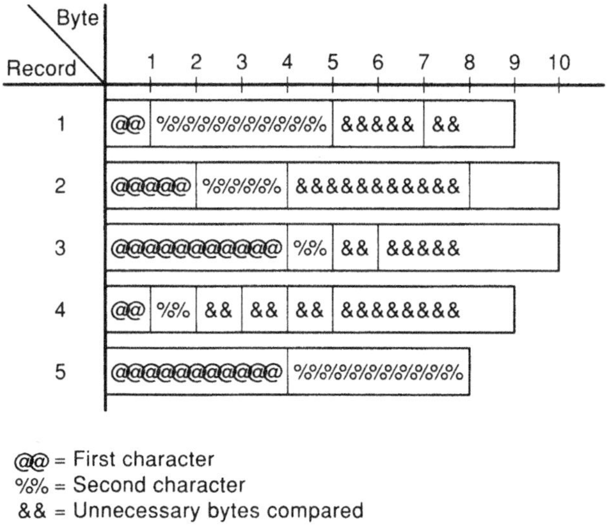

If the length of the sort key can only be specified by the number of bytes, in most cases the maximum possible length will be used. However, in a multi-byte character environment where a character occupies a variable number of bytes, specifying the maximum number of bytes causes the comparison of pad characters. This results in additional processing resources and unreliable results.

In a multi-byte character environment, processing should be carried out on a character-by-character basis. To sort data that involves multi-byte characters, users need a mechanism to specify the character position where a sort key is located and the length of the sort key in terms of the number of characters.

Chapter 10

Supporting Localization

This chapter describes the support that a central engineering group at Digital provides to an engineering group located in another country. Such support is often facilitated by an intermediary group operating between two groups.

The central engineering group's support for product localization should begin as soon as the decision to localize a product is made and should include development plans for the product. Internationalization issues should be considered in each phase of product planning, design, and development.

The central engineering group must also work to ensure that the appropriate deliverables are provided to the engineering groups in other countries. The deliverables fall into five categories:

- Planning

  A successful localization effort depends on effective organization and scheduling. This goal is best reached through collaboration between the central engineering group and the groups in the countries localizing the product. Planning should:

  — Define the scope of localization support to be provided for the particular product

  — Define the kinds of support to be provided, such as training

  — Define the contents of the localization kit (see Section 10.3)

  — Provide schedules

- Design

  The central engineering group should provide a modular design (see Chapter 4) as well as the following aids to localization:

  — System flags for localizable software modules

  — Bottom-up, incremental releases of code (see Section 10.3.1)

- Bottom-up, incremental, and translatable test procedures (see Section 10.3.5)
    - Incremental release of software builds, and build procedures (see Section 10.3.2)
    - Baselevel notes (see Section 10.3.4)
    - Tools to support specific tests (see Section 10.3.7)
- Translation

  The central engineering group should provide the following support to ease the translation effort:
    - Software translation markup (see Section 10.1)
    - Estimates for translation (see Section 10.2)
    - Ongoing consulting resources
- Engineering

  The central engineering group should provide the product itself, and the tools needed to facilitate localizing the product:
    - Localizable source files
    - Internals documentation (see Section 10.3.6)
    - Installable localization baselevels, including translatable installation procedures (see Section 10.3.3)
    - Modular, translatable build procedures (see Section 10.3.2)
    - Translatable test procedures (see Section 10.3.5)
    - A build environment to compile translated code
    - Kit build tools
    - Validation tools and translatable test suites
- Training

  The central engineering group is most knowledgeable about the product and is therefore best suited to lead training efforts and provide ongoing assistance to the engineering groups in other countries.

10.1 Translation Markup

It is not always obvious to translators which portions of a software product require translation. This section describes how to help translators locate the translatable text. At Digital, for reasons of simplicity, we use the term translatable text to refer to any area in a file that is subject to translation or localization. This section also gives examples of translation markup, that is, comments in application files that assist the translator in locating translatable and localizable items.

It is important to pay careful attention to detail during the markup of a product. Incomplete translation markup makes the translators' task unnecessarily difficult and delays the entire localization process. It is good practice to review the translation markup at least once to detect and correct errors or omissions.

Text to be translated can take the following forms:

- Natural language text used in prompts and messages
- Menu items
- Language-dependent keywords
- Strings used for validating user input
- Positioning information for display text (coordinates and sizes)

10.1.1 Objectives and Advantages of Markup

Translation markup in software files serves two objectives:

- It identifies the textual portions of a software product that have to be localized. The flags placed by the markup allow the translator to quickly find the translatable text.
- It helps developers understand how localization affects the product and where changes in the product could affect localization.

Translation markup is best done in the original files, rather than in a separate file or document, for the following reasons:

- Engineering groups in other countries can start translation with any baselevel, which allows translation to start early.
- Every baselevel contains markup from previous baselevels. Complete records of previous activities are preserved, providing an opportunity to refine and upgrade the translation at each pass.

- Markup is easier to update between baselevels. It takes less effort to make changes to text that has already been translated than to create an original translation for every baselevel.
- Because online markup is faster and more manageable than hardcopy markup, translation is easier to do on line than in hardcopy.
- Distribution is easier: if your translation agencies have network access, marked up files can be sent over the network.

10.1.2 Guidelines for Markup

The person best suited for providing translation markup is the product developer, since he or she knows the product best. The developer should mark up the original files at development time, and this set should be the only markup files produced.

Observe the following guidelines when performing source file markup:

- Start the section that requires translation with a comment:

  ```
  !++ Begin translation
  ```

- Terminate the section that requires translation with a comment:

  ```
  !-- End translation
  ```

- Mark up files using a comment line preceding the line that contains a translatable item.

  This practice enables the translators and software specialists to ignore comments outside the translatable section. It also makes it possible to automate the recognition of translatable portions.
- Include translation comments on the following subjects:
  - Restrictions on the length of text strings
  - Origin and context of text strings

Sample translation markup of VMS message files and ULTRIX files is shown in the sections that follow.

10.1.3 Markup of VMS Message Files (.MSG)

In VMS message files, there is no need to draw the translator's attention to translatable messages because it is assumed that all messages should be translated. However, it is essential that markup identify any messages that are *not* to be translated.

Place the comments pertaining to a particular message or group of messages on the line before the messages. It is good practice to start comments with the !+ and terminate them with the !- characters, for example:

```
!+
! This is a comment on the following message(s)...
!-
```

Where possible, put short comments at the end of the code line.

Guidelines

Observe the following guidelines when creating new messages in a message file or when transferring messages from code into a message file.

- Include meaningful comments on any messages that are not self-explanatory.
- State the origin of the message, that is, the part or parts of the source code that call the message.
- State the context in which the message appears on the screen.
- When a message is removed from source code and put into a message file, be sure that the message symbol or key points to the name of the file from which the message has been removed. If this cannot be done, include the file name in a comment.

In Example 10–1 the markup informs the translator about string format requirements and date convention formats, and it explains the meaning of an appended message when an error message overlays a prompt.

Example 10–1. Translation Comments in a VMS Message File

```
!+
! Printer destination "DOCUMENT" from SMPRINTER.DAT.  Only translate
! if you have changed the name of the destination:
!-
WP_PRNTDOCDEST      <DOCUMENT>
      .
      .
      .
!+
! The following must match the string supplied by the help
```

(Example 10–1 continues on next page)

Example 10–1 (Cont.). Translation Comments in a VMS Message File

```
! librarian in your language:
!-
ADDINFO    <Additional information available:>
     .
     .
     .
CMCAPITALA  <A> !Appointment
CMCAPITALB  <B> !Both
CMCAPITALC  <C> !Conflict
CMCAPITALD  <D> !Day
CMCAPITALM  <M> !Meeting
CMCAPITALP  <P> !Personal
CMCAPITALS  <S> !Schedule
CMCAPITALR  <R> !Reminders
CMCAPITALT  <T> !Two calendars
CMCAPITALW  <W> !Week
     .
     .
     .
!  The following date formats should be changed to represent the
!  standard way of displaying a date format.  The separators used for
!  the date formats in OALLV.BLI should be applied to these formats also.
!    MM stands for up to 2 numbers for the month
!    DD stands for up to 2 numbers for the day
!    YY stands for 2 numbers for the year (90)
!    MMM stands for three letters for the month (APR for APRIL)
!    YYYY stands for 4 numbers representing the year and century (1990)
!
DATE_LOAD_NU1                   <MM/DD/YY>
!                                ---20---
DATE_LOAD_NU2                   <DD/MM/YY>
!                                ---20---
DATE_LOAD_NU3                   <YY/MM/DD>
!                                ---20---
DATE_LOAD_AN1                   <DD-MMM-YYYY>
!                                ----40-----
DATE_LOAD_AN2                   <YYYY-MMM-DD>
!                                ----40-----
DATE_LOAD_ANDEFAULT             <Default date format for this language>
!                                ---------------40--------------------
!+
!  The following message is appended to the end of any error
!  message which overlays a prompt.
!-
PRET            <...Press RETURN >
```

10.1.4 Markup of ULTRIX Files

The following example shows a manpage from the ULTRIX man program that displays information about the operation of a program, much like the VMS utility.

Example 10–2. Translation Comments in an ULTRIX File

```
.\" SCCSID: @(#)man.1    2.13    8/23/90
.TH man 1
.SH NAME
man \- print manual pages
.SH SYNTAX
.br
.B man
\fB\-k\fR \fIkeyword...\fR
.br
.B man
\fB\-f\fR \fIfile...\fR
.br
.B man
[\fB\-\fR] [\fB\-t\fR] [\fB\-s\fR] [\|\fIsection\fR\|] \fItitle...\fR
.SH DESCRIPTION

./"++ Begin translation
./"+
./" Translate the command lines.
./"-

.NXR "man command"
.NXA "man command" "man macro package"
.NXAM "man command" "catman command"
.NXR "command" "locating on-line information"

./"+
./"Translate and change the manual's name, if necessary.
./"-

.NXR "Programmer's Manual" "accessing on line"
.NXR "Programmer's Manual" "printing"

./"+
./" Translate the program's description.
./"-

The
.PN man command is a program which gives information from the
programmers manual. It can be asked for one line descriptions of
commands specified by name, or for all commands whose description
contains any of a set of ds.  It can also provide on-line access
to the sections of the printed manual.
.SH OPTIONS
```

(Example 10–2 continues on next page)

Example 10–2 (Cont.). Translation Comments in an ULTRIX File

```
./"+
./" Translate the command line.
./"-

.NXR "man command" "options"

./"-- End translation
```

Example 10–3 shows comments associated with the translation of dates.

Example 10–3. Date Conventions in an ULTRIX File

```
/*
 * The following abbreviations should be changed to represent your
 * standard way of displaying them. The second number between
 * parenthesis stands for the number of characters in the
 * abbreviation of both month and day.  If necessary, change the
 * number [3] to the number of characters that you are using.
 *
 * ++ Begin translation
 */

 char     month[12][3] = {
         "Jan","Feb","Mar","Apr",
         "May","Jun","Jul","Aug",
         "Sep","Oct","Nov","Dec"
};
char     days[7][3] = {
         "Sun","Mon","Tue","Wed",
         "Thu","Fri","Sat"

/* -- End translation */
```

10.1.5 Files Not Requiring Markup

No translation markup is required for files where the translatable portion is obvious, such as the text file shown below, or where the respective file format does not require comments, as is the case with the help file.

Example 10–4. Text File—No Markup Required

```
This means that a number of user interface options are
available for the product.  The options may be bundled
into the product, or available by order to be installed
separately at a later time.  Users can select from language
interface and functionality options during execution of
the program, perhaps even moving from one user interface
option to another while using the product.  This implies
that two users of the same software product on the same
system can use different user interfaces for that product.
```

Example 10–5. Help File—No Markup Required

```
PRINT

  Queues one or more files for printing, either to the default
  system printer queue or to a specified queue.

  Format:

          PRINT  file-spec[,...]

  Additional information available:

  Parameters Command_Qualifiers
  /AFTER    /BACKUP  /BEFORE  /BURST   /BY_OWNER /CHARACTERISTICS
  /CONFIRM /COPIES   /CREATED /DELETE /DEVICE    /EXCLUDE   /EXPIRED
                .
                .
                .
```

10.2 Translation Estimates

To assist foreign engineering groups, Digital's central engineering groups supply estimates on the amount of translatable text contained in a corporate product. Incorrect counts of lines in text files and incorrect page counts can seriously hinder a translation project. It is important that these counts be as accurate as possible. Engineering groups in other countries base their resource planning and scheduling on these estimates, and production groups use these estimates to schedule equipment and prepare materials. Central engineering must provide accurate and up-to-date information about the items listed in Table 10–1.

Table 10–1. Page and Screen Counts

Software files	Line counts Number of translatable lines (do not include code, comment, and markup lines)
Online help, menus	Number of screens Number of dialog boxes Number of screen messages
Hardcopy documentation	Page and line counts in original documentation

For all manuals and other hardcopy documentation to be translated, central engineering must provide estimated page counts.

For all menus and online help files, central engineering must provide an estimated number of screens (24-line displays).

For other translatable software (for example, message files), central engineering must provide a realistic estimate of the number of lines to be translated.

10.3 Localization Kit

Digital's central engineering groups provide a localization kit to the product teams in the other countries. The localization kit contains all the elements that the teams need to localize the software; it results from collaboration of the central and local groups during the product planning and preliminary design phase.

The localization kit should include an installable baselevel that verifies the way the product is built and tested and that conforms to specifications.

A complete localization kit includes the components described in the following sections.

10.3.1 Source Software Modules

The localization kit should provide the source code, messages, and help modules that need to be translated. The kit includes the modules that

- Display text
- Solicit input from the user

- Process user input to make decisions and take actions
- Generate error messages
- Produce device-specific output

10.3.2 Modular Build Procedures

Product development includes incremental integration of code and incremental release of builds. Modular build procedures help put together those modules of the software product that are required for a given incremental release. Each modular build procedure should contain all the necessary instructions to complete one incremental integration of code. The central engineering group should strive to create build procedures that can be used by engineering groups in other countries.

10.3.3 Installable Baselevel

Central engineering groups collaborate with local engineering groups by supplying installable baselevel kits that demonstrate how the product functions, and how it appears to the user. The availability of installable baselevels at every phase enables the engineering groups in other countries to produce a product version with the same appearance as the original product. This baselevel will be used by the local engineering groups in other countries for reference only. It must *not* be used directly for translation.

10.3.4 Baselevel Notes

For larger localization projects, Digital has found it useful to provide engineering groups in other countries with additional baselevel notes. Baselevel notes typically consist of collected Internal Change Orders (ICOs), or Engineering Change Orders (ECOs), used by engineering teams for reporting and controlling engineering changes.

10.3.5 Test Procedures

When writing test procedures, the central engineering group should keep in mind that its international product will be tested in each country localizing the product.

Guidelines

To simplify the localization process, central engineering groups at Digital follow these guidelines for developing tests:

- Design test procedures that execute automatically. Include all input to the tests and all expected output from the tests.
- Collaborate with groups in other countries to create translatable test suites, including regression tests.
- Create test procedures that can be modified to test product variants.
- Make the test procedure easily translatable to other languages.
- Provide test procedures with each baselevel.
- Include, for each new release, detailed information on any changes made.

10.3.6 Internals Documentation

Digital's central engineering group provides the engineering groups in other countries with all applicable internals documentation, which includes the following:

- List of localizable modules
- Functional specifications
- Development plans
- Procedures manuals
- Quality evaluation plans
- Data definition documents

At Digital, central engineering groups should provide the teams in other countries with the latest revisions as they become available.

10.3.7 Tools and Utilities

It is important that software tools and utilities created specifically to test the international product be made available to the groups in other countries, and that the group members be familiar with their use. Include the following test tools:

- Product-specific test tools
- Compilers

- Linkers
- Filters
- Command procedures
- Verification programs

10.4 Digital's Localization Platform

Internationalization efforts are easier when the process begins by localizing the operating system. A localized operating system provides a common platform and architecture for the application programs. For example, many of the Asian character and data manipulation issues discussed in Chapter 9 can be handled by the localized Asian terminal drivers and specialized multi-byte handling utilities that Digital packages with the various Asian VMS operating systems. Similar facilities are also available in the Asian ULTRIX operating systems.

Besides the localized operating systems for European and Asian languages, Digital offers other localized hardware and software to assist with the localization of software applications. Digital's localized Asian products include hardware and software for

- Localized operating systems to provide a common platform to handle multi-byte characters and to support localized applications
- Input and output devices such as terminals, workstations, and printers for handling multi-byte Asian characters input and output
- Input methods to enter Asian characters
- Localized information management tools to facilitate development and run-time support of the Asian language by the application (currently only available under the Asian VMS platform)
- Other software engineering tools and languages such as VAXset and VAX SCAN can aid developers throughout the software localization process

Appendix A

Digital's Asian Products

Digital has made a significant investment in the development of both hardware and software platforms to facilitate international software products in native languages in Asia. This appendix lists Digital's available hardware and software that currently support the Chinese, Japanese, and Korean languages.

A.1 Hardware Platform

Most VAX and RISC processors, in conjunction with their respective VMS and ULTRIX operating systems, provide varying degrees of support for the local language processing of Chinese, Japanese, and Korean. Together with the available local language terminals and printers, Digital provides a complete hardware platform for users who have needs for data processing in Chinese, Japanese, or Korean.

Some of Digital's terminals and printers provide a complete local language processing architecture for a number of Asian languages. This effort includes a series of VT382 terminals supporting various Asian languages. Currently, Digital terminals and printers listed in Table A–1 and Table A–2 support the Traditional Chinese (Taiwan), Simplified Chinese (PRC), Japanese, and Korean languages.

Table A–1. Available Asian Terminals

Traditional Chinese	Simplified Chinese	Japanese	Korean
VT382-D	VT382-C	VT382-J	VT382-K
Mitac CT282	VT82	VT286-J	Doosan 220C
Mitac CPS50 (with terminal emulation software)		VT284-J	
		VT282-J	

Table A–2. Available Asian Printers

Traditional Chinese	Simplified Chinese	Japanese	Korean
Mitac CPC70 (printer controller)	LA380	LA380	LA380
	LA280	LA280	
	LA86	LA86	
		LN03	
		DEClaser 2300	
		LPS40	
		LPS20	

A.2 Software Platform

Digital provides a local language processing environment in the VAX architecture with localized VMS operating systems. Many utilities facilitating the processing of Asian characters are available with the localized VMS operating system; many of the data management tools and development tools have also been localized to support the processing of Asian characters. These utilities and tools make application localization a much easier task and also minimize the maintenance efforts required due to changes in standards adopted for a particular language.

The localization of the VMS operating system has brought about the development of a number of utilities specific to the processing of particular languages. Table A–3 lists these utilities. Some of them may not be included in all Asian VMS operating systems. Consult the Software Product Descriptions and System Support Addendums of individual Asian VMS operating systems for the specific information. In addition to these localized software products, some standard software products are available as useful tools in the Asian language multi-byte processing environment.

Similar local language processing capabilities are being developed for the RISC architecture.

Table A–3. Digital's Asian Software Platform

Capability	Asian Language
	Traditional Chinese
Operating System	VMS/Hanyu ULTRIX/Hanyu UWS/Hanyu
Networking	PCSA/Hanyu DECnet
Data Management	Rdb/Hanyu DTR/Hanyu DBMS/Hanyu CDD/Plus
Development Tools	DECforms/Hanyu FMS/Hanyu RALLY/Hanyu MACRO BASIC BLISS-32 C COBOL FORTRAN PASCAL PL/1
Application Integration	VMS DECwindows/Hanyu ALL-IN-1/Hanyu
Applications	DECwrite/Hanyu

(Table A–3 continues on next page)

Table A–3. Digital's Asian Software Platform (cont.)

Capability	Asian Language
	Simplified Chinese
Operating System	VMS/Hanzi ULTRIX/Hanzi UWS/Hanzi
Networking	PCSA/Hanzi DECnet
Data Management	Rdb/Hanzi DTR/Hanzi CDD/Plus
Development Tools	DECforms/Hanzi FMS/Hanzi RALLY/Hanzi MACRO BASIC BLISS-32 C COBOL FORTRAN PASCAL PL/1
Application Integration	VMS DECwindows/Hanzi ALL-IN-1/Hanzi
Applications	DECwrite/Hanzi VWS/Hanzi MANMAN/Hanzi

(Table A–3 continues on next page)

Table A–3. Digital's Asian Software Platform (cont.)

Capability	Asian Language
	Japanese
Operating System	VMS/Japanese ULTRIX/Japanese UWS/Japanese
Networking	PCSA/Japanese DECnet
Data Management	Rdb/Japanese DTR/Japanese CDD/Plus
Development Tools	DECforms/Japanese FMS/Japanese MACRO BASIC BLISS-32 C COBOL FORTRAN PASCAL PL/1
Application Integration	ALL-IN-1/Japanese VWS/Japanese VMS DECwindows/Japanese
Applications	DECwrite/Japanese MANMAN/Japanese
Graphic Tools	GKS/Japanese PHIGS/Japanese

(Table A–3 continues on next page)

Table A–3. Digital's Asian Software Platform (cont.)

Capability	Asian Language
	Korean
Operating System	VMS/Hangul ULTRIX/Hangul UWS/Hangul
Networking	PCSA/Hangul DECnet
Data Management	Rdb/Hangul DTR/Hangul CDD/Plus
Development Tools	DECforms/Hangul FMS/Hangul RALLY/Hangul MACRO BASIC BLISS-32 C COBOL FORTRAN PASCAL PL/1
Application Integration	VMS DECwindows/Hangul ALL-IN-1/Hangul
Applications	DECwrite/Hangul

A.3 Chinese and Korean VMS Components

Some Digital utilities and routines in Chinese and Korean VMS provide a computing environment for these two languages. They include the terminal driver, HEDT, and HTPU:

- Terminal driver

  The terminal driver within the VMS operating system has been enhanced to handle multi-byte character input and output. The following advanced line editing features are also available to support Asian characters:

  — Cursor movement over Asian characters

  — Deletion of Asian characters

  — Insertion of Asian characters in the middle of a line

— Wrapping at the end of a line containing Asian characters
— Overstriking of Asian characters
— READ verification

- HEDT and HTPU

  The HEDT and HTPU editors supplied with the Asian VMS operating system provide advanced editing features to support multi-byte Asian character editing.

- HSORT and HMERGE

  HSORT/HMERGE supports both the sorting of data according to collating sequences specific to the supported language and multiple collating sequences on the same sort key, a requirement of sorting in Asian languages.

- Callable SORT/MERGE Interfaces

  Callable interfaces for the Asian language SORT/MERGE facility is provided.

- HDUMP

  HDUMP supports the proper handling of multi-byte characters in DUMP output.

- HSYSHR

  HSYSHR, a multi-byte run-time library, facilitates application development in Asian languages. The run-time library routines perform various Asian language processing functions, such as string manipulation, read/write operations, and character conversions.

- HMAIL

  HMAIL, the local mail facility, supports both the editing and viewing of mail text with multi-byte Asian characters and Asian character folder names.

- Bilingual HELP messages

  The VMS operating system's HELP messages are provided in both English and the specific language of the particular Asian VMS operating system.

- Font utilities

  For some Asian VMS operating systems, users can define their own characters.

A.4 Japanese VMS Operating System's Components

Some Digital utilities and routines in Japanese provide a computing environment for this language.

- Terminal driver

  The terminal driver in VMS/Japanese has been enhanced to handle the following capabilities:

  — On demand loading of glyph

    In case the current terminal device does not have some glyphs, the terminal driver sends them to the terminal to meet the requests. Thus the terminal can display characters that the terminal does not have as a default. Users can enable and disable this feature by using the KANJIGEN utility.

  — JIS78 to JIS83 conversion

    The JIS78 to JIS83 conversion feature in the terminal drivers allows users with JIS78 terminals to also use JIS83 terminals. Users can specify the terminal version by using the KANJIGEN utility.

  — Input/Output flags

    Users can use the KANJIGEN utility to determine if the current device is a Kanji terminal.

- JTPU

  JTPU/JEVE is an editor supplied with VMS/Japanese that provides advanced editing features to support Japanese character editing.

- SORT/MERGE

  SORT/MERGE supports both the sorting of data according to collating sequences specific to the Japanese language, and supports multiple collating sequences on the same sort key, which is a requirement of sorting in the Japanese language.

- KDUMP

  KDUMP is a utility that supports the proper handling of multi-byte characters in DUMP output.

- JSYSHR

  JSYSHR is a shareable image that facilitates application development in Japanese. The run-time library routines perform a variety of Japanese language processing functions such as string manipulation, read/write operations, Kana-Kanji conversion, and so on.

- JSYLIB

  JSYLIB is an object library that has the same functionality as JSYSHR, but also contains code conversion routines.

- JSY$SMGSHR

  JSY$SMGSHR is a shareable image of enhanced SMGSHR that supports the Japanese language.

- JMAIL

  JMAIL is the local mail facility that supports both the editing and viewing of mail text with Japanese characters.

- VMS Local language (VMSL)

  VMS HELP messages, system messages, and some utilities' messages are provided in both English and Japanese. Users can choose the language displayed in messages by using the SET LANGUAGE command.

- KCODE

  This utility converts a DEC Kanji file to a file in another vendor's Kanji files and vice versa.

- JDICEDIT

  JDICEDIT maintains a personal dictionary for users performing Kana-Kanji conversions.

- Font Utilities

  Font utilities are provided with the VMS/Japanese operating system so that users can define their own characters.

A.5 Japanese ULTRIX Components

Digital provides a local language processing environment in its VAX and RISC architectures with a localized ULTRIX operating system. Many utilities that facilitate the processing of Asian characters have been provided with the localized ULTRIX operating system.

For specific information, consult the Software Product Descriptions and System Support Addendums for individual Asian ULTRIX software.

Digital provides a number of utilities and routines in the Japanese ULTRIX operating system to provide a computing environment for this language.

- **Tty** subsystem

  The **tty** subsystem handles multi-byte characters input and output and offers the following features:

  - Code conversion between terminal code and internal code
  - Kana-Kanji conversions
  - Soft-ODL capability
  - History capability

- **Csh**

  The Japanese csh handles Japanese characters in the command argument, shell script, and history list.

- Text editor

  The Japanese **Vi** and Japanese **Emacs** editors provide advanced editing features to support Japanese character editing.

- **Nroff**

  The Japanese **Nroff** supports Japanese characters and includes the Japanese specific KINSOKU-SYORI. **Nroff** also supports Japanese **tbl.**

- Libraries

  The libraries included with the ULTRIX/Japanese operating system include Kana-Kanji conversion libraries and code conversion libraries.

- On-line manuals

  Digital provides on-line manuals in Japanese for all supported Japanese products.

- Font utilities

  The **fedit** utility is provided with the ULTRIX/Japanese operating system so that users can define their own characters. The fonts created by **fedit** are used for VT terminals and Kanji printers.

- Code conversion

  In the **tty** subsystem, the supported terminal codes are shift-JIS, 7 bit-JIS, DEC Kanji 1978, and DEC Kanji 1983. And the **jcode** utilities and libraries convert one code to the other among those terminal codes.

- Other utilities

  Digital also supports Japanese printer filters, Japanese **grep,** Japanese **od,** Japanese **ed,** and Japanese **sed.**

A.6 Japanese DECwindows

Application developers should use Japanese DECwindows software to support Japanese characters. Japanese DECwindows software is available as part of VMS/Japanese and Japanese ULTRIX Worksystem Software (UWS). It consists of localized versions of the original DECwindows components such as a server, fonts, XUI Toolkit and several bundled applications as described below:

- Japanese DECwindows server

  The X Window System specifies Kana key symbols to be used for identifying Kana keyboard events. Japanese DECwindows software provides the keymap file which defines mapping between Digital's LK201-AJ (Kana keyboard) key codes and Kana key symbols.

  In addition, the Japanese version of the DECwindows server can control Kana input mode.

- Japanese fonts

  The DEC-Kanji character set consists of more than 7,000 Japanese characters. Four families (grouped by size) of Japanese fonts are available. Each family contains a set of Hankaku font files and a Zenkaku font file. Hankaku fonts (ASCII, JIS-Roman, JIS-Katakana, ISO Latin-1, DEC-Supplemental and DEC-Technical) have the same height and half-width as Zenkaku fonts (DEC-Kanji) in the same family.

  Each font file has a unique logical font description compliant with the X Logical Font Description (XLFD) convention.

As part of the Kanji character set, users can define new characters. VMS/Japanese provides the facilities called FEDIT/FDESIGN (fedit) to define and maintain the user-defined characters. Since the above facilities are designed to be used for character terminals, Japanese DECwindows software provides a font file converter which converts FEDIT/FDESIGN (fedit) generated font files to DECwindows server native format (SNF) font files.

- Japanese Xlib

  The original Xlib includes basic 16-bit character handling routines. The following six functions have their 16-bit counterparts.

8-Bit Functions	16-Bit Functions
XDrawString	XDrawString16
XDrawImageString	XDrawImageString16
XDrawText	XDrawText16
XTextWidth	XTextWidth16
XTextExtents	XTextExtents16
XQueryTextExtents	XQueryTextExtents16

  Xlib does not provide a built-in mechanism to handle the mixture of 8-bit and 16-bit characters.

- Japanese XUI Toolkit

  The original XUI Toolkit supports DDIF and incorporates a set of functions to handle it. Some widgets accept compound strings as values of their resources. Users can use DEC-Kanji or JIS-Katakana with those widgets.

  The Japanese version of XUI Toolkit is a superset of the original XUI Toolkit. It changes its behavior according to the language specified by the session manager. This language switching mechanism is subject to change.

  In the Japanese version of XUI Toolkit, the following widgets are localized in terms of default labels, propagation mechanisms of font lists, and so on.

  — ColorMix

  — FileSelection

  — Help

  — MessageBox

  — Scale

— Selection
— SText

The SText widget includes a built-in Japanese input method (Kana-to-Kanji conversion). The FileSelection and Help widgets contain some SText widgets.

A.7 Japanese Multi-Byte Run-Time Library

JSYSHR, the multi-byte run-time library, is a collection of commonly used routines that perform a wide variety of multi-byte Japanese language processing operations. The library is a valuable tool in the localization of software supporting Kanji data.

The library is available as part of the VMS/Japanese operating system. All routines provided in this library can be called from any programming language supported in the VMS/Japanese environment. Routines in JSYSHR are prefixed by either 'JLB$' or 'JSY$' and are divided into the following four groups according to the task they perform. Table A–4 lists the four routine groups.

Table A–4. JSYSHR Routines

Routines	Task Performed
General	Japanese processing library routines that are called with standard interface from VAX programming languages.
Preliminary	Basic routines to process details such as character manipulation.
Kana-Kanji conversion	A set of routines that perform the Kana-Kanji conversion.
Kanji code conversion	A set of routines to convert code between Digital's Kanji code and other vendors' Kanji code.

A.8 Chinese and Korean Multi-Byte Run-Time Library

HSYSHR, the multi-byte run-time library, is a collection of commonly used routines that perform a wide variety of multi-byte Asian language processing operations. The library is a valuable tool in the localization of single-byte software to multi-byte software.

The HSYSHR library is available as part of the Asian VMS operating system. All of the routines in this library follow the same VAX Procedure Call Standard and can be called from any programming language supported in the Asian VMS environment. Routines in HSYSHR are prefixed by either 'JLB$' or 'JSY$'; they are divided into nine groups according to the task they perform, see Table A–5.

Table A–5. HSYSHR Routines

Routine	Task Performed
Conversion	Multi-byte character conversion
String	Manipulate multi-byte character strings
Read/Write	Read/write of multi-byte characters in user buffers
Pointer	Manipulate multi-byte character pointers
Comparison	Compare strings that contain multi-byte characters
Search	Search for substrings containing multi-byte characters
Count	Count bytes and characters in strings containing multi-byte characters
Character Type	Identify the type and class of symbols and characters in multi-byte character processing
Date/Time	Convert the date/time format into the local language format

A.9 Japanese Screen Management Run-Time Library (JSY$SMGSHR)

JSY$SMGSHR is also a run-time library that can be called from any language supported in the Japanese VMS environment; supporting both Japanese Kanji and Katakana characters.

Appendix B

Digital's International Market

Digital localizes software products to provide users with interfaces in languages other than American English. Digital currently supports products with various user interface languages including British English, Chinese (traditional and simplified scripts), Danish, Dutch, Finnish, French, German, Hebrew, Icelandic, Italian, Japanese, Korean, Norwegian, Portuguese, Spanish, Swedish, and Thai.

Digital is also adapting products to support character sets other than the ISO Latin-1 character set, providing products that support languages such as Arabic, Chinese, Greek, Hebrew, Japanese, Korean, Thai, and Turkish. Languages supported by the ISO Latin-2 character set, such as Czech, (Serbo-)Croatian, Hungarian, Polish, Romanian, Slovak, and Slovene could be added to this list in the future.

Table B–1 provides an overview of countries to which these localizations apply and where Digital is currently selling localized products. For most of the countries listed, the product localization goes beyond language support to include other areas, such as support of various keyboards, various data input and display conventions, as well as various collating sequences.

The character sets listed are, where applicable, ISO standards. The keyboards listed are specific to a particular language. For example, a country like Belgium may use more than one keyboard to accommodate the various languages of its citizens. The labels, *Modified xxx, VT28x, VT38x, LA8x,* and *LAx80*, in the keyboard column indicate that more than just a local keyboard is required to adequately support the country and its languages.

Table B–1 lists languages used in the country, whether they are used in business or not. Some minority languages with no official status in the country are listed in parentheses.

The user interface languages of Digital's products include the important business languages for the countries listed. English is the most widely used language in business in many countries. Digital has offices in most of the countries listed in the table and also in some not listed, such as Fiji, India, Malaysia, and the Philippines.

Table B–1. Countries and Languages

Country	Character Set	Keyboard	Languages
Algeria	Latin-Arabic	Modified Arabic	Arabic, French (Berber)
Australia	ISO Latin-1	North American	English
Austria	ISO Latin-1 German NRC	German	German (Croatian, Slovenian)
Belgium	ISO Latin-1 French NRC	French/Belgian, Flemish	German, French, Dutch
Brazil	ISO Latin-1	North American	Portuguese (German, Spanish, Italian, Japanese, Polish)
Canada	ISO Latin-1 Canadian NRC	North American, French Canadian	English, French (Italian, Ukranian)
China (PRC)	Simplified Chinese Script	VT28x, VT38x, LA8x, LAx80	Chinese (Tibetan, Kazakh, Korean, Mongolian, Uighur, Yi, Zhuang)
Cyprus	Latin-Greek ISO Latin-5	Greek, Turkish	Greek, Turkish
Denmark	ISO Latin-1 Norwegian NRC	Danish	Danish (German)
Egypt	Latin-Arabic	Modified Arabic	Arabic
Finland	ISO Latin-1 Finnish NRC	Finnish	Finnish, Swedish
France	ISO Latin-1 French NRC	French/Belgian	French, Breton, Corsican, Basque, Occitan (Catalan, German, Dutch)
Germany	ISO Latin-1 German NRC	German	German (Danish, Frisian)
Greece	Latin-Greek	Modified Greek	Greek (Macedonian, Albanian, Turkish)

(Table B–1 continues on next page)

Table B–1. Countries and Languages (cont.)

Country	Character Set	Keyboard	Languages
Hong Kong	ISO Latin-1 Chinese	VT28x, VT38x, LA8x, LAx80	English, Chinese
Iceland	ISO Latin-1	Icelandic	Icelandic, Danish
Ireland	ISO Latin-1 United Kingdom NRC	United Kingdom	English, Irish Gaelic
Israel	Latin-Hebrew	Modified Hebrew	Hebrew, Arabic
Italy	ISO Latin-1 Italian NRC	Italian	German, Italian, French (Rhaeto-Romance, Sardinian, Albanian)
Japan	Kanji and Kana	VT28x, VT38x, LA8x, LAx80	Japanese (Korean)
Luxembourg	ISO Latin-1	Swiss	German, French, Luxembourgian
Mexico	ISO Latin-1	Spanish	Spanish (Indian)
Morocco	Latin-Arabic	Modified Arabic	Arabic, French (Berber, Spanish)
Netherlands	ISO Latin-1 Dutch NRC	Netherlands	Dutch, Frisian
New Zealand	ISO Latin-1	North American	English, Maori
Norway	ISO Latin-1 Norwegian NRC	Norwegian	Norwegian
Portugal	ISO Latin-1 Portuguese NRC	Portuguese	Portuguese
Republic of Korea (South)	Hangul and Hanja	VT28x, VT38x, LA8x, LAx80	Korean
Saudi Arabia	Latin-Arabic	Modified Arabic	Arabic, English
Singapore	Simplified Chinese Script	(Not sold by Digital)	English, Malay, Tamil, Chinese
Spain	ISO Latin-1 Spanish NRC	Spanish	Catalan, Spanish, Basque, Galician, Valencian (Mallorcan)

(Table B–1 continues on next page)

Table B–1. Countries and Languages (cont.)

Country	Character Set	Keyboard	Languages
Sweden	ISO Latin-1 Swedish NRC	Swedish	Swedish
Switzerland	ISO Latin-1 Swiss NRC	Swiss (German), Swiss (French)	German, French, Italian, Rhaeto-Romance
Taiwan (ROC)	Traditional Chinese Script	VT28x, VT38x, LA8x, LAx80	Chinese
Thailand	Thai ISO Latin-1	VT28x, VT38x, LA8x, LAx80	Thai (English, Malay, Chinese)
Tunisia	Latin-Arabic	Modified Arabic	Arabic (French)
Turkey	ISO Latin-5	Modified Turkish	Turkish (Kurdish)
United Kingdom	ISO Latin-1 United Kingdom NRC	United Kingdom	English, Welsh (Irish Gaelic, Scots Gaelic)
United States	ISO Latin-1	North American	English, Spanish (German, French, Italian, Chinese)
Yugoslavia	ISO Latin-2 Latin-Cyrillic	Modified Croatian	Croatian, Macedonian, Slovenian, Serbian (Albanian, German, Hungarian)

Appendix C

Language-Specific Collating Sequences

This appendix contains tables listing the collating sequences for the following languages:

Danish
English
Finnish
French
German
Greek
Icelandic
Italian
Norwegian
Portuguese
Spanish
Swedish

The tables are intended as a source of information for applications developers. They show how characters should be collated to obtain alphabetical output according to dictionary order.

The Arabic, Chinese, Hebrew, Japanese, Korean, Taiwanese, and Thai collating sequences are not included here because of the numerous characters involved and the variety of possible collating methods.

Refer to Table C–1 to find out which collating sequence a country uses. Tables C–2 through C–4 list the collating sequences for each language.

Table C–1. Collating Sequences Used by Different Countries

Country	Collating Sequences Used
Australia	English
Austria	German
Belgium	English, French
Canada	English, French
Denmark	Danish
Finland	Finnish
France	French
Germany	German
Greece	Greek
Hong Kong	English
Iceland	Icelandic
Ireland	English
Israel	Hebrew
Italy	Italian
Luxembourg	French, German
Mexico	Spanish
Netherlands	English[1]
New Zealand	English
Norway	Norwegian
Portugal	Portuguese
Puerto Rico	English, Spanish
Spain	Spanish
Sweden	Swedish
Switzerland	French, German, Italian
United Kingdom	English
United States	English

[1]The English collating sequence is used for Digital's Dutch products.

When reading Tables C–2 through C–4, keep the following points in mind:

- Letters are grouped in sets. Each set consists of variants of a basic letter; all letters in a set have the same basic collating value, which means that sorting is performed as if the variants were replaced by the basic letter.
- Within any set, the variants are in a specific order; this order is used for tie-breaking. For example, with the English collating sequence, a sorted list could contain the following elements:

    key
    Keynesian
    kg
    KG
    khaddar

Table C–2. Danish, English, Finnish, and French Collating Sequences

Danish	English	Finnish	French
a A à	a A	a A	a A æ[2] Æ[2] á[1] Á[1] à À â Â å[1]
b B	b B	b B	Å[1] ä[1] Ä[1] ã[1] Ã[1]
c C	c C	c C	b B
d D	d D	d D	c C ç Ç
e E é É	e E	e E é	d D
f F	f F	f F	e E é É è È ê Ê ë Ë
g G	g G	g G	f F
h H	h H	h H	g G
i I	i I	i I	h H
j J	j J	j J	i I í[1] Í[1] ì[1] Ì[1] î Î ï Ï
k K	k K	k K	j J
l L	l L	l L	k K
m M	m M	m M	l L
n N	n N	n N	m M
o O	o O	o O	n N ñ[1] Ñ[1]
p P	p P	p P	o O œ[2] Œ[2] ó[1] Ó[1] ò[1] Ò[1] ô
q Q	q Q	q Q	Ô ö[1] Ö[1] õ[1] Õ[1] ø[1] Ø[1]
r R	r R	r R	p P
s S	s S	s S	q Q
t T	t T	t T	r R
u U	u U	u U	s S
v V	v V	v V w W	t T
w W	w W	x X	u U ú[1] Ú[1] ù Ù û Û ü Ü
x X	x X	y Y ü Ü	v V
y Y ü Ü	y Y	z Z	w W
z Z	z Z	å Å	x X
æ Æ		ä Ä	y Y ÿ Ÿ
ø Ø		ö Ö	z Z
å Å			

[1]For French, these letters occur only in borrowed words.

[2]æ, Æ, œ, and Œ are collated as if they were ae, AE, oe, OE; for tie-breaks they collate between a and á, o and ó. For example, the order would be: *aède, ægosome, aérage, ærage, æschne, aétite*.

Table C–3. German, Greek, Icelandic, and Italian Collating Sequences

German	Greek	Icelandic	Italian
a A ä Ä	α A	a A	a A à À
b B	β B	á Á	b B
c C	γ Γ	b B	c C ç Ç
d D	δ Δ	c C	d D
e E	ϵ E	d D	e E è È é É
f F	ς Z	(eth)	f F
g G	η H	e E	g G
h H	θ Θ	é É	h H
i I	ι I	f F	i I ì Ì
j J	κ K	g G	j J
k K	λ Λ	h H	k K
l L	μ M	i I	l L
m M	ν N	í Í	m M
n N	ξ Ξ	j J	n N
o O ö Ö	ο O	k K	o O ò Ò
p P	π Π	l L	p P
q Q	ρ P	m M	q Q
r R	σ ς Σ	n N	r R
s S ß[1]	τ T	o O	s S
t T	υ Υ	ó Ó	t T
u U ü Ü	φ Φ	p P	u U ù Ù
v V	χ X	q Q	v V
w W	ψ Ψ	r R	w W
x X	ω Ω	s S	x X
y Y		t T	y Y
z Z		u U	z Z
		ú Ú	
		v V	
		w W	
		x X	
		y Y	
		(y acute)	
		z Z	
		(thorn)	
		æ Æ	
		ö Ö	

[1]ß is treated as if it were the 2-letter sequence *ss* when compared with other characters. When it is compared with the characters *ss*, it is sorted after *ss*; for example, the order would be: *Maßarbeit, Masse, Maße, massieren.*

Table C–4. Norwegian, Portuguese, Spanish, and Swedish Collating Sequences

Norwegian	Portuguese	Spanish	Swedish
a A	a A à À á Á â Â ã Ã	a A á	a A
b B	b B	b B	b B
c C	c C ç Ç	c C	c C
d D	d D	ch[1] Ch[1]	d D
e E	e E é É ê Ê	d D	e E é
f F	f F	e E é	f F
g G	g G	f F	g G
h H	h H	g G	h H
i I	i I í Í	h H	i I
j J	j J	i I í	j J
k K	l L	j J	k K
l L	m M	k K	l L
m M	n N	l L	m M
n N	o O ó Ó ô õ Õ	ll[1] Ll[1]	n N
o O	p P	m M	o O
p P	q Q	n N	p P
q Q	r R	ñ Ñ	q Q
r R	s S	o O ó	r R
s S	t T	p P	s S
t T	u U ú Ú	q Q	t T
u U	v V	r R	u U
v V	x X	s S	v V
w W	z Z	t T	w W
x X		u U ú üw	x X
y Y		v V	y Y
z Z		w W	z Z
æ Æ		x X	å Å
ø Ø		y Y	ä Ä
å Å		z Z	ö Ö

[1]Collate the two-letter combinations as if they were one letter; for example, the order would be: *curva, chasquido, daño* for *ch* and *falta, falla, familia* for *ll*.

Appendix D

Local Data Formats

This appendix presents the formats used by countries shown in Table D–1 for the following types of data:

- Names and abbreviations for weekdays (Table D–2)
- Names and abbreviations for months (Table D–3)
- Dates (Table D–4)
- Translations for yesterday, today, tomorrow (Table D–5)
- Personal titles and forms of address (Table D–6)
- Postal addresses (Table D–7)
- Representations of currency (Table D–8)
- Expressions of time (Table D–9)
- Ordinal numbers (Table D–10)
- Telephone numbers (Table D–11)

Table D–1. Countries and Their Major Business Languages

Country	Country Name in Local Language	Local Languages	ISO 3166 Country Code
Austria	Österreich	Deutsch	AT
Belgium	België Belgique	Français Nederlands	BE
Canada	Canada	English Français	CA
Denmark	Danmark	Dansk	DK
Finland	Suomi	Suomian	FI
France	France	Français	FR
Germany	Deutschland Bundesrepublik Deutschlands (BRD)	Deutsch	DE
Iceland	Ísland	Íslenska	IS
Ireland	Eire Republic of Ireland	English	IE
Italy	Italia	Italiano	IT
Netherlands	Nederland	Nederlands	NL
Norway	Norge	Norsk	NO
Portugal	Portugal	Português	PT
Spain	España	Español	ES
Sweden	Sverige	Svensk	SE
Switzerland	Schweiz Suisse Svizzera	Deutsch: Schweiz Français: Suisse Romande Italiano: Svizzero	CH
United Kingdom	United Kingdom	English	GB
United States	United States	English	US

Table D–2. Abbreviations of Weekdays

Austria		Belgium: Flanders		Belgium: French-speaking	
Sonntag	Son	zondag	zon/zo	dimanche	dim/di
Montag	Mon	maandag	maa/ma	lundi	lun/lu
Dienstag	Die	dinsdag	din/di	mardi	mar/ma
Mittwoch	Mit	woensdag	woe/wo	mercredi	mer/me
Donnerstag	Don	donderdag	don/do	jeudi	jeu/je
Freitag	Fre	vrijdag	vri/vr	vendredi	ven/ve
Samstag	Sam	zaterdag	zat/ za	samedi	sam/sa

Canada: English-speaking		Canada: French-speaking		Denmark	
Sunday	Sun	dimanche	dim.	søndag	søn
Monday	Mon	lundi	lundi	mandag	man
Tuesday	Tue	mardi	mardi	tirsdag	tir
Wednesday	Wed	mercredi	mercr.	onsdag	ons
Thursday	Thu	jeudi	jeudi	torsdag	tor
Friday	Fri	vendredi	vendr.	fredag	fre
Saturday	Sat	samedi	sam.	lørdag	lør

Finland		France		Germany	
maanantai	ma	dimanche	dim/di	Sonntag	So
tiistai	ti	lundi	lun/lu	Montag	Mo
keskiviikko	ke	mardi	mar/ma	Dienstag	Di
torstai	to	mercredi	mer/me	Mittwoch	Mi
perjantai	pe	jeudi	jeu/je	Donnerstag	Do
lauantai	la	vendredi	ven/ve	Freitag	Fr
sunnuntai	su	samedi	sam/sa	Samstag	Sa

Iceland		Ireland		Italy	
sunnudagur	sunnud./su.	Sunday	Sun	domenica	(Abbreviations not used)
mánudagur	mánud./má.	Monday	Mon	lunedì	
tridjudagur	tridjud./tri.	Tuesday	Tue	martedì	
midvikudagur	midv.d./mi	Wednesday	Wed	mercoledì	
fimtudagur	fimmtud./fi.	Thursday	Thu	giovedì	
föstudagur	föstud./fö.	Friday	Fri	venerdì	
laugardagur	laugard./lau.	Saturday	Sat	sabato	

(Table D–2 continues on next page)

Table D–2. Abbreviations of Weekdays (cont.)

Netherlands		Norway		Portugal	
zondag	zo/zon	søndag	søn/sø	domingo	dom.
maandag	ma/maa	mandag	man/ma	segunda-feira	seg.
dinsdag	di/din	tirsdag	tir/ti	terça-feira	ter.
woensdag	wo/woe	onsdag	ons/on	quarta-feira	qua.
donderdag	do/don	torsdag	tor/to	quinta-feira	qui.
vrijdag	vr/vri	fredag	fre/fr	sexta-feira	sex.
zaterdag	za/zat	lørdag	lør/lø	sábado	sáb.

Spain		Sweden		Switzerland: French-speaking	
lunes	lun/L (mil)	söndag	sön	dimanche	di
martes	mar/M (mil)	måndag	mån	lundi	lu
miércoles	mie/X (mil)	tisdag	tis	mardi	ma
jueves	jue/J (mil)	onsdag	ons	mercredi	me
viernes	vie/V (mil)	torsdag	tors	jeudi	je
sábado	sa /S (mil)	fredag	fre	vendredi	ve
domingo	do /D (mil)	lördag	lör	samedi	sa

Switzerland: German-speaking		Switzerland: Italian-speaking		United Kingdom	
Sonntag	So	domenica	(Abbrevia-	Sunday	Sun
Montag	Mo	lunedì	tions not	Monday	Mon
Dienstag	Di	martedì	used)	Tuesday	Tue
Mittwoch	Mi	mercoledì		Wednesday	Wed
Donnerstag	Do	giovedì		Thursday	Thu
Freitag	Fr	venerdì		Friday	Fri
Samstag	Sa	sabato		Saturday	Sat

United States	
Sunday	Sun./Sund./S.
Monday	Mon./Mo. /M.
Tuesday	Tue./Tu. /T.
Wednesday	Wed./We. /W.
Thursday	Thu./Th. /Thurs.
Friday	Fri./Fr. /F.
Saturday	Sat./Sa.

Table D–3. Abbreviations of Months

Austria		Belgium: Flanders		Belgium: French-speaking	
Januar	Jan	januari	jan	janvier	jan
Februar	Feb	februari	feb	février	fév
März	Mär	maart	mrt	mars	mar
April	Apr	april	apr	avril	avr
Mai	Mai	mei	mei	mai	mai
Juni	Jun	juni	jun	juin	juin
Juli	Jul	juli	jul	juillet	juil
August	Aug	augustus	aug	août	aoû
September	Sep	september	sep	septembre	sep
Oktober	Okt	oktober	okt	octobre	oct
November	Nov	november	nov	novembre	nov
Dezember	Dez	december	dec	décembre	déc

Canada: English-speaking		Canada: French-speaking		Denmark	
January	Jan	janvier	janv.	januar	jan
February	Feb	février	févr.	februar	feb
March	Mar	mars	mars	marts	mar
April	Apr	avril	avr.	april	apr
May	May	mai	mai	maj	maj
June	Jun	juin	juin	juni	jun
July	Jul	juillet	juil.	juli	jul
August	Aug	août	août	august	aug
September	Sep	septembre	sept.	september	sep
October	Oct	octobre	oct.	oktober	okt
November	Nov	novembre	nov.	november	nov
December	Dec	décembre	déc.	december	dec

(Table D–3 continues on next page)

Table D–3. Abbreviations of Months (cont.)

Finland		France		Germany	
tammikuu	tammi	janvier	jan.	Januar	Jan
helmikuu	helmi	février	fév.	Februar	Feb
maaliskuu	maalis	mars	mar.	März	Mär
huhtikuu	huhti	avril	avr.	April	Apr
toukokuu	touko	mai	mai	Mai	Mai
kesäkuu	kesä	juin	juin	Juni	Jun
heinäkuu	heinä	juillet	juil.	Juli	Jul
elokuu	elo	août	aoû.	August	Aug
syyskuu	syys	septembre	sep.	September	Sep
lokakuu	loka	octobre	oct.	Oktober	Okt
marraskuu	marras	novembre	nov.	November	Nov
joulukuu	joulu	décembre	déc.	Dezember	Dez

Iceland		Ireland		Italy	
janúar	jan.	January	Jan	gennaio	GEN
febrúar	feb.	February	Feb	febbraio	FEB
marz	mar.	March	Mar	marzo	MAR
apríl	apr.	April	Apr	aprile	APR
maí	maí.	May	May	maggio	MAG
júní	jún.	June	Jun	giugno	GIU
júlí	júl.	July	Jul	luglio	LUG
ágúst	ág.	August	Aug	agosto	AGO
september	sept.	September	Sept	settembre	SET/7bre
október	okt.	October	Oct	ottobre	OTT/8bre
nóvember	nóv.	November	Nov	novembre	NOV/9bre
desember	des.	December	Dec	dicembre	DIC/10bre

(Table D–3 continues on next page)

Table D–3. Abbreviations of Months (cont.)

Netherlands		Norway		Portugal	
januari	jan	januar	jan	janeiro	jan./JAN
februari	feb	februar	feb	fevereiro	fev./FEV
maart	mrt	mars	mar	março	mar./MAR
april	apr	april	apr	abril	abr./ABR
mei	mei	mai	mai	maio	mai./MAI
juni	jun	juni	jun	junho	jun./JUN
juli	jul	juli	jul	julho	jul./JUL
augustus	aug	august	aug	agosto	ago./AGO
september	sep	september	sept	setembro	set./SET
oktober	okt	oktober	okt	outubro	out./OUT
november	nov	november	nov	novembro	nov./NOV
december	dec	desember	des	dezembro	dez./DEZ

Spain		Sweden		Switzerland: French-speaking	
enero	eno	januari	jan	janvier	janv.
febrero	fbro	februari	feb	février	févr.
marzo	mzo	mars	mar	mars	mars
abril	ab	april	apr	avril	avr.
mayo	may/my (mil)	maj	maj	mai	mai
junio	jun	juni	juni	juin	juin
julio	jul	juli	juli	juillet	juil
agosto	agto	augusti	aug	août	août
septiembre	sbre	september	sept	septembre	sept.
octubre	obre	oktober	okt	octobre	oct.
noviembre	nbre	november	nov	novembre	nov.
diciembre	dbre	december	dec	décembre	déc.

(Table D–3 continues on next page)

Table D–3. Abbreviations of Months (cont.)

Switzerland: German-speaking		Switzerland: Italian-speaking		United Kingdom	
Januar	Jan.	gennaio	GEN	January	Jan
Februar	Febr.	febbraio	FEB	February	Feb
März	März	marzo	MAR	March	Mar
April	Apr.	aprile	APR	April	Apr
Mai	Mai	maggio	MAG	May	May
Juni	Juni	giugno	GIU	June	Jun
Juli	Juli	luglio	LUG	July	Jul
August	Aug.	agosto	AGO	August	Aug
September	Sept.	settembre	SET/7bre	September	Sept
Oktober	Okt.	ottobre	OTT/8bre	October	Oct
November	Nov.	novembre	NOV/9bre	November	Nov
Dezember	Dez.	dicembre	DIC/10bre	December	Dec

United States	
January	Jan./Ja.
February	Feb./F.
March	Mar./Mr.
April	Apr./Apl.
May	May /My.
June	Jun./Je.
July	Jul./Jy.
August	Aug./Ag.
September	Sep./S./7ber
October	Oct./O./8ber
November	Nov./N./9ber
December	Dec./D./10ber

Table D–4. Dates

Austria	Belgium: Flanders	Belgium: French-speaking
Gregorian calendar 2.Januar 1990 2.1.90 900102 2.Jan.1990 2 Jan 1990 **Note:** Abbreviations of months are used in date formats in data processing. Roman numerals: no	**Gregorian calendar** 31-12-90 31-jan-90 31/12/90 31 januari 1990 31.12.90 31 jan 90 Roman numerals: no	**Gregorian calendar** 31-12-90 31-jan-90 31/12/90 2 janvier 1990 2 jan 90 **Note:** Zeroes are optional in date formats. Roman numerals: optional

Canada: English-speaking	Canada: French-speaking	Denmark
Gregorian calendar January 2, 1991 2-jan-91 1/02/90 (mm/dd/yy)	**Gregorian calendar** 2 janvier 1990 90-01-02 (yy-mm-dd) 90 01 02 (yy mm dd) 2 janv. 1990 **Note:** It is recommended to use the full name of the month or to use the numeric form, rather than an abbreviated form such as "2 janv. 1990." In text, the abbreviated form should never be used.	**Gregorian calendar** 31. januar 1990 1990-01-31 1990 01 31 31/1-90 **Note:** The standard EEC date format 90-12-31 is rarely used in Danish and is being adopted reluctantly. The exception also applies to the date format in Finland. Roman numerals: optional

(Table D–4 continues on next page)

Table D–4. Dates (cont.)

Finland	France	Germany
Gregorian calendar 2.1.1990 2.1.90 1990-01-02 2. tammikuuta 1990 **Note:** The standard EEC format 1990-01-02 is rarely used. Roman numerals: no	**Gregorian calendar** 2 janvier 1990 2 jan 90 02.01.90 02/01/90 02-01-90 **Note:** Zeroes are optional. The first two figures for year are optional, 1990 or simply 90. Roman numerals: yes	**Gregorian calendar** 2. Januar 1990 2. Jan. 1990 2.1.90 02.01.90 2.1.1990 Roman numerals: no

Iceland	Ireland	Italy
Gregorian calendar 2. janúar 1990. 2. 1. 1990. 2. 1. '90. 020190 900102 90 01 02 **Note:** The last two examples are based on ISO 2014 (data formats) which lists an Icelandic standard for dates, but these formats are rarely used. Roman numerals: no	**Gregorian calendar** 2-January-1990 2.1.90 020190 Roman numerals: optional	**Gregorian calendar** 2-GEN-90 2/1/90 2 Gennaio 1990 29.1.90 Roman numerals: no

(Table D–4 continues on next page)

Table D–4. Dates (cont.)

Netherlands	Norway	Portugal
Gregorian calendar 31-12-90 31-jan-90 31/12/90 31 januari 1990 31.12.90 31 jan 90 Roman numerals: no	**Gregorian calendar** 2. januar 1990 2.1.90 020190 02.01.90 Roman numerals: no	**Gregorian calendar** 90.01.02 2.1.90 02.01.90 2.JAN.90 2/1/90 02/01/90 2/JAN/90 2/1/1990 Roman numerals: no
Spain	**Sweden**	**Switzerland: French-speaking**
Gregorian calendar 02-01-90 (civil) 02.01.90 (military) Roman numerals: no	**Gregorian calendar** 2 januari 1990 2/1-90 900102 (Swedish standard) 90-01-02 Roman numerals: no	**Gregorian calendar** 2 janvier 1990 2.1.90 2 jan. 90 2 janv. 90 Roman numerals: no
Switzerland: German-speaking	**Switzerland: Italian-speaking**	**United Kingdom**
Gregorian calendar 2. Januar 1990 2.1.90 2. Jan. 90 Roman numerals: no	**Gregorian calendar** 2-GEN-90 2/1/90 2 Gennaio 1990 29.1.90 Roman numerals: no	**Gregorian calendar** 2nd January 1990 2-January-1990 2/1/90 2.1.90 020190 2 Jan 90 Roman numerals: yes

(Table D–4 continues on next page)

Table D–4. Dates (cont.)

United States
Gregorian calendar
02-Jan-90 January 2, 1990
1/02/90 second of January '90
31-Month-1990 (military) 90/12/31 (military)
Roman numerals: no

Table D–5. Yesterday, Today, Tomorrow

Country	Yesterday	Today	Tomorrow
Austria	gestern	heute	morgen
Belgium: Flanders	gisteren	vandaag	morgen
Belgium: French-speaking	hier	aujourd'hui	demain
Canada: English-speaking	yesterday	today	tomorrow
Canada: French-speaking	hier	aujourd'hui	demain
Denmark	i går	i dag	i morgen
Finland	eilinen	tänään	huomenna
France	hier	aujourd'hui	demain
Germany	gestern	heute	morgen
Iceland	í gær	í dag	á morgun
Italy	ieri	oggi	domani
Netherlands	gisteren	vandaag	morgen
Norway	i går	i dag	i morgen
Portugal	ontem	hoje	amanhã
Spain	ayer	hoy	mañana
Sweden	i går	i dag	i morgon
Switzerland: French-speaking	hier	aujourd'hui	demain
Switzerland: German-speaking	gestern	heute	morgen
Switzerland: Italian-speaking	ieri	oggi	domani
United Kingdom	yesterday	today	tomorrow
United States	yesterday	today	tomorrow

Table D–6. Personal Titles and Forms of Address

Austria	Title
Male	Hr. Alfred Maier
Female, married	Fr. Helga Maier
Female, unmarried	Frl. Helga Maier (no longer used officially)
Medical doctor	Hr. Dr. Alfred Maier

Note: The difference between Fräulein and Frau depends on age, rather than marital status. Frau is most commonly used in addresses. Austria does not use middle initials in personal names.

Belgium: Flanders	Title
Male	De heer Emile Dubois (abbr. Dhr./ de Hr.)
Female	Mevrouw Charlotte Van De Woestijne (abbr. Mevr./Mw.)
Medical doctor	Dokter Peeters (abbr. Dr.)
Academic titles	prof. D'Hertoghe ir. René Smedts
Legal profession	Mr. De Clercq

Note: Indication of marital status is no longer used in addresses.

Belgium: French-speaking	Title
Male	Monsieur P. Dupont (abbr. M.)
Female, married	Madame M. Dupont (abbr. Mme)
Female, unmarried	Mademoiselle L. Dupont (abbr. Mlle)
Medical doctor only	Docteur G. Durand (abbr. Dr.)
Medical or academic title	Professeur G. Durand (abbr. Prof.)
Legal profession	Maître G. Durand (abbr. MO)

Note: The title Mademoiselle is rarely used; Madame now replaces it.

(Table D–6 continues on next page)

Table D–6. Personal Titles and Forms of Address (cont.)

Canada: English-speaking	Title
Male	Mr. John Smith (Mister is rarely used, abbr. to Mr. is normally used)
Female, married	Mrs. Jane-Anne Smith
Female, unmarried	Miss Jane-Anne Smith
Female, without indication of marital status	Ms. A. Smith
Medical doctor only	John F. Smith, MD (periods and comma required)
Professor: medical or academic	Professor John Smith (abbr. to Prof.)

Canada: French-speaking	Title
Male	Monsieur Jean Tremblay (abbr. to M.)
Female, married	Madame Jeannine Tremblay (abbr. to Mme)
Female, unmarried	Mademoiselle Jeannine Tremblay (abbr. to Mlle)
Female, without indication of marital status	Madame Jeannine Tremblay (abbr. to Mme)
Lawyer	Maître J.L. Durand (abbr. to M^{e})
Medical doctor only	Docteur J.L. Durand (abbr. to D^{r})
Professor: medical or academic	Professeur J.L. Durand (abbr. to Prof.)

Note: The title "Mademoiselle" is rarely used; the title "Madame" now replaces it.

Denmark	Title
Male	Hr. John F. Hansen
Female, married	Fru Charlotte Jensen
Female, unmarried	Frk Charlotte Jensen
Female, no indication of marital status	Fr Charlotte Jensen
Medical doctor	John F. Hansen, Dr. Med.
Chartered accountant	Charlotte Jensen, Statsaut. Rev.

Note: Fru, Frk, and Fr are normally omitted if the addressee's professional qualifications are added to a name.

(Table D–6 continues on next page)

Table D–6. Personal Titles and Forms of Address (cont.)

Finland	Title
Male	Kari Koikkalainen (the name only)
Female	Anja Koikkalainen (the name only)
	Kari Koikkalainen, ekonomi (comma required) (Ekonomi is a degree equivalent to MSc. Economic Sciences)

Note: Degrees and professional qualifications, if used, are placed either before or after the name.

France	Title
Male	Monsieur H. Martin (abbr. M.)
Female, married	Madame J. Dupont (abbr. Mme)
Female, unmarried	Mademoiselle M. Durand (abbr. Mlle)
Medical doctor only	Docteur M. G. Laurent (abbr. Dr)
Professor: medical or academic	Professeur J. B. Balzac (abbr. Prof)
Lawyer	Maître J. L. Lorin (abbr. Me)

Germany	Title
Male	Herr Josef Meier (no abbreviation)
Female, married	Frau Irmgard Mainz (no abbreviation)
Female, unmarried	Fräulein Irmgard Mainz (rarely used) (abbr. Frl.)
Female, no indication of marital status	None (Frau may be used)
Medical doctor	Herrn Dr. med. Klaus Kunkel
Engineer	Herrn Dipl. Ing. Uwe Kniep

Note: The difference between Fräulein and Frau depends on age, rather than marital status. Frau is most commonly used in addresses.

(Table D–6 continues on next page)

Table D–6. Personal Titles and Forms of Address (cont.)

Iceland	Title
Male	Hr. (Herr) Gísli Sigurdsson
Female, married	Frú Vigdis Sigurdsson
Female, unmarried	Frk. (Frúken) V. Sigurdsson
Female, no indication of marital status	Fr. M. Sigurdsson
Business manager	Hr. framkvæmdastjóri, Gísli Sigurdsson

Note: If addressing a person with a professional qualification, the name is always placed after the personal title and in lowercase letters followed by a comma.

Ireland	Title
Male	Mr. John Smith
	John Smith Esq. (used only for correspondence from business sources)
Female, married	Mrs. Lisa Smith
Female, unmarried	Miss Lisa Smith
Female, no indication of marital status	Ms. L. Smith
Medical doctor	Dr John F. Smith, MD (period and comma optional)
Chartered accountant	Lisa Smith, FCA (comma optional)

Note: Mr., Mrs., and Ms. are usually omitted if professional qualifications are added.

Italy	Title
Male	Signor Giovanni Sabatini
	Egr. Sig. Giovanni Sabatini (sometimes used to address correspondence from business or professional sources)
Female, married	Signora Roberta Verri
Female, unmarried	Signorina Roberta Verri
Female, no indication of marital status	Sig.ra Roberta Verri
Medical doctor	Egr. Dott. Piero Savoni
Academic degree	Rag. Roberta Verri

(Table D–6 continues on next page)

Table D–6. Personal Titles and Forms of Address (cont.)

Netherlands	Title
Male	De Heer C.J.M. Bosch (abbr. Dhr.)
Female, married	Mevrouw M. Westerhout (abbr. Mw)
Female, no indication of marital status (abbr. Mw)	Mevr. M. Westerhout
Medical doctor	De Heer C.J.M. Bosch, arts
Academic titles	De Heer Prof. Dr. C.J.M. Bosch
Profession, peerage, and academic titles	Brigade-generaal b.d. Jhr. Mr. C.J.M. Bosch

Note: Many other valid variants of Brigade-generaal exist.

Norway	Title
Male	Herr Per Johansen (abbr. Hr.)
Female, married	Fru Kari Haugen
Female, unmarried	Fr. Kari Haugen
Female, no indication of marital status	Fr. Kari Haugen
Medical doctor	Prof.dr.med. Per Johansen
Chartered accountant	Siv.øk. Kari Haugen

Portugal	Title
Male	Senhor Jorge Manuel de Sousa (abbr. Sr.)
Female, married	Senhora Maria Isabel de Sousa (abbr. Sra)
Female, unmarried	Senhora M. Isabel de Sousa
Medical doctor	Senhor Dr. Jorge Manuel de Sousa
Medical doctor, female	Senhora Dra. Maria Isabel de Sousa

(Table D–6 continues on next page)

Table D–6. Personal Titles and Forms of Address (cont.)

Spain	Title
Male	Señor Don Carlos Bustamante López (abbr. Sr. D.)
Female, married	Señora María Jiménez (abbr. Sra.)
Female, unmarried	Señorita Doña María Jiménez (abbr. Srta, Dña.)
Female, no indication of marital status	Doña María Jiménez
Advanced academic degree	Señor Don Rubén Cerdán, Doctor en Físicas
Medical doctor	Dr. Carlos Bustamante López

Note: Professional titles are not often appended to names. In this case, Dr. (Doctor) is substituted for Sr. D.

Sweden	Title
Male	Herr Lars G Andersson
Female, married	Fru Eva Svensson
Female, unmarried	Frk Eva Svensson
Female, no indication of marital status	Fr Eva Svensson
Medical doctor	Dr Lars G. Andersson

Note: Qualifications and titles are usually added before the name, without a comma or period.

Switzerland: French-speaking	Title
Male	Monsieur Alain Delon (abbr. M.)
Female, married	Madame Brigitte Chaval (abbr. Mme)
Female, unmarried	Mademoiselle Brigitte Chaval (abbr. Mlle)
Female, no indication of marital status	Mademoiselle Brigitte Chaval
Medical doctor	De en medicine
Legal profession	Dr en droit Alain Delon

(Table D–6 continues on next page)

Table D–6. Personal Titles and Forms of Address (cont.)

Switzerland: German-speaking	Title
Male	Herr Hans F. Schmid (abbr. Hr. or Herrn if in address on a letter)
Female, married	Frau Dora Meier (abbr. Fr.)
Female, unmarried	Fräulein Dora Meier (abbr. Frl.)
Female, no indication of marital status	Frau Dora Meier (abbr. Fr.)
Medical doctor	Herrn Dr. med. K.Wieland
Academic doctor	Frau Dr. rer. pol. K. Wieland

Notes: In professional qualifications, Herr (Herrn), Frau and Fräulein are placed one line before the profession and the personal name.

The difference between Fräulein and Frau depends on age, rather than marital status. Frau is most commonly used in addresses.

Switzerland: Italian-speaking	Title
Male	Signor Giovanni Sabatini
	Egr. Sig. Giovanni Sabatini (sometimes used to address correspondence from business or professional sources)
Female, married	Signora Roberta Verri
Female, unmarried	Signorina Roberta Verri
Female, no indication of marital status	Sig.ra Roberta Verri
Medical doctor	Egr. Dott. Piero Savoni
Academic degree	Rag. Roberta Verri

(Table D–6 continues on next page)

Table D–6. Personal Titles and Forms of Address (cont.)

United Kingdom	Title
Male	Mr. John F. Smith (Mister is rarely used, abbr. Mr. is normally substituted) J. F. Smith Esq. (used only to address formal correspondence from a business or professional source)
Female, married	Mrs. Jane Smith
Female, unmarried	Miss Jane Smith
Female, no indication of marital status	Ms. J. Smith
Medical doctor	John F. Smith Esq., MD (period and comma optional)
Chartered accountant	Jane Smith, CA (comma optional)
Titled person with civil decoration and membership in a learned society	Sir John Smith-Smythe, CBE, FRS

Notes: Mr., Mrs., and Ms. are usually omitted if the addressee's professional qualifications are added to a name.

The middle initial in personal titles is optional. The courtesy title Esq. is now rarely used except in formal or legal correspondence.

United States	Title
Male	Mr. Robert L. Jones (Mister is rarely used; abbr. Mr. is normally substituted)
Female, married	Mrs. Patricia Jones (no abbr.)
Female, unmarried	Miss Patricia Jones
Female, no indication of marital status	Ms. P. Jones (no abbr.)
Medical doctor	Robert L. Jones, M.D. (periods and comma required)
Certified public accountant	Patricia M. Jones, C.P.A. (periods and comma required)
Military title	Maj. Gen. John F. Schwartz

Note: U.S. scholastic, military and civil titles are commonly abbreviated when they are used before or after a proper name. Such abbreviations consist of capital letters separated by periods without spaces between the letters and periods.

Table D–7. Addresses

Austria	Format
Personal address:	
Amtsrat Dipl.Ing. Eric Maier	[title] [degrees] [name] [surname]
	[blank line]
Ackerweg 3	[street name] [number]
A-4711 Bad Vöslau	[country code] [postal code] [county]
Österreich	[country]
Business address:	
Sonnenuhren Ges.m.b.H	[company name]
z.Hd. Amtsrat Dipl.Ing. Eric Maier	[attention] [title] [name] [surname]
	[blank line]
Amtsweg 31	[street] [number]
A-4711 Niederndorf	[country code] [postal code] [county]
Österreich	[country]

Belgium: Flanders	Format
Personal address:	
De Heer C.J.M. Bosch	[title] [name]
Stationsstraat 124	[street name] [number]
B-2000 Antwerpen	[country code] [postal code] [town]
BELGIË	[country]
Business address:	
Windmolen N.V.	[company name]
T.a.v. Mevrouw T. De Lange	[attention addressee]
Afd. Public Relations	[department]
Waterweg 3	[street name] [number]
B-2000 Antwerpen	[country code] [postal code] [town]
BELGIË	[country]

(Table D–7 continues on next page)

Table D–7. Addresses (cont.)

Belgium: French-speaking	Format
Personal address:	
M. Ph. Delacroix Av. Léopold II 123 B-1140 Bruxelles BELGIQUE	[title] [name] [surname] [street name] [number] [country code] [postal code] [town] [country]
Business address:	
Madame Delvaux abs Windmolen S.A. Dépt. Public Relations Bd. Brand Whitlock 12 B-1140 Bruxelles BELGIQUE	[title] [surname] [company] [department] [street name] [number] [country code] [postal code] [town] [country]
or:	
Windmolen S.A. à l'att. de Madame Delvaux Dépt. Public Relations Bd. Brand Whitlock 12 B-1140 Bruxelles BELGIQUE	[company] [attention addressee] [department] [street name] [number] [country code] [postal code] [town] [country]

(Table D–7 continues on next page)

Table D–7. Addresses (cont.)

Canada: English-speaking	Format
Personal address:	
Louise Adams	[name] [surname]
304 Oak Street	[number] [street name]
Kanata, Ontario	[town] [province]
Canada	[country] (optional if letter is mailed within Canada)
J7Y 4D5	[postal code]
Business address:	
Mrs. Louise Adams	[title] [name] [surname]
Regional Sales Manager	[job title]
ABC Company	[company]
Suite 400	[location details]
304 Elm Street	[number] [street name]
Kanata, Ontario	[town] [province]
J7X 3Z2	[postal code]

Canada: French-speaking	Format
Personal address:	
M. Jean Durand	[title] [name] [surname]
1228, rue Kirouac	[number] [,] [street name]
St-Jean (Québec)	[town] [province]
Canada	[country] (optional if letter is mailed within Canada)
J3V 5V9	[postal code]
Business address:	
À l'attention de M. Jean Durand	[attention] [title] [name] [surname]
Directeur du personnel	[job title]
Entreprises Canadiennes	[company]
6506, autoroute transcanadienne	[number] [,] [street name]
Bureau 900	[location details]
Saint-Laurent (Québec)	[town] [province]
H4T 9X6	[postal code]

(Table D–7 continues on next page)

Table D–7. Addresses (cont.)

Denmark	Format
Personal address:	
Hr. A. Jensen Sandtoften 9 DK-2820 Gentofte Danmark	[title] [initial] [surname] [street name] [number] [country code] [postal code] [town] [country]
Business address:	
Administrerende direktør Digital Equipment Corp. Sandtoften 9 DK-2820 Gentofte Danmark	[job title] [company name] [street name] [number] [country code] [postal code] [town] [country]

Finland	Format
Personal address:	
Ekonomi Pekka Paukku Mannerheimintie 12 SF-00100 Helsinki Finland	[title or degree] [name] [surname] [street name] [number] [country code] [postal code] [town] or [municipality] [country]
Business address:	
Toimitusjohtaja Pekka Paukku Computop Oy Koulutie 6 SF-02200 Espoo Finland	[job title] [name] [company name] [street name] [number] [country code] [postal code] [town] [country]

Note: The business or company name may also come before the job title and personal name.

(Table D–7 continues on next page)

Table D–7. Addresses (cont.)

France	Format
Personal address:	
M. J. Martin	[title] [initial] [surname]
25, rue de la Poste	[number] or [name] [,] [street name]
Thoué	[town] (if not postal town)
F-38560 Le Versoud	[country code] [postal code] [postal town]
France	[country]
Business address:	
Compagnie des Eaux	[company name]
M. J. Durand-Dupond,	[personal title] [initial] [surname]
Directeur des recherches	[job title]
25, rue de la Poste	[number] [,] [street name]
Thoué	[town]
F-38560 Le Versoud	[country code] [postal code] [postal town]
France	[country]
or:	
A l'attention de:	[attention]
M. le Directeur du personnel	[personal title] [job title]
Compagnie des Eaux	[name of company]
25, rue de la Poste	[number] [,] [street name]
Thoué	[town]
F-38560 Le Versoud	[country code] [postal code] [postal area]
France	[country]

(Table D–7 continues on next page)

Table D–7. Addresses (cont.)

Germany	Format
Personal address:	
Ingrid Boderke Säbener Str. 32 D-8000 München Germany	[name] [surname] [degrees] [street name] [number] [country code] [postal code] [postal town] [country code]
Business address:	
Hd.d August GmbH and Co KG. Geschäftsleitung Sommerstr. 41 D-7639 Winterdorf Germany	[company name] [street name] [number] [country code] [postal code] [town] [country]

Iceland	Format
Personal address:	
Hr. framkvæmdastjóri, Gísli Sigurdsson, Austurstræti 18, 1. hæd t.h., 101 Reykjavík Ísland	[personal title and profession] (optional) [name] [surname] [street name] [number] [floor] (optional) [post number] [city] [country]
Business address:	
Hr. framkvæmdastjóri, Gísli Sigurdsson, Framkvæmdabanki Íslands, Hafnarstræti 10, 3. hæd t.h., IS 101 Reykjavík, ICELAND	[personal title] [profession] [name] [surname] [name of company] [street name] [number] [floor] [country code] [postal code] [city] [country]

(Table D–7 continues on next page)

Table D–7. Addresses (cont.)

Ireland	Format
Personal address:	
Mr L.M. O'Grady	[personal title] [initial] [surname]
16 Thomas Street	[number] or [name of house] [street name]
Carrickfergus	[postal town]
Co. Antrim	[country code] [county]
Northern Ireland	[country]
Business address:	
L.M. O'Grady PhD	[initials] [surname] [degrees]
	[blank line]
The Managing Director	[job title]
Gaelic Software Ltd	[company name]
Unit 5, Industrial Estate	[location details]
Carrickfergus	[postal town]
Co. Antrim	[country code] [county]
Northern Ireland	[country]

Italy	Format
Personal address:	
Egr. Dott. Silvano Mattei	[courtesy adjective] [title] [name] [surname]
Via Piave, 23	[street name] [,] [street number]
I-20052 Monza (MI)	[country code] [postal code] [town] [county]
Italia	[country]
Business address:	
Spett. le DIGITAL SpA	[courtesy adjective] [company name]
Direttore Generale	[job title]
Via Italia, 32	[street name] [,] [street number]
I-20100 Milano (MI)	[country code] [postal code] [town] [county code]
Italy	[country]

(Table D–7 continues on next page)

Table D–7. Addresses (cont.)

Netherlands	Format
Personal address:	
De Heer P.L. Bosch Reigerskamp 1024 3345 TE Amsterdam The Netherlands	[title] [initials] [surname] [street name] [number] [country code] [postal code] [town] [country]
Business address:	
Windmolen B.V. Mw drs. T. de Lange, Public Relations Waterweg 3 2187 WU De Kwakel The Netherlands	[company name] [personal title] [surname] [department] [street name] [number] [country code] [postal code] [town] [country]

Norway	Format
Personal address:	
Herr Per Hansen Drammensveien 20 N-0271 OSLO 2 Norge	[title] [name] [surname] [street name] [number] [country code] [postal code] [postal town/area code] [country]
Business address:	
Direktør Per Hansen Western Computer Company A/S Drammensveien 20 N-0271 OSLO 2 Norway	[title] [name] [surname] [company name] [street name] [number] [country code] [postal code] [postal town/area code] [country]

(Table D–7 continues on next page)

Table D–7. Addresses (cont.)

Portugal	Format
Personal address:	
Exmo. Senhor Dr. Jorge Manuel de Sousa	[title] [degrees] [surname] [name]
Rua dos Douradores, nº 14	[street name] [,] [number]
P-1200 LISBOA	[country code] [postal code] [town]
Portugal	[country]
Business address:	
Exmo. Senhor Dr. Jorge Manuel de Sousa	[courtesy adjective] [title] [degrees] [name] [surname]
Director-Geral da Philips Portuguesa	[job title]
Philips Portuguesa	[company name]
Rua dos Douradores, nº 14	[street name] [number]
P-1200 LISBOA	[country code] [postal code] [town]
Portugal	[country]

Spain	Format
Personal address:	
Sr. R.J. Bustamante García	[title] [name] [surname] [degrees]
Avenida de la Constitución, 45,	[street name] [number]
E-28045 Madrid (España)	[country code] [city postal code] [town]
Business address:	
Sr. R.J. Bustamante García	[title] [name] [surname] [degrees]
Director Técnico,	[job title]
Aleph Systems Inc.	[name of company]
Avenida de la Constitución, 45,	[street name] [number]
E-28045 Madrid (España)	[country code] [city postal code] [town]

(Table D–7 continues on next page)

Table D–7. Addresses (cont.)

Sweden	Format
Personal address:	
Dr John Andersson	[title] [first name or initial] [surname]
Villagatan 45 II	[street name] [number] [optional floor number]
S-114 57 Stockholm	[country code] [postal code] [town]
Sweden	[country] (optional if letter is mailed within Sweden)
Business address:	
Digital Equipment AB	[name of company]
Att: John Andersson	[attention] [job title] [addressee]
SWAS	[department]
Box 34567	[postal address]
S-114 37 Stockholm	[country code] [postal code] [town]
Sweden	[country] (optional if letter is mailed within Sweden)

Switzerland: French-speaking	Format
Personal address:	
Monsieur	[title]
Robert Tissot	[name] [surname]
25, rue Jacques Martin	[number] [,] [street name]
CH-1200 Genève	[country code] [postal code] [town]
Suisse	[country]
Business address:	
Monsieur	[title]
Robert Tissot	[name] [surname]
Lombards SA	[company]
25, rue Jacques Martin	[number] [,] [street name]
CH-1200 Genève	[country code] [postal code] [town]
Switzerland	[country]

(Table D–7 continues on next page)

Table D–7. Addresses (cont.)

Switzerland: French-speaking	Format
or:	
Lombard SA	[company]
à l'att. M. Robert Tissot	[attention addressee]
25, rue Jacques Martin	[number] [,] [street name]
CH-1200 Genève	[country code] [postal code] [town]
Switzerland	[country]

Switzerland: German-speaking	Format
Personal address:	
Herrn	[title]
Dr. K. Diggelmann	[degrees] [initial] [surname]
Bahnhofstr.41	[street name] [number]
CH-3000 Bern	[country code] [postal code] [town]
Schweiz	[country]
Business address:	
Hasler AG	[company]
z.H. Herrn Dr. K. Diggelmann	[attention addressee]
Bahnhofstr.41	[street name] [number]
CH-3000 Bern	[country code] [postal code] [town]
Switzerland	[country]
or:	
Herrn	[title]
Dr. K. Diggelmann	[degrees] [initial] [surname]
Hasler AG	[company]
Bahnhofstr.41	[street name] [number]
CH-3000 Bern	[country code] [postal code] [town]
Switzerland	[country]

(Table D–7 continues on next page)

Table D–7. Addresses (cont.)

Switzerland: Italian-speaking	Format
Personal address:	
Egr. Dott. Silvano Mattei Via Piave, 23 I-20052 Monza (MI) Svizzera	[courtesy adjective] [title] [name] [surname] [street name] [,] [street number] [country code] [postal code] [town] [county] [country]
Business address:	
Spett. le DIGITAL SpA Direttore Generale Via Italia, 32 I-20100 Milano (MI) Switzerland	[courtesy adjective] [company name] [job title] [street name] [,] [street number] [country code] [postal code] [town] [county code] [country]

United Kingdom	Format
Personal address:	
Mr. J. L. Smith 15 Evergreen Street Camberley Surrey GR2 5TT England	[title] [initial] [surname] [number] or [house name] [street name] [postal town] [county] [postal code] [country]
Note: Commas after the number or house name and at the end of each line (except for the last line) are optional.	
Business address:	
The Managing Director Western Computer Co. Ltd Peyton House 235 Commercial Road Croydon CR8 4GA UK	[job title] [company] [location] [number] [street or road name] [county] [postal code] [country]

(Table D–7 continues on next page)

Table D–7. Addresses (cont.)

United Kingdom	Format
For mail sent from outside the United Kingdom, the country name and postal code must be in this form:	
The Managing Director	[job title]
Western Computer Co. Ltd	[company]
Peyton House	[location]
235 Commercial Road	[number] [street or road name]
Croydon CR8 4GA	[county] [postal code]
UK	[country]
Note: The first part of a postal code in the U.K. is from two to four characters. The first character of the code is always alphabetic; the other characters can be letters or numbers. A space is always allowed within the number. Examples are: WC1V 6HB, M60 8AS, B1 2HE.	

United States	Format
Personal address:	
Susan J. Avril, Ph.D.	[name] [surname] [degrees]
11 Hancock Street	[number] or [name] [street name]
Lexington	[city]
MA 02173	[state] [postal code]
U.S.A.	[country]
Business address:	
Richard J. Blickstein Jr.	[Name of addressee]
Vice-President, Marketing	[job title]
Western Computer Corporation	[company name]
Peyton House	[location name]
654 Commercial Boulevard	[number] [street name]
Merrimack, New Hampshire 03054	[town name] [,] [state name] [postal code]
U.S.A.	[country]
Note: For mail sent to the U.S.A. from overseas, the country name and postal code must be in the above format.	

Table D–8. Currency

	Austria	Belgium: Flanders
Currency unit	Austrian schilling	Belgian franc (frank)
Fraction	groschen x 100 (g)	centime x 100
ISO 4217 symbol	ATS	BEF
ISO 4217 numeric code	040	056
International symbol	A$	BF
EEC symbol	AS	BEF
Internal symbols	öS Sch ÖS S	F fr.
Formats	A$2.50 AS 2,50 Sch 2.50 ATS 2.50 öS 2,50 öS 0,50	F 22,50 BEF 2.50 BF 2,50 12,5 fr. BFr 12,75
Separators	Period and comma öS -,50 öS 1,- öS 1,50 öS 5,- öS 50,- öS 500,- öS 5.000,- öS 50.000,- öS 500.000,- öS 5.000.000,- 30 groschen -,30 **Note:** The groschen has no symbol of its own. The Austrian currency symbol uses öS (O-umlaut) in German, but is written AS in English.	Period and comma 0,5 fr. 1 fr. 1,5 fr. 5 fr. 50 fr. 500 fr. 5.000 fr. 50.000 fr. 500.000 fr. 5.000.000 fr.

(Table D–8 continues on next page)

Table D–8. Currency (cont.)

	Belgium: French-speaking	Canada: English-speaking
Currency unit	Belgian franc	Canadian dollar
Fraction	centime x 100	cent x 100
ISO 4217 symbol	BEF	CAD
ISO 4217 numeric code	056	124
International symbol	FB	$
EEC symbol	BEF	$
Internal symbols	F	$
Formats	12,5 fr. BF 12,5 BEF 12,5 FB 2.50	$2.50 $ 2.50 0.50 $
Separators	Comma and period F 0,5 F 1 F 1,5 F 5 F 50 F 500 F 5.000 F 50.000 F 500.000 F 5.000.000	Comma and period - $1 - $1.50 $5 $50 $500 $5,000 $50,000 $500,000 $5,000,000 $13K $50M **Notes:** Thousands or millions of dollars are often expressed by placing an uppercase K or M immediately after the numerals indicating the number. When there is no decimal value, the decimal separator and zeroes are not used, except in tables where you find numbers with and without decimal values.

(Table D–8 continues on next page)

Table D–8. Currency (cont.)

	Canada: French-speaking	Denmark
Currency unit	Canadian dollar	Danish krone (DKr)
Fraction	cent x 100	øre x 100
ISO 4217 symbol	CAD	DKK
ISO 4217 numeric code	124	208
International symbol	$	Dkr
EEC symbol	$	DKR
National symbols	$	Kr. kr Dkr
Formats	2,50 $ 0,50 $	Kr. 2,50 Dkr 2.50 2,50 Kr 2,- Kr Kr. 2,50 DKR 2.50 DKK 2.50 1 krone 1,50 kr. 5 kr. 10 kroner og 50 øre
Separators	Space and comma - 1 $ - 1,50 $ 5 $ 50 $ 500 $ 5 000 $ 50 000 $ 500 000 $ 5 000 000 $	Period and comma 0,5 kr. 1 kr. 1,5 kr. 5 kr. 50 kr. 500 kr. 5.000 kr. 50.000 kr. 500.000 kr. 5.000.000 kr.

(Table D–8 continues on next page)

Table D–8. Currency (cont.)

	Finland	France
Currency unit	Finnish markka (the finnmark)	French franc
Fraction	penni x 100 (Pia)	centime x 100
ISO 4217 symbol	FIM	FRF
ISO 4217 numeric code	246	250
International symbol	FMK	FFR
EEC symbol	FMK	FFR
National symbols	FIM mk Fmk	F or FF centime c, ct, or cs
Formats	65 penniä 2.50 FIM FMK 2.50 FIM 2.50	20F50 FF 2.50 2,50 F 2,50 FF F 2,50 FFR 2.50 FRF 2.50
Separators	Space and comma 5,00 mk or: 5 mk 10,75 mk 500 mk 5000 mk or: 5 000 mk 5 000 000 mk 10 080,50 mk **Notes:** Finland has many speakers of Swedish but the currency remains the Finnish markka, sometimes referred to as the finnmark. A period is sometimes used for the sake of clarity, but is encountered in normal usage only for very large quantities, for example 5.000.000 mk.	Space, period, and comma F 0,50 F 1 F 1,5 F 5 F 50 F 500 F 5 000 F 50 000 F 5000 000 or: F 5 000 000 or: F 5.000.000 **Notes:** The period and a space are used for convenience, not as a compulsory standard. Currency symbols can be placed before or after the figure. FF is distinct from FS (Swiss francs) and FB (Belgian francs).

(Table D–8 continues on next page)

Table D–8. Currency (cont.)

	Germany	Iceland
Currency unit	deutsche mark	Icelandic króna (plural: krónur)
Fraction	pfennig (Pf) x 100	eyrir x 100 (plural: aurar)
ISO 4217 symbol	DEM	ISK
ISO 4217 numeric code	280	352
International symbol	DM	ICK
EEC symbol	DM	ÍSK
National symbols	DM	Kr. kr.
Formats	DM 2,50 DM 2,- 2,50 DM DM 2,50 DEM 2,50 DM 2,-	ÍSK 2,50 Kr. 2,50 ISK 2,50 kr. 2,- ICK 2,50
Separators	Period and comma 65 Pf DM 5,00 or: DM 5,- DM 10,75 (10 deutsche marks and 75 pfennig) DM 500 DM 5.000 DM 5.000.000 DM 10.080,50	Period and comma ,65 (65 aurar) Kr. 5,00 Kr. 5 Kr. 5,75 Kr. 5.080,50 Kr. 500,00 Kr. 5.000,- Kr. 5.000.000 Kr. 5.080,50 (5,080 krónur, 50 aurar)

(Table D–8 continues on next page)

Table D–8. Currency (cont.)

	Ireland	Italy
Currency unit	Irish pound (or punt)	Italian lire (plural: lira)
Fraction	penny x 100	centesimo (ctmo)
ISO 4217 symbol	IEP	ITL
ISO 4217 numeric code	372	380
International symbol	IR£	LIT
EEC symbol	IR£	LIT
National symbols	£	L. Lit
Formats	IR£2.50 £2.50 IEP 2.50	Lit 250 LIT 250 L 250 L. 250 ITL 2,500
Separators	Period and comma 65p (65 pence) IR£5.00 IR£10.75 (10 pounds and 75 pence) IR£5 IR£500 IR£5,000 IR£5,000,000 IR£10,080.50	Period and space L. 50 L. 500 L. 1.000 L. 10.000 L. 1.000.000 L. 100 000 000 **Note:** The L. for Italian lire is similar to the U.K. pound-sterling sign. It is not included in the MNC, so 'L' should suffice. Lire do not have a decimal point; the quantity is always an integer. Periods are not used as separators for quantities greater than 1.000.000.

(Table D–8 continues on next page)

Table D–8. Currency (cont.)

	Netherlands	Norway
Currency unit	Dutch (Netherlands) guilder (f.)	Norwegian krone (plural: kroner)
Fraction	cent x 100	øre x 100
ISO 4217 symbol	NLG	NOK
ISO 4217 numeric code	528	578
International symbol	Dfl.	NKR
EEC symbol	NLG	NKr.
National symbols	FL fl F f Hfl gld DFL	Kr.
Formats	FL 15,47 FL 15,- fl 15,47 fl 15,- f 15,47 f 15,- Hfl 15,47 Hfl 15,- fl. 15,47 fl. 15,- NLG 2.50	kr. 2,50 NKr 2.50 Kr. 2,50 NKR 2.50 NOK 2.50
Separators	Period and comma 65 cents FL 5,00 or: FL 5 FL 10,75 (10 guilders and 75 cents) FL 500 FL 5.000 FL 5.000.000 FL 10.080,50	Space, period, and comma NKr. 0,65 (65 øre) NKr. 5,00 NKr. 10,75 NKr. 500,00 NKr. 5 000,00 or NKr. 5.000,00 NKr. 10 080,50 (10,080 kroner, 50 øre) **Note:** A comma is always used as decimal point between kroner and øre. A period or space may be used as a thousands separator.

(Table D–8 continues on next page)

Table D–8. Currency (cont.)

	Portugal	Spain
Currency unit	Portuguese escudo	Spanish peseta
Fraction	centavo x 100	céntimo (cts)
ISO 4217 symbol	PTE	ESP
ISO 4217 numeric code	620	724
International symbol	ESC	PTA
EEC symbol	ESC	Pts.
National symbols	Esc. or a $ with two dashes	Pta, plural: Pts
Formats	1$50 Esc. 2.50 1$50 ESC 2.50 PTE 2.50	2.50 Pts 2,50 Pts PTA 2,50 ESP 2,50
Separators	Period 5.00 (5$00) 500.00 (500$00) 5.000.00 (5.000$00) ESC 5.000.000.00 (5.000.000$00) 10.50 (10$50) (10 escudos and 50 centavos) Portugal has the word *conto* (C) meaning 1.000 escudos. 5.000$00 = 5,000 escudos, 5 contos, or 5C. 100.000$00 = 100,000 escudos, 100 contos, or 100C. **Note:** The $ symbol for escudos is always placed after the quantity it is signifying. Price tags use the $ symbol instead of a period.	Period and comma, apostrophe for céntimos alone 0'65 Pts (65 céntimos) 5,00 Pts or 5 Pts 10,75 Pts 500 Pts 5.000 Pts 5.000.000 Pts 10.080,50 (10,080 pesetas, 50 céntimos) **Note:** Céntimos generally tend to be expressed as a fraction of pesetas (0'75 pesetas = 75 céntimos). There are no coins for the céntimo, as it is only a theoretical division without physical representation.

(Table D–8 continues on next page)

Table D–8. Currency (cont.)

	Sweden	Switzerland: French-speaking
Currency unit	Swedish krona (plural: kronor)	Swiss franc
Fraction	öre x 100	centime x 100 (ct.)
ISO 4217 symbol	SEK	CHF
ISO 4217 numeric code	752	756
International symbol	SKR	SFR
EEC symbol	SKR	SFR
National symbols	Kr kr	F SFr fr.
Formats	-:50 (50 öre) 50:- (50 kronor) Kr 10:- 10 Kr 5 Kr. SEK 2.50 2,50 kr SKR 2,50 In accounting: Kr. 2,50 Kr. 2:50	2.50F SFr 2.50 SFR 2.50 CHF 2.50
Separators	Colon, period, and comma -:50 öre 2,50 kr. (often used) 10:75 Kr. 500 Kr. 5.000 Kr. 50.000.000 Kr. 10.080:50 Kr. (10,080 kronor, 50 öre) Special conventions to express quantities of currency: 13 000 kr. or 13 tkr. (13,000 kronor) 50 milj kr. or 50 mkr. (50,000,000 kronor)	Period and apostrophe fr.s. 5.00 fr.s. 5.- fr 5.00 fr 5.- fr 10.75 fr 500.00 fr 5'000.00 fr 50'000.50 fr 50'000'000.-

(Table D–8 continues on next page)

Table D–8. Currency (cont.)

	Switzerland: German-speaking	Switzerland: Italian-speaking
Currency unit	Swiss franken	Swiss franchi
Fraction	centime x 100 (ct.)	centisimo
ISO 4217 symbol	CHF	CHF
ISO 4217 numeric code	756	756
International symbol	SFR	SFR
EEC symbol	SFR	SFR
National symbols	F Fr.	F SFr fr.
Formats	F 2,50 Fr. 2.50 SFR 2.50 CHF 2.50 SFr. 5.00 SFr. 5.- 5.- Fr. 500.- Fr.	2.50F SFr 2.50 SFR 2.50
Separators	Period and apostrophe Fr. 5.00 Fr. 5.- Fr. 10.75 Fr. 500.00 Fr. 5'000.00 Fr. 5'000.- Fr. 5'000'000.- Special conventions to express quantities of currency: 50 Mio Fr. (50 million francs)	Period and apostrophe fr.s. 5.00 fr.s. 5.- fr 5.00 fr 5.- fr 10.75 fr 500.00 fr 5'000.00 fr 50'000.50 fr 50'000'000.-

(Table D–8 continues on next page)

Table D–8. Currency (cont.)

	United Kingdom	United States
Currency unit	British pound (pound-sterling)	U.S. dollar
Fraction	new penny x 100 (p) (plural: pence)	cent x 100 (plural: cents)
ISO 4217 symbol	GBP	USD
ISO 4217 numeric code	826	840
International symbol	GB£	US$
EEC symbol	GB£	USA
National symbols	£	$ (dollars) ¢ (cents)
Formats	75p £2.50 £0.25 GB£2.50 GBP 2.50	65¢ 65¢ $50 $50.65¢ $500 US$5000 USD5000
Separators	Comma, decimal point, and center dot 65p (65 pence) (no separator or decimal point is used) £5.00 or £5 £5.75 £500 £5,000 £5,000,000 £5,000.50 (5,000 pounds and 50 pence) £50M (50,000,000 pounds-sterling) Millions of pounds-sterling are often expressed by placing an uppercase M immediately after the numerals indicating the number of millions.	Comma and period $0.65 or .65 or 65¢ (sixty-five cents) $5 or $5.00 $500.00 $5,000 $5,000.50 $5,550.50 $5,000,000 $ 13K (thirteen thousand dollars) $ 50 M (fifty million dollars) **Note:** Thousands or millions of dollars are often expressed by placing an uppercase K or M immediately after the numerals indicating the number.

Table D–9. Expressions of Time

Austria	9:45 19:45 9:45 Uhr 23:15 Uhr 9:45:17 08:15 08:15:10 08:05:10.75
Belgium: Flanders	14.15 u. 9 u. 15 min. 30 sec. (in everyday writing) 14:15 09:15:30.75 (in data processing)
Belgium: French-speaking	18.18 18h27 6 h 3 min 4 s (in everyday writing) 09:15 9:15:30.25 (in data processing)
Canada: English-speaking	9:45 AM (12-hour clock) 11:15 PM (12-hour clock) 9:45 (24-hour clock) 23:15 (24-hour clock) 23:15:30.75 (hours, minutes, seconds, fractions of seconds format)
Canada: French-speaking	9 h 45 (24-hour clock) 23 h 15 (24-hour clock) 9:18:14 (hours, minutes, seconds, fractions of seconds are usually not represented) 9:45 (this format should be used in a scientific or technical context only, usage of the 24-hour clock still applies)

(Table D–9 continues on next page)

Table D–9. Expressions of Time (cont.)

Denmark	09:45 23:15 23:15:30.75
Finland	9.45 23.15 23.15.30,75
France	18.18 18h 18mn 18 h 27 04.15 **Note:** These formats may be written with or without spaces. 09:00:02.03 23:15:30.75 23 h 15 min 30 s 75/100ème 23 h 15 mn 30 s 75/100ème **Note:** Formats for hours, minutes, seconds, and hundredths of a second require spaces.
Germany	9.45 Uhr 9.30 - 13.30 (24-hour clock) 9:45 Uhr (24-hour clock) 23:15 Uhr (24-hour clock) 23:15:30.75
Iceland	9.45 f.h. (equivalent to a.m. for the 12-hour clock) 11.15 e.h. (equivalent to p.m. for the 12-hour clock) 09:45 (24-hour clock) 23:15 (24-hour clock) 23:15:30.75

(Table D–9 continues on next page)

Table D–9. Expressions of Time (cont.)

Ireland	9.45 AM (12-hour clock) 11.15 PM (12-hour clock) 09:45 hrs (24-hour clock) 23:15 hrs (24-hour clock) 23:15:30.75
Italy	9.45 09.45 13:15 23:15:30.75 **Note:** The English style for writing hours, minutes, seconds and fractions of seconds is generally used in computing; otherwise, the style 23 15' 30" e 75 is used in science and commerce.
Netherlands	14.15 (in everyday writing) 14:15 (in data processing) 09.15.30 uur 09:15:30 uur 23:15:30.75 in data processing 09.00.02 03 in everyday use
Norway	kl 09.45 (24-hour clock) kl 23.15 23.15.30,75 09.00.02,03
Portugal	09H45m (24-hour clock) 23H15m (24-hour clock) **Note:** Portugal uses seconds and fractions of a second in scientific and medical applications. 23:15:30.75 09:00:02.03

(Table D–9 continues on next page)

Table D–9. Expressions of Time (cont.)

Spain	09:45 (24-hour clock) 21:45 (24-hour clock) 09H45' 21H45' 23:15:30.75 or: 23:15:30:00 (preferred) 09:00:02.03 or: 09:00:02:03 (preferred) **Note:** Seconds apostrophes are always shown in military specifications.
Sweden	kl. 9.45 (24-hour clock) kl 23.45 (24-hour clock) 23.15.30,75 1.15.30,75
Switzerland: French-speaking	09.45 h 23.15 h 23:15:30.75
Switzerland: German-speaking	9.45 h 09.45 h 23.15 h 9.45 Uhr 23.15 Uhr 23:15:30.75
Switzerland: Italian-speaking	9.45 h 09:45 23:15 23:15:30.74

(Table D–9 continues on next page)

Table D–9. Expressions of Time (cont.)

United Kingdom	9.45 am (12-hour clock) 11.15 pm (12-hour clock) 09:45 hrs (24-hour clock) 23:15 hrs (24-hour clock) 2 o'clock 23:15:30.75 **Note:** Ante meridiem (AM) indicates morning (before noon); post meridiem (PM) indicates after midday (after noon). These suffixes are used in 12-hour clock systems only.
United States	9:45 AM (12-hour clock) 11:15 PM (12-hour clock) 0945 hrs (24-hour clock) 2315 hrs (24-hour clock) 23:15:30.75 **Note:** No punctuation or abbreviations are used in standard military 24-hour time-systems, for example, 0630, 1645, 1900.

Table D–10. Ordinal Numbers

Austria				**Belgium: Flanders**			
1.	2.	3.	4.	1ste	2de	3de	4de
5.	6.	7.	8.	5de	6de	7de	8ste
9.	10.	11.	12.	9de	10de	11de	12de
13.	14.	15.	16.	13de	14de	15de	16de
17.	18.	19.	20.	17de	18de	19de	20ste
21.	22.	23.	24.	21ste	22ste	23ste	24ste
25.	26.	27.	28.	25ste	26ste	27ste	28ste
29.	30.	31.		29ste	30ste	31ste	

(Table D–10 continues on next page)

Table D–10. Ordinal Numbers (cont.)

Belgium: French-speaking

1er	2ème[1]	3ème	4ème
5ème	6ème	7ème	8ème
9ème	10ème	11ème	12ème
13ème	14ème	15ème	16ème
17ème	18ème	19ème	20ème
21ème	22ème	23ème	24ème
25ème	26ème	27ème	28ème
29ème	30ème	31ème	

Canada: English-speaking

1st	2nd	3rd	4th
5th	6th	7th	8th
9th	10th	11th	12th
13th	14th	15th	16th
17th	18th	19th	20th
21st	22nd	23rd	24th
25th	26th	27th	28th
29th	30th	31st	

Canada: French-speaking

1er[2]	2^{e}	3^{e}	4^{e}
5^{e}	6^{e}	7^{e}	8^{e}
9^{e}	10^{e}	11^{e}	12^{e}
13^{e}	14^{e}	15^{e}	16^{e}
17^{e}	18^{e}	19^{e}	20^{e}
21^{e}	22^{e}	23^{e}	24^{e}
25^{e}	26^{e}	27^{e}	28^{e}
29^{e}	30^{e}	31^{e}	

Denmark

1.	2.	3.	4.
5.	6.	7.	8.
9.	10.	11.	12.
13.	14.	15.	16.
17.	18.	19.	20.
21.	22.	23.	24.
25.	26.	27.	28.
29.	30.	31.	

Finland

1.	2.	3.	4.
5.	6.	7.	8.
9.	10.	11.	12.
13.	14.	15.	16.
17.	18.	19.	20.
21.	22.	23.	24.
25.	26.	27.	28.
29.	30.	31.	

France

1er	2ème[1]	3ème	4ème
5ème	6ème	7ème	8ème
9ème	10ème	11ème	12ème
13ème	14ème	15ème	16ème
17ème	18ème	19ème	20ème
21ème	22ème	23ème	24ème
25ème	26ème	27ème	28ème
29ème	30ème	31ème	

[1]The feminine form of 1er is 1re. The plural form for the three notations is 1ers, 1res, and X^{es}.
[2]If there are more than two choices, 2ème is used; if there are only two choices, 2nd is used.

(Table D–10 continues on next page)

Table D–10. Ordinal Numbers (cont.)

Germany

1.	2.	3.	4.
5.	6.	7.	8.
9.	10.	11.	12.
13.	14.	15.	16.
17.	18.	19.	20.
21.	22.	23.	24.
25.	26.	27.	28.
29.	30.	31.	

Iceland

1.	2.	3.	4.
5.	6.	7.	8.
9.	10.	11.	12.
13.	14.	15.	16.
17.	18.	19.	20.
21.	22.	23.	24.
25.	26.	27.	28.
29.	30.	31.	

Ireland

1st	2nd	3rd	4th
5th	6th	7th	8th
9th	10th	11th	12th
13th	14th	15th	16th
17th	18th	19th	20th
21st	22nd	23rd	24th
25th	26th	27th	28th
29th	30th	31st	

Italy

1º	2º	3º	4º
5º	6º	7º	8º
9º	10º	11º	12º
13º	14º	15º	16º
17º	18º	19º	20º
21º	22º	23º	24º
25º	26º	27º	28º
29º	30º	31º	

Netherlands

1ste	2de	3de	4de
5de	6de	7de	8ste
9de	10de	11de	12de
13de	14de	15de	16de
17de	18de	19de	20ste
21ste	22ste	23ste	24ste
25ste	26ste	27ste	28ste
29ste	30ste	31ste	

Norway

1.	2.	3.	4.
5.	6.	7.	8.
9.	10.	11.	12.
13.	14.	15.	16.
17.	18.	19.	20.
21.	22.	23.	24.
25.	26.	27.	28.
29.	30.	31.	

(Table D–10 continues on next page)

Table D–10. Ordinal Numbers (cont.)

Portugal

1º	2º	3º	4º
5º	6º	7º	8º
9º	10º	11º	12º
13º	14º	15º	16º
17º	18º	19º	20º
21º	22º	23º	24º
25º	26º	27º	28º
29º	30º	31º	

Spain

1º	2º	3º	4º
5º	6º	7º	8º
9º	10º	11º	12º
13º	14º	15º	16º
17º	18º	19º	20º
21º	22º	23º	24º
25º	26º	27º	28º
29º	30º	31º	

Sweden

1	2	3	4
5	6	7	8
9	10	11	12
13	14	15	16
17	18	19	20
21	22	23	24
25	26	27	28
29	30	31	

Switzerland: French-speaking

1er	2	3	4
5	6	7	8
9	10	11	12
13	14	15	16
17	18	19	20
21	22	23	24
25	26	27	28
29	30	31	

Switzerland: German-speaking

1º	2º	3º	4º
5º	6º	7º	8º
9º	10º	11º	12º
13º	14º	15º	16º
17º	18º	19º	20º
21º	22º	23º	24º
25º	26º	27º	28º
29º	30º	31º	

Switzerland: Italian-speaking

1.	2.	3.	4.
5.	6.	7.	8.
9.	10.	11.	12.
13.	14.	15.	16.
17.	18.	19.	20.
21.	22.	23.	24.
25.	26.	27.	28.
29.	30.	31.	

(Table D–10 continues on next page)

Table D–10. Ordinal Numbers (cont.)

United Kingdom				United States			
1st	2nd	3rd	4th	1st	2nd	3rd	4th
5th	6th	7th	8th	5th	6th	7th	8th
9th	10th	11th	12th	9th	10th	11th	12th
13th	14th	15th	16th	13th	14th	15th	16th
17th	18th	19th	20th	17th	18th	19th	20th
21st	22nd	23rd	24th	21st	22nd	23rd	24th
25th	26th	27th	28th	25th	26th	27th	28th
29th	30th	31st		29th	30th	31st	

Table D–11. Telephone Numbers

Austria	Belgium: Flanders	Belgium: French-speaking
84 86 11 84 86 11/DW. 1230 0222 84 86 11 84.86.11 0222 84 86 11/DW. 1230 (complete number and extension)	02-734 50 95 051-32 18 60	02-734 50 95 051-32 18 60 02/35.56.78
Canada: English-speaking	**Canada: French-speaking**	**Denmark**
473-9064 (518) 473-9064 1-800-473-9000 1 800-473-9000	473-9064 (518) 473-9064 1-800-473-9000 1 800-473-9000	02 88 96 66
Finland	**France**	**Germany**
90-474 6481 90 4746481 (90) 474 6481 921-307 570 921 307570 (921) 307 570	(16-1)60-75-54-01 (16) 84-48-52-13 (16.1) 60.75.54.01 (16) 84.48.52.13	(089)3 59 37 10 089/ 3 59 37 10 (089)3593710 (089)3.59.37.10

(Table D–11 continues on next page)

Table D–11. Telephone Numbers (cont.)

Iceland[1]	Ireland	Italy
1357	(0903) 29631	(06) 5209021
13579	0903-29631	06/5209021
135791		06-5209021
	010-353-903-29631	06-52-09-21
92-1357	(from outside Ireland)	
96-13579		
99-135791		

Netherlands	Norway	Portugal
(015) 56789	02 30 35 00	068-233 22
015-56789	(073) 24 226	068-22 22 22
	073 24 226	068-222 22 22
02134-53265		017-351-96
020-7432567		
020-625432		

Spain	Sweden	Switzerland: French-speaking
(91) 734 70 02	08/765 49 83	01/398-79-78
(91) 734-70-02	08/27 87 54	(01) 398-79-78
(91)734.70.02	0155/276 51	031/24-66-96
		(031) 24-66-96
	or preferred,	01/398'79'78
		(01) 398'79'78
	08-765 49 83	
	08-27 87 54	
	0155-27 657	

[1]Icelandic telephone numbers consist of only four, five, or six numeric characters if the number is being called inside a zone. From outside a zone, two numeric characters (of the series 91 through 99) are added in front of the number.

(Table D–11 continues on next page)

Table D–11. Telephone Numbers (cont.)

Switzerland: German-speaking	Switzerland: Italian-speaking	United Kingdom
01/398-79-78	01/398-79-78	(071) 398 7978
(01) 398-79-78	(01) 398-79-78	031-246 6965
031/24-66-96	031/24-66-96	0255 716509
(031) 24-66-96	(031) 24-66-96	Farnham (0252) 718645
01/398'79'78	01/398'79'78	
(01) 398'79'78	(01) 398'79'78	(071) = inner city London
		(081) = suburban London

United States
398-7979
601-398-7978
(601)398-7978
1-800-398-7979

Appendix E

Creating a Bidirectional Text Editor

Using symmetric programming techniques, it is possible to develop a text editor that will accommodate two language directions. This bidirectional capability is useful with Hebrew, for example, which is written from right to left, but has embedded numbers and text from other languages, such as English, that are written from left to right.

Figure E–1 shows the mirror symmetry of a simple text editor that works as well for languages that are written consistently in one direction—either from left to right or from right to left—as it does for bidirectional languages. In this figure, the x axis represents the writing direction and the y axis represents the line position. The two-dimensional text editor shown in Figure E–1 has the following characteristics:

- An entered character is inserted at the cursor position and the cursor advances one position in the writing direction.
- Pressing the Delete key removes the character adjacent to the cursor in a direction opposite to the writing direction, that is to the left in a left-to-right language, to the right in a right-to-left language.
- Pressing the Tab key advances the cursor in the writing direction to the next tab position, inserting a single tab character in the text.
- Pressing the Return key inserts a carriage return into the text and moves the cursor to the first position on the next line.
- Pressing the Backspace key moves the cursor one position in the direction opposite the writing direction.
- Pressing the Arrow keys moves the cursor one position in the direction of the arrow; this works the same way for right-to-left or left-to-right languages.

Figure E–1. Mirror Symmetry for a Simple Text Editor

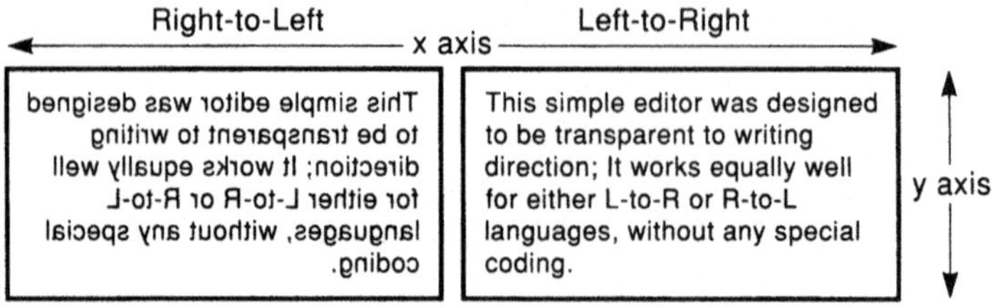

Following the principles of symmetric programming, the designer of a bidirectional text editor needs to:

- Design the editor so that its internal function remains the same, regardless of the writing direction, but the external view shows the appropriate view of the text data being entered.
- Treat the logical flow of text data in the same way for either language writing direction. The data has to be processed internally, for example, for searches, and stored permanently in files in the same way.
- Use mirror symmetry (left-to-right reversal) so that the amount of function conditioned by parameters is minimal; with the choice of virtual coordinates illustrated in Figure E–1, no conditionalized coding is required until the final virtual-to-physical mapping is made.
- Use virtual coordinates internally to establish positions and increment/decrement positions on the virtual screen. For example, adding 1 to the X position always advances the cursor one character position in the writing direction; adding 1 to the Y position advances the cursor to the next line.
- Transform from the internal virtual display coordinate to actual positions and movements (left and right) on the physical screen as the last step prior to physical input and output to the terminal.

Regardless of the language direction, the editor works the same way in accepting input, moving the cursor, and deleting and displaying text. While the logical text entered and saved on file is organized the same way for either language direction, the editor operates under the control of the writing direction attribute of the language to produce a distinctly different display of the text.

The details of the mapping of virtual coordinates to physical coordinates, under writing direction control, depend on the control primitives of the particular physical device—video display terminal or bit-mapped workstation display. It is possible to build a terminal that can be set up as a right-to-left terminal, effectively changing its coordinate system to agree with the characteristics of the language. The origin would be in the upper right corner for right-to-left languages, and upper left corner for left-to-right languages.

Figure E–2 shows that using appropriate parameters can extend the applicability of the editor. In fact, taking full advantage of symmetry, the editor could be used to edit languages that include combinations of all the line layout and character layout directions: 0, 90, 180, and 270 degrees. For example, a right-to-left (character layout) and bottom-to-top (line layout) writing direction with origin (1,1) at the bottom right-hand corner of the display would be permitted, even though no language actually uses that combination.

Figure E–2. Editing Vertical Writing with the Symmetric Editor

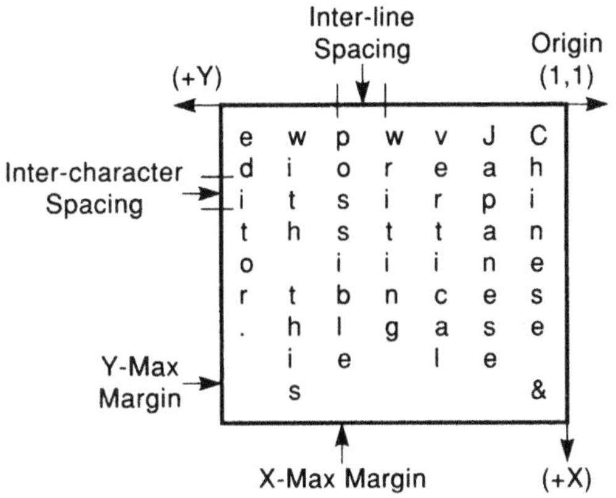

It is possible to mix text requiring different writing directions, such as inserting an Arabic number or English text into Hebrew or Arabic text. However, additional programming is required to do so.

E.1 Bidirectional Editing

It is necessary to understand the following terms when creating a bidirectional editor.

- Chronological order

  The order in which a stream of characters is typed in. This is the order in which the stream is intended to be read. Chronological order is sometimes referred to as logical order.

- Display order

  The order in which a stream of characters is displayed. In bilingual situations this order is not the same as the chronological order of the stream. In the example below, the *h* in the word *werbeh* and the *M* in the word *MORE* are physically next to each other. However, when the text is read, as illustrated below, the chronological order is different. Display order is sometimes referred to as physical order.

```
                               +--------------------------------------+
order in which displayed :     |ENGLISH TEXT txet werbeh MORE ENGLISH |
                               +--------------------------------------+
order in which read:               1      2     4     3      5     6
(chronological order)
```

- Segmentation

  When representing bidirectional text, divide it into smaller portions, called segments, which can be nested. An entire document is a segment that consists of other segments. If a segment does not contain other segments, the text it contains must be of a single direction. In other words, a segment that contains text of different directions must be broken into smaller segments, each containing either right-to-left text or left-to-right text. Within each segment, character data is stored in logical order.

- Bidirectional data storage

  A bidirectional document can be viewed as a group of segments, each having its own direction. Additionally, an attribute signifies the orientation or direction of the document.

- Document direction

  The value of document direction determines the global formatting behavior, such as starting and ending margins, juxtaposing of segments, how the document is to be bound, and placing of page headers and page numbers. For example, when the document direction is left-to-right, the starting margin is the left margin, the ending margin is the right margin, and each segment is placed to the right of the previous one. When the document direction is right-to-left, the starting margin is right, the ending margin is left, and each segment is placed to the left of the previous one.

- Segment direction

  The value of segment direction determines the juxtaposition of characters within the segments.

Figure E–3 contains a document with a left-to-right document direction consisting of three segments.

Figure E–3. Left-to-Right Document Direction

```
segment 1:
     segment direction: left-to-right
     segment data: "ENGLISH TEXT "

segment 2:
     segment direction: right-to-left
     segment data: "hebrew text"

segment 3:
     segment direction: left-to-right
     segment data: "MORE ENGLISH"

After formatting this will be:

+-------------------------------------------------------+
|ENGLISH TEXT txet werbeh MORE ENGLISH                  |
+-------------------------------------------------------+
```

Figure E–4 contains a document with a right-to-left document direction consisting of three segments.

Figure E–4. Right-to-Left Document Direction

```
segment 1:
     segment direction: right-to-left
     segment data: "hebrew text "

segment 2:
     segment direction: left-to-right
     segment data: "ENGLISH TEXT"

segment 3:
     segment direction: right-to-left
     segment data: "more hebrew"

After formatting this will be:

+------------------------------------------------------+
|                 werbeh erom ENGLISH TEXT txet werbeh|
+------------------------------------------------------+
```

E.2 Hebrew Text Entry and Editing

Word processing in a bidirectional environment must support the following two features:

- Text entry and editing in one of the two main text paths, left-to-right and right-to-left. The left-to-right text path is used for languages based on Latin characters and the right-to-left text path is used in accordance with right-to-left based languages (such as Hebrew or Arabic).
- Text entry and editing in a secondary segment within a document to allow inclusion of left-to-right text within right-to-left text and vice versa.

Direction-based editing is implemented by setting direction attributes (segment tags) that are maintained and manipulated by the editor. This attribute of the main text path could be implemented as a tag of a segment within the document. The user can then have sections with different main direction paths in a single document. The main text path determines the editing direction and the alignment of the text.

The Direction Switching Key (DSK), or Toggle key, can be used to insert a portion of text in a direction opposite to the main text path. Pressing the DSK opens a new editing window where the editing is done according to the rules of the secondary direction.

If the text at the insertion point was inserted originally in the secondary direction, this secondary segment is moved to the new window and formatted according to the secondary path, as if it were the main path in that window. If the insertion point is inside the main segment, the new editing window is empty. The text editing in this window is done normally.

When the user finishes editing in the secondary segment window and presses the DSK, the secondary segment is inserted in the document at the insertion point and formatted according to the main text path.

Appendix F

Database Source Language Syntax Description

This appendix describes the database source language used in the ULTRIX operating system to create a source file for a language support database. The appendix explains the syntax elements of the source files and gives an Extended Backus-Naur Form (EBNF) notation of the syntax recognized by the ULTRIX **ic** compiler.

F.1 Rules for Building Identifiers

The rules for building an identifier (Ident) are as follows:

- Each identifier must start with a letter or a hyphen.
- An identifier can be any length and can contain letters (*a* to *z* and *A* to *Z*), digits (1–9), hyphens, and periods.
- If you use a period in an identifier, at least one letter, digit, or hyphen must follow the period.

F.2 Rules for Building Strings

The rules for building a string (String) are as follows:

- No string can contain more than 255 characters.
- Each string must be enclosed in quotation marks (" ").
- Each string must be on one line in the source file.

- A string can contain the following escape sequences:

Description	Symbol	Sequence
Newline	NL (LF)	\n
Horizontal tab	HT	\t
Vertical	VT	\v
Backspace	BS	\b
Carriage return	CR	\r
Form feed	FF	\f
Backslash	\	\\

F.3 Rules for Building Constants

A constant can be any of the following forms:

- A character constant, such as one character enclosed in single quotation marks (' '). You can use constant by following the C language rules for using escape sequences.
- A hexadecimal constant of the form 0x*nnnn*, where *n* designates a hexadecimal digit (0–9, *a* to *f*, and *A* to *F*). The hexadecimal constant must be in the range of 0 to 0x7FFF. You can omit leading null valued digits.
- An octal constant of the form 0*nnnn*, where *n* designates an octal digit (0-7). The octal constant must be in the range of 0 to 077777. You can omit leading null valued digits.
- A character in ISO notation n/n, where *n* designates a decimal number in the range of 0 to 15.
- A decimal number *n*, where n is a positive integer in the range 0 to 32,767.

F.4 Rules for Separating Tokens, Specifying Comments, and Using Directives

Separate tokens with spaces or horizontal tabs. You must not include blank space within tokens. White space (for example, " ", newline, horizontal tab) is significant only as a token separator. The **ic** compiler ignores blank space that you use to make your source file readable.

As in the C language, comments are delimited by pairs of slashes and asterisks (/*comment*/). You can include comments anywhere in the source file except within tokens. If you use a comment within a token, the **ic** compiler considers the token to end where the comment begins. Any text that follows the comment begins a new token.

Because the database source file is preprocessed by the C preprocessor, you can use the preprocessor directives, such as **#include, #define,** and **#if,** throughout the source file.

F.5 EBNF Description

Example F–1 contains the EBNF description of the database source language.

Example F–1. EBNF Description of the Database Source Language

```
intl_data_base
        : codeset_table data_tables

data_tables
        : data_table | data_tables data_table

data_table
        : property_table
        | collation_table
        | format_table
        | conversion_table

codeset_table
        : CODESET Ident ':' code_definition_list END '.'

code_definition_list
        : code_definition
        | code_definition_list ';' code_definition

code_definition
        : Ident '=' code_value ':' property_list
        | Ident '=' code_value
        | property_definition

code_value
        : code | code_value ',' code
```

(Example F–1 continues on next page)

Example F–1 (Cont.). EBNF Description of the Database Source Language

```
code
        : Constant | Ident

property_list
        : property | property_list ',' property

property_table
        : PROPERTY Ident ':' property_definition_list END '.'

property_definition_list
        : property_definition
        | property_definition_list ';' property_definition

property_definition
        : Ident ':' property_list

property
        : ARITH | BLANK | CTRL | CURENCY | DIACRIT
        | DIPHTONG | DOUBLE | FRACTION | HEX | ILLEGAL
        | LOWER | MISCEL | NUMERAL | PUNCT
        | SPACE | SUPSUB | UPPER

collation_table
        : COLLATION ':' collation_list END '.'
        | COLLATION Ident ':' collation_list END '.'

collation_list
        : collation | collation_list ';' collation

collation
        : PRIMARY ':' code_value_list
        | PRIMARY ':' Ident '-' Ident
        | PRIMARY ':' REST
        | EQUAL ':' code_value_list
        | EQUAL ':' Ident '-' Ident
        | EQUAL ':' REST
        | Ident '=' '(' Ident ',' Ident ')'
        | PROPERTY ':' Ident

code_value_list
        : Ident | code_value_list ',' Ident

format_table
        : STRINGTABLE ':' format_list END '.'
        | STRINGTABLE Ident ':' format_list END '.'

format_list
        : format | format_list ';' format

format
        : Ident '=' format_value

format_value
        : code_or_string | format_value ',' code_or_string
```

(Example F–1 continues on next page)

Example F–1 (Cont.). EBNF Description of the Database Source Language

```
code_or_string
        : code | String


conversion_table
        : CONVERSION Ident ':' conversion_list END '.'
        | CODE CONVERSION Ident ':' conversion_list END '.'

conversion_list
        : conversion | conversion_list ';' conversion

conversion
        : DEFAULT '->' default_value
        | Ident '->' conversion_value
        | Ident '-' Ident '->' Ident '-' Ident

default_value
        : VOID | SAME | conversion_value

conversion_value
        : code_or_string
        | conversion_value ',' code_or_string
```

Appendix G

Example Source Language File

Example G–1 illustrates the file structure of a source file for a language support database using the ULTRIX operating system. The example is only a portion of a source file.

Example G–1. Example of a Language Support Database Source File

```
/*
 * example annotated (partial) source for
 * a Language Support Database
 */
CODESET CH_ASCIIPLUS :
        /*  CH_ASCIIPLUS will be the name of the INTLINFO file */
#include "ISO646"
        /* include ISO646 as the predefined ASCII code definition */

        /*
         * additional definitions for demonstration purposes:
         *
         * first we have a range of secondary control codes.
         * This is not enforced by the ic compiler nor by
         * the language but is a common IS 2022 style
         * code set extension technique. Note that because
         * there are no properties defined below all these
         * codes are defined but not legal.
         */
        sc00 = 0x80; sc01 = 0x81; sc02 = 0x82; sc03 = 0x83;
        sc04 = 0x84; sc05 = 0x85; sc06 = 0x86; sc07 = 0x87;
        sc08 = 0x88; sc09 = 0x89; sc0a = 0x8a; sc0b = 0x8b;
        sc0c = 0x8c; sc0d = 0x8d; sc0e = 0x8e; sc0f = 0x8f;

        /*
         * NOTE: this gap in the source will prevent compilation.
         * This was done to shorten the example.
         */
```

(Example G–1 continues on next page)

Example G–1 (Cont.). Example of a Language Support Database Source File

```
/*
 * now come some more useful code definitions. These
 * definitions are taken from the ISO 8859-1
 * definition. Note the convention of writing
 * uppercase letters in all uppercase, lowercase
 * letters and special codes in all lowercase.
 * Here the codes are defined directly from their
 * ISO notation.
 */
A_GRAVE = 12/0   : UPPER;
A_AIGU = 12/1    : UPPER;
A_CIRCON = 12/2  : UPPER;
A_TILDE = 12/3   : UPPER;
DIA_A = 12/4     : UPPER;
A_CIRCLE = 12/5  : UPPER;
/*
 * The following declaration of AE as a diphthong enables
 * the correct treatment of diphthongs (one-to-two
 * collation) in the default collation.
 */
AE = 12/6        : UPPER, DIPHTHONG;

/*
 * NOTE: this gap in the source will prevent compilation.
 * This was done to shorten the example.
 */



/*
 * lowercase equivalents of the codes defined
 * in the last block
 */
a_grave = 14/0   : LOWER;
a_aigu = 14/1    : LOWER;
a_circon = 14/2  : LOWER;
a_tilde = 14/3   : LOWER;
dia_a = 14/4     : LOWER;
a_circle = 14/5  : LOWER;
ae = 14/6        : LOWER, DIPHTHONG;

/*
 * special double letters for Spanish
 * Note that these "characters" are not defined by
 * any standard! They represent an extension
 * useful to handle the following problems:
 *      \*- two to one collation
 *      \*- conversions toupper and tolower
 */
Ll = L, l : DOUBLE, UPPER;
ll = l, l : DOUBLE, LOWER;
```

(Example G–1 continues on next page)

Example G–1 (Cont.). Example of a Language Support Database Source File

```
END.

/*
 * Collation table that shows most of the possible
 * problems in collation but does not make very much
 * sense in the real world:
 *
 * Uppercase and lowercase letters are intermixed and
 * within one letter the uppercase comes before the
 * lowercase letter.
 *
 * Accented characters sort after their corresponding
 * nonaccented base character.
 *
 */
COLLATION :
        PRIMARY : A, A_GRAVE, A_AIGU, A_CIRCON, A_TILDE,
                  DIA_A, A_CIRCLE;
        PRIMARY : a, a_grave, a_aigu, a_circon, a_tilde,
                  dia_a, a_circle;
        PRIMARY: B; PRIMARY: b; PRIMARY: C; PRIMARY: c;
        PRIMARY: D; PRIMARY: d; PRIMARY: E; PRIMARY: e;
        PRIMARY: F; PRIMARY: f; PRIMARY: G; PRIMARY: g;
        PRIMARY: H; PRIMARY: h; PRIMARY: I; PRIMARY: i;
        PRIMARY: J; PRIMARY: j; PRIMARY: K; PRIMARY: k;
        PRIMARY: L; PRIMARY: l;


        /*
         * TWO-TO-ONE COLLATION:
         *
         * For Ll and ll Spanish collation rule says that
         * this has to be collated after L or l.
         */
        PRIMARY: Ll; PRIMARY: ll;

        PRIMARY: M; PRIMARY: m; PRIMARY: N; PRIMARY: n;

        /*
         * ONE-TO-TWO COLLATION:
         *
         * The following two codes are diphthongs, that is
         * codes that collate as two characters.
         */
        AE = (A, E);                        ae = (a, e);

        /*
         * The rest of the codes defined in the codeset will
         * collate as don't care characters.
         */
```

(Example G–1 continues on next page)

Example G–1 (Cont.). Example of a Language Support Database Source File

```
END.

/*
 * This is a sample string table based on the German language.
 *
 * Note the mixed uses of ASCII strings and identifiers
 * specified in the codeset definition.
 *
 * The strings for CRNCYSTR, D_T_FMT, D_FMT, T_FMT are
 * typically specified as ASCII strings.
 *
 * Each of the items specified is required by the ic
 * compiler. Additional items can be specified if so
 * desired.
 */

STRINGTABLE :
        NOSTR       = "nein";
        EXPL_STR    = 'e';
        EXPU_STR    = 'E';
        RADIXCHAR   = comma;
        THOUSEP     = dot;
        YESSTR      = "ja";
        CRNCYSTR    = "+DM";

        D_T_FMT     = "%a, %d. %b %Y %H:%M:%S" ;
        D_FMT       = "%a, %d. %b %Y";
        T_FMT       = "%H:%M:%S";
        AM_STR      = "AM";
        PM_STR      = "PM";

        DAY_1       = "Sonntag";          DAY_2        = "Montag";
        DAY_3       = "Dienstag";         DAY_4        = "Mittwoch";
        DAY_5       = "Donnerstag";       DAY_6        = "Freitag";
        DAY_7       = "Samstag";

        ABDAY_1     = "So";               ABDAY_2      = "Mo";
        ABDAY_3     = "Di";               ABDAY_4      = "Mi";
        ABDAY_5     = "Do";               ABDAY_6      = "Fr";
        ABDAY_7     = "Sa";

        MON_1       = "Januar";           MON_2        = "Februar";
        MON_3       = M, dia_a, "rz";     MON_4        = "April";
        MON_5       = "Mai";              MON_6        = "Juni";
        MON_7       = "Juli";             MON_8        = "August";
        MON_9       = "September";        MON_10       = "Oktober";
        MON_11      = "November";         MON_12       = "Dezember";
```

(Example G–1 continues on next page)

Example G–1 (Cont.). Example of a Language Support Database Source File

```
        ABMON_1     = "Jan";            ABMON_2     = "Feb";
        ABMON_3     = M, dia_a, r;      ABMON_4     = "Apr";
        ABMON_5     = "Mai";            ABMON_6     = "Jun";
        ABMON_7     = "Jul";            ABMON_8     = "Aug";
        ABMON_9     = "Sep";            ABMON_10    = "Okt";
        ABMON_11    = "Nov";            ABMON_12    = "Dez";
END.

STRINGTABLE :
MON_1 = "January";
YESSTR = "oui";
END.
```

Appendix H
ISO Standards

Table H–1 lists the ISO standards that pertain to office and publishing processes, systems, interchange formats, data/text encodings.

Table H–1. ISO Standards

Standard	Description
ISO 646 : 1973	Information processing—7-bit coded character set for information interchange (ASCII is the US variant of ISO 646; ISO 646 also defines the framework for the National Replacement Character sets)
ISO 2022 : 1986	Information processing—ISO 7-bit and 8-bit coded character sets—Code extension techniques
ISO 4873:1983	Information processing—ISO 8-bit code for information interchange—structure and rules for implementation
ISO 6429 : 1988	Information processing—ISO 7-bit and 8-bit coded character sets—Additional control functions for character-imaging devices
ISO 8601	Data elements and interchange formats—Information interchange—Representation of dates and times
ISO 8613 : ODA/ODIF	Office Document Architecture, Office Document Interchange Format
ISO 8632 : 1987	Information processing systems—Computer graphics metafile (CGM) for the storage and transfer of picture description information, Part 1: Functional description, Part 3: Binary encoding
ISO 8824 : 1987	Information processing systems—Open System Interconnection (OSI)—Specification of Abstract Syntax Notation One (ASN.1)
ISO 8825 : 1987	Information processing systems—Basic encoding rules for Abstract Syntax Notation One (ASN.1)

(Table H–1 continues on next page)

Table H–1. ISO Standards (cont.)

Standard	Description
ISO 8859–1: 1987	Information processing—8-bit single-byte coded graphic character sets. Part 1: ISO Latin-1 character set
ISO 8859–2: 1987	Information processing—8-bit single-byte coded graphic character sets. Part 2: ISO Latin-2 character set
ISO 8859–3: 1988	Information processing—8-bit single-byte coded graphic character sets. Part 3: ISO Latin-3 character set
ISO 8859–4: 1988	Information processing—8-bit single-byte coded graphic character sets. Part 4: ISO Latin-4 character set
ISO 8859–5: 1988	Information processing—8-bit single-byte coded graphic character sets. Part 5: Latin-Cyrillic Alphabet character set
ISO 8859–6: 1987	Information processing—8-bit single-byte coded graphic character sets. Part 6: Latin-Arabic Alphabet character set
ISO 8859–7: 1987	Information processing—8-bit single-byte coded graphic character sets. Part 7: Latin-Greek Alphabet character set
ISO 8859–8: 1988	Information processing—8-bit single-byte coded graphic character sets. Part 8: Latin-Hebrew Alphabet character set
ISO 8859–9: 1988	Information processing—8-bit single-byte coded graphic character sets. Part 9: Latin Alphabet No. 5 (Western Europe variation)
ISO 8879 : 1986	Information processing—Standard Generalized Markup Language (SGML)
ISO 9069	Information processing—SGML support facilities, SGML Document Interchange Format (SDIF)
ISO DIS 9541	Information processing—Font and character information interchange. Part 1: Introduction, Part 2: Registration and naming procedures, Part 5: Font attributes and character model
ISO DIS 10646	Information processing—Multiple-octet coded character set (MOCCS)—Aim is to permit the representation of the written form of the languages of the world

Appendix I

Addresses of Standards Organizations

This appendix lists the addresses of standards organizations.

International Organization for Standardization (ISO)
1, Rue de Varembé
Case postale 56
CH-1211 Genève 20
Suisse/Switzerland

European Standards

European Computer Manufacturers Association (ECMA)
114, Rue du Rhône
CH-1204 Genève
Suisse/Switzerland

Arab States

Arab Standards and Metrology Organisation (ASMO)
P.O. Box 926161
Amman
Jordan

Australia

Standards Association of Australia (SAA)
Standards House
80-86 Arthur Street
North Sydney - N.S.W. 2060

Austria

Österreichisches Normungsinstitut (ON)
Heinestraße 38
Postfach 130
A-1021 Wien

Belgium

Institut Belge de Normalisation (IBN)
Belgisch Instituut voor Normalisatie (BIN)
Av. de la Brabançonne - Brabançonnelaan 29
B-1040 Bruxelles - Brussel

Canada

Standards Council of Canada (SCC)
International Standardisation Branch
2000 Argentia Road, Suite 2-401
Mississauga
Ontario
L5N 1V8

China

China State Bureau of Standards (CSBS)
P.O. Box 820
Beijing
People's Republic of China

Denmark

Dansk Standardiseringsraad (DS)
Aurehøjvej 12
Postbox 77
DK-2900 Hellerup

Finland

Suomen Standardisoimisliitto (SFS)
P.O. Box 205
SF-00121 Helsinki

France

Association Française de Normalisation (AFNOR)
Tour Europe
Cedex 7
F-92080 Paris

Germany

DIN
Deutsches Institut für Normung
Burggrafenstraße 6
Postfach 1107
D-1000 Berlin 30

Greece

Hellenic Organisation for Standardisation (ELOT)
Didotou 15
106 80 Athens

Hong Kong

Hong Kong Standards and Testing Centre
10 Dai Wang Street
Taipo Industrial Estate
Taipo, N.T.

Iceland

Technological Institute of Iceland
Standards Division
Keldnaholt
IS-112 Reykjavik

Ireland

National Standards Authority of Ireland (NSAI)
Ballymun Road
Dublin-9

Israel

Standards Institution of Israel (SII)
42 University Street
Tel Aviv 69977

Italy

Ente Nazionale Italiano di Unificazione (UNI)
Piazza Armando Diaz, 2
I-20123 Milano

Japan

Japanese Industrial Standards Committee (JISC)
c/o Standards Department
Agency of Industrial Science and Technology
Ministry of International Trade and Industry
1-3-1, Kasumigaseki
Chiyoda-ku
Tokyo 100

Mexico

Dirección General de Normas (DGN)
Calle Puente de Tecamachalco N° 6
Lomas de Tecamachalco
Sección Fuentes
Naucalpan de Juárez
53 950 Mexico

The Netherlands

Nederlands Normalisatie-instituut (NNI)
Kalfjeslaan 2
P.O. Box 5059
2600 GB Delft

New Zealand

Standards Association of New Zealand (SANZ)
Private Bag
Wellington

Norway

Norges Standardiseringsforbund (NSF)
Postboks 7020 Homansbyen
N-0306 Oslo 3

Portugal

Instituto Português da Qualidade (IPQ)
Rua José Estêvão, 83-A
P-1199 Lisboa

Spain

Instituto Español de Normalización (IRANOR)
Calle Fernandez de la Hoz, 52
28010 Madrid

Sweden

SIS—Standardiseringskommissionen i Sverige
Box 3295
S-103 66 Stockholm

Switzerland

Swiss Association for Standardisation (SNV)
Kirchenweg 4
Postfach
CH-8032 Zúrich

United Kingdom

British Standards Institution (BSI)
2 Park Street
London
W1A 2BS

United States of America

American National Standards Institute (ANSI)
1430 Broadway
New York
NY 10018

Appendix J

Additional Reading

This appendix lists documentation associated with the material in this guide and also provides the order number for each document or document set. A table at the end of this appendix shows you how to order documentation from Digital.

- *The Digital Guide to Software Development*
  Order No. EY–C178E–DP
- *DECforms Document Set*
  Order No. QA–VCHAA–GZ; includes the following:

  DECforms Guide to Developing Forms
  DECforms Guide to Programming
  DECforms Reference Manual
  DECforms Guide to Converting VAX FMS Applications
  DECforms Guide to Converting VAX TDMS Applications
  DECforms Summary Card
  DECforms Keypad Card
- *Guide to Creating VMS Modular Procedures*
  Order No. AA–FB84A–TE
- *Guide to VAX DEC/Code Management System*
  Order No. AI–KL03A–TE
- *Guide to VAX DEC/Module Management System*
  Order No. AI–P119C–TE
- *Guide to VAX Language-Sensitive Editor and VAX Source Code Analyzer*
  Order No. AI–FY24B–TE
- *Input Method Manual (for Traditional Chinese)*
  Order No. EK–VT38D–IM
- *Input Method User's Guide (for Simplified Chinese)*
  Order No. EK–IMUGC–UG–001

- *A Technical Guide to Asian Language Software Localization*
  Order No. EF–B2551–50
- *ULTRIX-32 (DECwindows) Document Set*
  Order No. QA–0JQAA–GZ; includes the following:

  UWS (ULTRIX Workstation Software) V2.0 Release Notes
  UWS Advanced Installation Guide
  UWS Guide to UWS Window Manager
  UWS Reference Pages, Section 1
  UWS Introduction to UWS User Environment
  UWS DECwindows User's Guide
  UWS DECwindows Desktop Applications Guide
  UWS Guide to DXDIFF VS DIFF Programming
  UWS XUI Programming Overview
  UWS Guide to Writing Applications for Widgets
  UWS Guide to Porting Xlib Applications
  UWS Guide to DXDB Debugger
  UWS Guide to XUI User Interface
  UWS Guide to XUI Toolkit Widgets
  UWS Guide to Toolkit Intrinsics
  UWS Guide to Xlib Library
  UWS X Window System Protocol
  UWS Reference Pages, Section 3
  UWS Guide to X Toolkit Widgets
  UWS User Interface Style Guide
- *ULTRIX–32 Guide to Internationalization*
  Order No. AA–LY26A–TE
- *ULTRIX Worksystem Software / Japanese Documentation Set*[1]
  Order No. QA–VYUJA–GZ (H–kit, VAX)
  Order No. QA–YEQJA–GZ (H–kit, RISC)
- *ULTRIX / Japanese V4.0 Documentation Set* [1]
  Order No. QA–VWGJA–GZ (H–kit, VAX)
  Order No. AQ–YERJA–GZ (H–kit, RISC)
- *VAX GKS / 0b Document Set*
  Order No. QA–810AA–GZ; includes the following:

  VAX GKS Reference Manual Volume 1
  VAX GKS Reference Manual Volume 2
  VAX GKS User Manual
  Writing VAX GKS Handlers
  VAX GKS Pocket Guide

---

[1] This documentation is available in Japanese.

- *VAX PHIGS Document Set*
  Order No. QA–0KBAA–GZ; includes the following:

  VAX PHIGS$ Binding Manual
  VAX PHIGS FORTRAN Binding Manual
  VAX PHIGS C Binding Manual
  VAX PHIGS Reference Manual

- *VMS / ULTRIX Compound Document Architecture Manual*
  Order No. AA–MG30A–TE
- *VMS Command Definition Utility Manual*
  Order No. AA–LA60A–TE
- *VMS Debugger Manual*
  Order No. AA–LA59A–TE
- *VMS DECwindows User Kit*
  Order No. QA–09SAB–GZ; includes the following:

  VMS DECwindows User's Guide
  VMS DECwindows Desktop Applications Guide
  Overview of VMS DECwindows

- *VMS DECwindows Programming Kit*
  Order No. QA–001AM–GZ; includes the following:

  XUI Style Guide
  VMS DECwindows Guide to Application Programming
  VMS DECwindows User Interface Language Reference Manual
  VMS DECwindows Toolkit Routines Reference Manual Part 1
  VMS DECwindows Toolkit Routines Reference Manual Part 2
  VMS DECwindows Guide to Xlib Programming: MIT C Binding
  VMS DECwindows Guide to Xlib Programming: VAX Binding
  VMS DECwindows Xlib Routines Reference Manual Part 1
  VMS DECwindows Xlib Routines Reference Manual Part 2
  VMS DECwindows Device Driver Architecture Manual

- *VMS Message Utility Manual*
  Order No. AA–LA63A–TE
- *VMS Record Management Services Reference Manual*
  Order No. AA–LA83A–TE
- *VMS RTL Screen Management (SMG$) Manual*
  Order No. AA–LA77A–TE
- *VMS Run-Time Library Routines Manual*
  Order No. AA–76A–TE
- *VMS Utility Routines Manual*
  Order No. AA–LA67A–TE

- *VT382–K User Guide (for Korean)*
  Order No. EK–VT38K–UG–001
- *XLIB Programming Volume 1*
  Order No. QA–001A6–GZ

Table J–1. How to Order Documentation from Digital

From	Call	Write
Alaska, Hawaii, or New Hampshire	603-884-6660	Digital Equipment Corporation P.O. Box CS2008 Nashua, NH 03061
Rest of United States and Puerto Rico*	1-800-DIGITAL	Digital Equipment Corporation P.O. Box CS2008 Nashua, NH 03061 U.S.A.
Canada	800-267-6219	Digital Equipment of Canada Ltd. 100 Herzberg Road Kanata, Ontario, Canada K2K 2A6 Attn: Direct Order Desk
United Kingdom	0101-800-DIGITAL	Digital Equipment Corporation P.O. Box CS2008 Nashua, NH 03061 U.S.A.
Countries other than Canada, U.S., or U.K.	001-800-DIGITAL	Digital Equipment Corporation P.O. Box CS2008 Nashua, NH 03061 U.S.A.

*For prepaid orders from Puerto Rico, call Digital's local subsidiary (809-754-7575).

Glossary

ABCD model: For ease of reference, Digital often uses the letters A, B, C, and D to refer to the four international product model components, and calls the entire model the ABCD model. *See* product.

American National Standards Institute (ANSI): A group that represents most foreign country specifications and supplies all types of standards.

American Standard Code for Information Interchange (ASCII): A character set that uses seven bits to code a character. It includes the standard 26 letters of the English alphabet but none of the national characters used by non-English speaking countries.

ANSI: *See* American National Standards Institute.

application profile: A data structure that defines the values of options and attributes that control or condition the performance of a product.

Arabic character sets: There are a number of Arabic character sets, some of which are 7-bit and some of which are 8-bit. The most common Arabic sets are ASMO-449 and ASMO-662 (defined by the Arabic Standards and Metrology Organization) and ECMA-114 (defined by the European Computer Manufacturers Association). ECMA-114 includes Latin and Arabic characters.

architecture: A precise specification of all data structures and functional interfaces of a computer system or solution. For example, the VAX hardware architecture specifies internal data structures and instructions operating on those data structures. The VMS software architecture specifies rules for writing VMS applications that operate within the VAX hardware framework.

ASCII: *See* American Standard Code for Information Interchange.

bourne shell: A standard command interpreter.

byte: A 7-bit or 8-bit unit of information used to represent control or graphic information.

C shell: A command interpreter that provides a number of convenient features for interactive use including filename completion, command aliasing, history substitution, job control, and a number of built-in commands.

case conversion: Information identifying the possible other cases of each legal character code. Used by character conversion functions to shift characters from uppercase to lowercase and vice versa.

CCITT: *See* Consultative Committee of the International Telegraph and Telephone.

CDA: *See* Compound Document Architecture.

CDG: *See* country development group.

character: A member of the set of elements used for the organization, control, or representation of text. Distinct from *coded character* in that no coding or one-to-one relationship is implied.

character cell: A matrix of pixels used to display a single glyph, most often a fixed-size matrix, but may vary with proportional fonts and/or character sets.

character set: A set of alphabetic or other characters used to construct the words and other elementary units of a national language or a computer language.

CLD: *See* Command Language Definition.

code conversion: The process of taking source data coded according to a particular coded character set and producing destination data coded according to another character set.

coded character: A member of the coded character set; often confused with *character*.

coded character set: A set of unambiguous rules that establish a set of named characters and the one-to-one relationships between the characters and their unique bit combinations.

collating sequence: The sequence in which characters are ordered for string comparison and sorting. Depending on character encodings, this sequence can be very complicated, as when uppercase and lowercase characters must be sorted together in order (A, a, B, b, and so on), for example: *aldehyde, al dente, Alderney, aleph.*

Command Language Definition (.CLD): A type of file format. The command definition for the VAX RALLY command is provided in Command Language Definition (CLD) format.

compose sequence: A series of keystrokes that creates a character.

composite graphic symbol: A graphic symbol consisting of a combination of two or more other graphic symbols in a single character position, such as a diacritical mark and a basic letter.

compound document: A file that can include all or some of the following elements: text, graphics, images, or spreadsheets, and, in the future, voice and video. Books, magazines, and newspapers are all examples of traditional compound documents.

Compound Document Architecture (CDA): The core technology for a new area of networked documents. This technology provides the means to universally interchange and link all types of information and to create and manage compound documents across a network and between multiple platforms and applications. CDA is an architecture, or set of rules for dynamic compound documents.

compound string: A DDIF data type that enables applications to specify attributes in text, graphics, images, or data. Compound strings make it possible for text in a DECwindows user interface to be translated into any language for which a font supported by the DECwindows interface is available.

configuration data: Identifies the locale supported by a system in terms of permitted locale-name settings. This name is a composite text string identifying the associated language, cultural data, and coded character set.

Consultative Committee of the International Telegraph and Telephone (CCITT): A committee that sets international communications usage standards, which include facsimile, mail, and image compression.

control character: A character, other than a graphic character, that affects the recording, processing, transmission, or interpretation of text.

corporate engineering group: The Digital engineering group that produces an international product.

country development group (CDG): A group within Digital's European organization, located in Paris, whose mission is to develop business in new European markets. These markets now include the Eastern countries Yugoslavia, Turkey, and some Arabic countries.

country-specific information component: *See* product.

country-specific information: Information that is relevant only in a particular country or area, such as references to time, telephone numbers, warranties, and ordering information.

culture-specific information: Information that relates to specific cultural knowledge and experience.

DDIF: *See* Digital Document Interchange Format.

DDIS: *See* Digital Data Interchange Syntax.

dead key: A key used when composing characters. On certain keyboards some keys, such as the apostrophe, circumflex, and quotation mark are dead keys. When the key is pressed, the character is not sent to the program, but a compose sequence is started. If the next character completes a valid compose sequence, the composed character is sent.

DEC Multinational Character Set (DEC MCS): An 8-bit coded character set that includes all of the characters of most Western European languages. It does not include the additional characters used by Iceland, or any characters not based on the Latin alphabet.

DECwindows Resource Manager (DRM): The DECwindows Resource Manager interprets the output of the UIL compiler (a resource database) and generates argument lists for DECwindows widget creation routines. *See also* widget and User Interface Language.

development cycle: The cycle of events within engineering that starts with initial product conceptions and ends with the transfer of the completed product into manufacturing.

diacritical mark: A mark added to a letter or symbol to distinguish it in some way or to show its pronunciation.

diagnostics: A program that tests a product or system and reports performance and error correction. Diagnostics programs are also used to test hardware, firmware, peripheral operation, logic, or memory, and to report any faults detected.

dialog box: A special window that is displayed in response to user action in the DECwindows interface. Usually, the user must take an appropriate action (as indicated by the choices presented in the dialog box) to continue application activity.

Digital Data Interchange Syntax (DDIS): Digital's internal version of the ISO Abstract Syntax Notation One (ASN.1) which provides a means for Type-Length-Value (TLV) encoding of structured data. DDIS is a collection of notation and encoding rules for data, with a standard data type notation (analogous to C structure declaration), a standard data value notation (analogous to a C initialization statement), and standard data value encoding rules (analogous to CPU data representation).

Digital Document Interchange Format (DDIF): A syntax based on DDIS that serves as a document interchange format and conversion hub that is application- and system-independent. DDIF can express most known document semantics and combinations of text, graphics, images, and data.

Digital Table Interface Format (DTIF): A syntax based on DDIS that serves as a interchange format and conversion hub that is application- and system-independent.

diphthong: For the purposes of internationalization, a character for which 1-to-2 collation must be used. This implies an interdependence with the collation tables. The meaning of *diphthong* in internationalization is somewhat different from the definition used in the grammar of languages that use diphthongs.

ditroff: A text-formatting tool used on ULTRIX and other UNIX-based systems. The term *ditroff* stands for device-independent troff. *See also* troff.

DTIF: *See* Digital Table Interface Format.

end user: The ultimate consumer of a computer product, beyond the manufacturer or distributor; one who uses a computer system, as opposed to one who owns, manages, operates, or supports the computer system.

environmental interface: The ways a product interacts with the physical and electrical end-user environment in which it is placed. The product affects the local environment, and the local environment affects the product.

European area: In Digital's organization, Europe currently includes continental Europe, the British Isles, Israel, Iceland, parts of Northern Africa, and the Near East (Saudi Arabia, Turkey, and so on).

FDE: *See* Form Development Environment.

form: The total of all user-perceived characteristics of a product, including both the control interactions provided by the user and the resulting user-visible output of the system, that is, all user input and output.

Form Development Environment (FDE): A menu-driven form creation tool that enables developers to create or modify a form file or test a form file's functioning at run time. Application developers can use FDE to interactively design forms.

format: The shape, size, and general makeup, as of a printed document.

full-form characters: A set of 2-byte alphabetic characters defined in most of the multi-byte character sets.

function: The information processing (computing) carried out by a product in response to the user actions. This processing is not visible to the user.

geographical market: A market defined or bounded by a physical geography. A geographical market may be a country, a part of a country, or a collection of countries.

geometric information: Information used to position user interface objects such as prompts, menus, messages, and so on, on a video screen. Also referred to as positioning information.

global product: A product that functions properly in a usage environment that includes users throughout the world. Such a product performs equally well in any locale; it is either language- and locale-neutral (insensitive to language, country, and local convention) or it has all the necessary variants to provide localized function to its users.

glyph: An image, typically of a character in a font.

GMT: *See* Greenwich Mean Time.

graphic character: A character, other than a control character, that has a visual representation normally handwritten, printed, or displayed.

graphic symbol: The visual representation of a character (graphic or control) or control function on a character imaging device.

Greenwich Mean Time (GMT): Mean solar time of the meridian at Greenwich, England. Used for the basis of standard time throughout most of the world.

half-form characters: Single-byte alphabetic characters.

Hangul: The script used when writing Korean characters. Chinese characters are also used when writing Korean. They are then referred to as Hanja.

Hanja: Chinese characters used when writing Korean.

Hanyu: A Digital-specific term that refers to Chinese characters as defined by the (Taiwan) CNS standard.

Hanzi: A Digital-specific term that refers to Chinese characters defined by the (PRC) GB standard.

Hebrew character sets: There are three Hebrew character sets. These all contain both Latin and Hebrew characters. The DEC Hebrew 7-bit set, an adapted version of the ASCII character set, is essentially the Hebrew NRC set. The DEC Hebrew 8-bit set, based on DEC MCS, removes some of the characters and adds the Hebrew characters. Also, an 8-bit ISO Hebrew set, ISO Latin/Hebrew Alphabet, is based on the ISO Latin-1 character set.

HELP key: A key the user can press to view an explanatory message about the subsystem, form, or field the user is currently in.

help message: Explanatory message to help users to understand the product or to correct a problem or error.

Hiragana: The kana that is used to write all verbal and adjectival endings in the Japanese language. Hiragana is associated primarily with the representation of items that are regarded as native to the Japanese language.

hooks: Facilities in a product that allow a future addition or alteration of functions in order to allow it to interface with other products.

Kana: The Japanese set of written characters representing syllables.

Kanji: The script used when writing Japanese characters.

Katakana: The Japanese set of written characters representing syllables used primarily for writing words borrowed from foreign languages. For example, Katakana for *motorscooter* is *mootaasukuutaa* and Katakana for *Asia* is *Azia*.

icon: A pictorial representation of an object or function. Icons are used for software representations, and only a few icons are standard. *See also* symbol.

ideographic character: A character that symbolizes a specific thought or idea without actually expressing the name of the thing they represent. Generally consisting of many elements, some contain over 30 strokes of the pen or brush. Languages such as Japanese, Chinese, and Korean use ideographic characters.

IEEE: *See* Institute of Electrical and Electronics Engineers

IFDL: *See* Independent Form Description Language.

Independent Form Description Language (IFDL): The source language in which DECforms screens are written.

Institute of Electrical and Electronics Engineers (IEEE): A formal, ANSI-accredited, standards-developing organization. IEEE standards include the 802.x local-area network and POSIX 1003.x efforts.

international: Existing between or among nations or their citizens; participated in by two or more nations.

international base component: *See* product.

internationalization: A process that includes both the development of an international product and the localization of the international product for delivery into worldwide markets.

International Organization for Standardization (ISO) Latin Alphabets: The ISO Latin-1 character set has been developed by the International Organization for Standardization as the standard character set for Western European languages. It will eventually supersede DEC MCS. Other ISO character sets are being developed to cover European languages not based on the Latin alphabet. They cover Eastern Europe (ISO Latin-2), Southern Europe (ISO Latin-3), and the Northern European Countries (ISO Latin-4).

international product: An international product (also sometimes known as an international base product) is a product that can easily be localized. An international product consists of the following components:

- international base component
- user interface component
- market-specific component

- country-specific information component

international product development: The process of developing a product that can be easily localized. The design and development efforts ensure that the product conforms to:

- The general structure of the international product model
- Published guidelines and standards for producing international products

The result of this effort will be an international product.

ISO: *See* International Organization for Standardization

ISO 646: An ISO 7-bit coded character set for information interchange. The reference version of ISO 646 contains 95 graphic characters, which are identical to the graphic characters defined in the ASCII coded character set.

ISO 6937: An ISO 7-bit or 8-bit coded character set for text communication using public communication networks, private communication networks, or interchange media such as magnetic tapes and discs.

ISO 8859 - 1: An ISO 8-bit single-byte coded character set Part 1, Latin Alphabet No. 1. The ISO 8859/1 character set comprises 191 graphic characters covering the requirements of most of Western Europe.

LAN: *See* Local Area Network.

LANG: The environment variable used with the ULTRIX operating system to announce the user's requirements for national language, local customs, and coded character set to the computer system.

language-neutral: *See* locale-neutral.

language information: Refers to the localization data describing the format and setting of locale-specific cultural data.

language variant: A language variant of a software product consists of the international base component and a modified and/or translated user interface component.

linguistic aids: Software used for natural-language text processing. Examples of linguistic aids are spell-checking, grammar-checking, and automatic hyphenation tools.

Local Area Network (LAN): A data communication system that spans a physically limited distance, provides high bandwidth communication over inexpensive media, and is privately owned.

local conventions: The formats and separators used for certain types of data in a particular locale, such as formats for telephone numbers, date and time values, and currency values. These formats and separators vary from locale to locale.

local customs: The conventions of a geographical area or territory for such things as date, time, and currency formats.

local devices: The user-interface devices that are used in a particular locale, such as keyboards, input/output devices, communications equipment, and printers. These devices can vary from locale to locale.

local engineering group: A Digital engineering group within a country's software and applications support organization, that performs those engineering activities required to produce a product variant from an international (base) product for their local market.

local language: The primary language or languages spoken within a particular geographic area. Synonymous with *natural language* and *national language*.

local usage environment: A synonym for *locale*. *See* locale.

locale: The environment in which a product is used. This environment includes language, dialect, keyboard, data input and display conventions, collating sequence, and many other attributes, all of which directly affect the way users interact with the product. Note that the boundaries for a locale do not necessarily match country borders; a single country might include several different locales and vice versa.

locale-neutral: Independent of natural language and other attributes of the locale, such as keyboard type. Used to apply to locale-neutral test suites, locale-neutral data structures, or locale-neutral coding. By implication, locale-neutral components are equally valid, without change, in any specified locale.

localizable software: Software designed to be easily localized. Preferred to the term *translatable,* which is frequently and incorrectly used to mean *localizable*.

localization: The process that includes all activities required to create a product variant from the international product. Localization of the international product may, or may not, include translation of the product. Localization does not change the functionality of the international base component. If functionality changes, reengineering has been performed and a new product has been created.

localization components: Those components of an international product that vary in different markets. By contrast, the international base component, is invariant in all markets.

localization kit: A package containing all of the files and information a local engineering group needs to create a product variant. The localization kit typically consists of electronic and hardcopy files, documents (plans, specifications, and so on), and tools.

localization team: The group that performs the localization. The team may be part of a local engineering group, located in the country where the local version will be sold.

localized software: Software that functions effectively in a particular locale. To be effective, it should be as attractive and familiar to the user as software developed specifically for that environment.

logical name: A user-specified name for any portion of a VMS file specification. For example, the logical name INPUT can be assigned to a terminal device from which a program reads data entered by a user.

market-specific component: *See* product.

message catalog: A file or storage area containing program messages, command prompts, and responses to prompts for a particular national language, territory, and codeset.

mnemonics: Techniques that use established conventions, prior training, or memory aids, such as an abbreviation or symbol, to assist human memory. As mnemonics are usually specific to the language and culture they come from, they are best avoided in material to be translated.

monotoniko: A simplified transliteration of Greek writing in which the Latin alphabet is used in combination with Greek accent marks. For example, "where do you come from?" is written "apó poú eíste."

mouse: A peripheral pointing device that, when moved across any surface, causes a corresponding movement of the pointer on the screen. A mouse can have one or more buttons.

multilingual software: Software capable of supporting user interfaces in more than one natural language at a time.

multinational: Of, relating to, or involving more than one nation; usually applied to business activities. *International* is the preferred term.

multi-byte character: A single character represented by a series of one or more bytes in an underlying codeset.

National Character Set (NCS): The National Character Set Utility is available in Digital's VMS Version 5.0 Run-Time Library and assists developers writing software that uses collating sequences. This utility supports the ISO Latin-1 character set and allows specific collating sequences to be defined and then stored in an NCS library.

National Replacement Character (NRC) Set: A 7-bit coded character set that replaces certain ASCII characters with characters used in a specific country. Many NRC sets are specified by national standards; others have been created by Digital.

natural language: The primary language or languages spoken within a particular geographic area. Such languages are natural languages, as opposed to artificial languages such as C, Assembly, Ada, and so on. Synonymous with *local language* and *national language*.

NCS: *See* National Character Set.

NLSPATH: An environment variable used with the ULTRIX operating system to indicate the search path for message catalogs.

noninternational product: A product that does not conform to the guidelines and standards for creating an international product. Such products cannot be localized unless they are first reengineered.

NRC: *See* National Replacement Character set.

nroff: A tool used on ULTRIX and other UNIX-based systems for producing formatted text files that can be displayed on a terminal or workstation screen.

polytonic: A form of Greek writing in which a variety of diacritical marks are used. Today, these diacritical marks have only historic meaning; they do not change pronunciation. Similarly, accents in Greek only show which syllable is to be stressed. The form of the accent does not have an impact on pronunciation.

Portable Operating System Interface for Computer Environments (POSIX): A set of standards designed to provide applications portability that are being developed by the IEEE 1003.0-1003.9 working groups. POSIX is also commonly used to refer specifically to the 1003.1 Standard, which defines an operating system interface specification.

POSIX: *See* Portable Operating System Interface for Computer Environments.

product: A combination of components, developed in response to a market problem or opportunity, that is consistent with company strategy. An international product, whether hardware or software, consists of the following components.

- international base component

  The international base component consists of software functionality or hardware modules that will remain constant in all the worldwide markets where the product will be sold. This component is the common element in all variants of the product.

  For example, an international base component for a software product consists of code that does not require any changes for use in any market where the product is sold.

- user interface component

  The user interface component is the text and language processing component. It does not contain code. This is the component that typically gets translated or modified to meet the needs of specific languages or cultures.

  For example, the user interface component could include user messages, text control information, online help, symbols and icons, and documentation.

- market-specific component

  The market-specific component provides optional features that can be added to the international base component in response to a particular market need. This component provides additional or changed functionality for the specified market.

  For example, the general market requirements for an office system would be satisfied in the international base component; the various modem, printer, local interconnect, and power cords which tend to vary by area or country would be contained in the market-specific component. Specific dialects of languages could also be included in this component.

- country-specific information component

  The country-specific information component contains information that is specific to a particular country and is required for delivery of the product. This component does not contain software code.

  For example, warranty, service and ordering information, license certificates, VDE postcards, and terms and conditions are all examples of country-specific information components.

product variant: A variant of a software product produced as a result of localization. A product variant has the same international base component as the international product. It also includes

- user interface component
- optionally, a market-specific component
- country-specific information component

Product variants are complete and ready for delivery to the customer. Note that the process of creating a product variant (localization) does not change functionality in the international base component. If that functionality is changed, a new version of the product has been created.

radix character: The character that separates the integer of a number from the fraction.

reengineering: A process that includes any additional engineering activities required to make a product suitable for localization. Reengineering may include the following activities:

- Engineering activities required to create an international product from a noninternational product: redesign, writing of interface specifications, and other activities.
- Engineering activities required because of the unique requirements of particular languages: redesigning the product to handle additional character sets and screen display requirements for the Asian, Hebrew, and Arabic languages, for example.

Reengineering is still commonly performed to produce Asian, Hebrew and Arabic products. The result of reengineering is a base Asian, Hebrew, or Arabic version. Because reengineering is time-consuming, it adds to the cost of localizing software.

simultaneous ship: A strategy to ship a number of product variants on the same day as the first revenue shipment of the international product. *See also* synchronized ship.

single-byte format: An 8-bit character format used in the standard ASCII computing environment of European and English-speaking countries.

software architecture: *See* architecture.

Software Product Description (SPD): A document that defines the function of a Digital software product and minimum hardware needed to support it. It describes software, components, and service.

standard: 1. A precise rule, communication protocol, functional interface, data format specification, or environmental measure or interface that a product is expected to adhere to in order to claim conformance to that standard. 2. A set of minimum requirements upon which successful product designs may be based for products intended for worldwide markets. 3. Any rule, principle, or measure established by authority.

strategic market: A market in which Digital is making significant long term investments and where customers must be able to use the full functionality of a product regardless of the local standards, language environment, power, or regulatory environment.

symmetric programming: Programming techniques that allow you to develop text editors that accommodate two language directions. This bidirectional capability is useful with Hebrew, for example, which is written from right to left, but has embedded numbers and text from other languages, such as English, that are written from left to right.

synchronized ship: A strategy to ship a predetermined number of product variants within an agreed period of time after first revenue shipment of the international product. *See also* simultaneous ship.

telecommunications interface: The mechanism by which a product is connected to the telephone system.

Terminal Fallback Facility (TFF): A facility that provides table-driven character conversion for terminals. TFF allows you to compose characters not included on the keyboard. TFF allows users with NRC set terminals to use software developed with DEC MCS.

TFF: *See* Terminal Fallback Facility.

time-to-market: The time lapse between identifying a commercial opportunity for a new product and shipping the product to the first customer.

TLV: *See* Type-Length-Value.

translatability: A measure of the ease of translating user information into another language.

translatable text: Natural language text designed for ease of translation, for example, text that is structured in modules permitting selective translation, and free of culturally biased examples and acronyms that are not usually considered translatable.

translation: The process of rendering information presented in one natural language into another natural language. Translation is one part of localization.

translation markup: Comments in application files that assist the translator in locating translatable and localizable items.

translator: 1. A person who renders information presented in one natural language into another natural language and retains its original meaning. 2. A program or series of programs that changes statements from one machine language into another (for example, a compiler or assembler).

troff: A UNIX-based text-formatting tool similar to nroff. Files generated by troff can be used to drive a phototypesetter or laser printer. *See also* nroff.

type-length value (TLV): A type of software coding of structured data provided by DDIS.

UID: *See* User Interface Description.

UIL: *See* User Interface Language.

ULTRIX Worksystems Software (UWS): A Digital product based on two major components: the ULTRIX-32 operating system and an extensive X window-based environment that supports general users and graphics applications developers.

UPS: *See* User Preference Supplemental.

user interface: A mechanism through which the user makes the product perform its intended function. This mechanism takes into consideration the way user information is used, the way hardware is used, and the way user behaviors are integrated to solve a problem.

user interface architecture: The user's view of a software product consisting of all online command and control actions taken by the user, online and hardcopy documentation (error messages, help, and tutorials), labels and legends on control keys, and other controls and indicators, such as a mouse.

user interface component: *See* product.

User Interface Description (UID): File created when the DECwindow's user interface language (UIL) compiler translates the UIL module. Application and library use of user interface definition (UID) files then aid in the localization process.

User Interface Language (UIL): Definition files produced by the DECwindows UIL compiler containing the data necessary to separate form and function in the DECwindows applications and allowing DECwindows toolkit widgets and gadget detail to be stored separately from the toolkit and run-time code.

user profile: A data structure that defines the attributes of the local usage environment.

UWS: *See* ULTRIX Worksystems Software.

VDE Postcards: Cards used in Germany for registering high-frequency equipment with the telecommunications authority.

widget: A DECwindows interaction mechanism by which users give input to an application or receive messages from an application. Widgets are standard calls to the DECwindows windowing system that help to maintain a consistent look and feel across different applications.

worldwide product: A term that encompasses an international product and any product variants.

Xdefault files: DECwindows application resource databases that provide default values that define the basic attributes of an application user interface such as origin, height, width, background color, foreground color, and font. These values are stored in a customizable file and form a type of application profile for the software product.

Xlib: Digital's implementation of the X Window System's graphic programming library. Xlib provides low-level routines for creating windows, managing windows, and performing graphic functions.

X/Open: An international consortium of vendors whose purpose is to define the X/Open Common Applications Environment (CAE). The CAE is a comprehensive software environment designed to provide applications portability.

X Resource Manager: A feature of the DECwindows interface that aids in the localization process.

XRM: *See* X Resource Manager.

Xtoolkit: A package of tools for programmers that extends the basic functionality provided by the X Window System to support human interface construction within user applications. It does this by providing application programmers with a common set of intrinsics.

XUI: *See* X User Interface

X User Interface (XUI): The programmer and user interface developed by Digital for X-based workstations. The X User Interface is made up of the User Executive, the Session Manager, and the Window Manager. Each helps developers and end users to maintain a consistent user interface.

Index

A

B

C

D

E

F

G

H

I

J

K

L

M

N

O

P

U

V

W

X

Printed in Dunstable, United Kingdom

91340602R00226